CONTESTING STEREOTYPES
AND CREATING IDENTITIES

CONTESTING STEREOTYPES AND CREATING IDENTITIES

Social Categories, Social Identities, and Educational Participation

Andrew J. Fuligni

Editor

Russell Sage Foundation • New York

Library of Congress Cataloging-in-Publication Data

Contesting stereotypes and creating identities : social categories, social identities, and educational participation / edited by Andrew J. Fuligni

    p. cm.

    ISBN-13: 978-0-87154-298-4
    ISBN-10: 0-87154-298-6

    1. Educational sociology—United States. 2. Educational equalization—United States. 3. Minorities—Education—United States. 4. Stereotypes (Social psychology)—United States. 5. Group identity—United States. I. Fuligni, Andrew J.

    LC191.4.C665 2007

    306.43—dc22   2006038384

Text design by Suzanne Nichols.

RUSSELL SAGE FOUNDATION
112 East 64th Street, New York, New York 10021
10 9 8 7 6 5 4 3 2 1

Contents

Contributors   vii
Introduction   1
Andrew J. Fuligni

PART I   HOW SOCIAL CATEGORIES AND
THEIR MEANINGS SHAPE
EDUCATIONAL OPPORTUNITIES
AND BARRIERS

Chapter 1   Past as Present, Present as Past:
Historicizing Black Education and
Interrogating "Integration"   15
Anne Galletta and William E. Cross, Jr.

Chapter 2   Essentialism and Cultural Narratives:
A Social-Marginality Perspective   42
Ramaswami Mahalingam

Chapter 3   Relations Among Social Identities,
Intergroup Attitudes, and Schooling:
Perspectives from Intergroup
Theory and Research   66
*Meagan M. Patterson and
Rebecca S. Bigler*

PART II   HOW SOCIAL IDENTITIES
FACILITATE OR CHALLENGE
ACHIEVEMENT AND ENGAGEMENT
IN SCHOOL

Chapter 4   Racial-Ethnic Identity: Content
and Consequences for African
American, Latino, and LatinaYouths   91
*Daphna Oyserman, Daniel Brickman,
and Marjorie Rhodes*

Chapter 5   Social Identity, Stereotype Threat,
               and Self-Theories   115
               Catherine Good, Carol S. Dweck, and
               Joshua Aronson

Chapter 6   Ethnicity, Ethnic Identity, and School
               Valuing Among Children from
               Immigrant and Non-Immigrant
               Families   136
               Jason S. Lawrence, Meredith Bachman,
               and Diane N. Ruble

Chapter 7   Women of Color in College: Effects
               of Identity and Context on Contingent
               Self-Worth   160
               Julie A. Garcia and Jennifer Crocker

PART III   HOW SOCIAL RELATIONSHIPS
               MEDIATE THE EFFECTS OF SOCIAL
               CATEGORIES AND IDENTITIES

Chapter 8   The Meaning of "Blackness": How
               Black Students Differentially Align
               Race and Achievement Across Time
               and Space   183
               Carla O'Connor, Sonia DeLuca Fernández,
               and Brian Girard

Chapter 9   The Role of Peers, Families, and
               Ethnic-Identity Enactments in
               Educational Persistence and
               Achievement of Latino and
               Latina Youths   209
               Elizabeth Birr Moje and Magdalena
               Martinez

Chapter 10   Family Identity and the Educational
               Persistence of Students with Latin
               American and Asian Backgrounds   239
               Andrew J. Fuligni, Gwendelyn J. Rivera,
               and April Leininger

               Index   265

Contributors

Andrew J. Fuligni is professor in the Department of Psychiatry and Biobehavioral Sciences and the Department of Psychology at the University of California, Los Angeles.

Joshua Aronson is associate professor in the Department of Applied Psychology at New York University.

Meredith Bachman is survey research associate at Consumer Reports National Research Center.

Rebecca S. Bigler is a professor of psychology at the University of Texas at Austin.

Daniel Brickman is an NIMH Prevention Research Fellow and a doctoral student in social psychology at the University of Michigan.

Jennifer Crocker is Claude M. Steele Collegiate Professor of Psychology and research professor at the Research Center for Group Dynamics at the University of Michigan.

William E. Cross, Jr., is Professor and Head of the Doctoral Program in Social-Personality Psychology as well as the coordinator of the African American Studies Certificate Program at the Graduate Center of the City University of New York.

Carol S. Dweck is Lewis and Virginia Eaton Professor of Psychology at Stanford University.

Sonia DeLuca Fernández is a doctoral student in the School of Education at the University of Michigan.

Anne Galletta is assistant professor in the College of Education and Human Services at Cleveland State University.

Julie A. Garcia is assistant professor in the Department of Psychology at California Polytechnical State University, San Luis Obispo.

Brian Girard is a doctoral student in the School of Education at the University of Michigan.

Catherine Good is assistant professor in the Department of Psychology at Barnard College, Columbia University.

Jason S. Lawrence is assistant professor of psychology at the University of Massachusetts, Lowell.

April Leininger is a social worker with Los Angeles County–University of Southern California's Inpatient Psychiatry Services.

Ramaswami Mahalingam is assistant professor of psychology at the University of Michigan, Ann Arbor.

Magdalena Martinez is a doctoral candidate in the Center for the Study of Higher and Postsecondary Education at the University of Michigan.

Elizabeth Birr Moje is Arthur F. Thurnau Professor of Education at the University of Michigan.

Carla O'Connor is Arthur F. Thurnau Professor and associate professor of education at the University of Michigan.

Daphna Oyserman is a professor at the University of Michigan with joint appointments in the Department of Psychology, the School of Social Work, and the Institute for Social Research.

Meagan M. Patterson is a doctorial candidate in psychology at the University of Texas at Austin.

Marjorie Rhodes is an NIMH Prevention Research Fellow and doctoral student in developmental psychology at the University of Michigan.

Gwendelyn J. Rivera is a doctoral student in the Department of Psychological Studies in Education at University of California, Los Angeles.

Diane N. Ruble is emeritus professor at New York University.

Introduction

Andrew J. Fuligni

Educational achievement and opportunity often differ according to the social categories with which societies divide up their world, such as ethnicity, race, gender, or caste (Buchmann and Hannum 2001; Shavit and Blossfeld 1993). Within the United States, inequalities in attainment and opportunity continue to be an entrenched feature of the educational landscape in the twenty-first century. Although the high school completion rate of African American youths has improved over the last thirty years, a significant gap in the graduation rates of African American and white students has remained for the past ten to fifteen years (Laird et al. 2006). The graduation rate for Latino students has fluctuated over the last three decades, but it is essentially unchanged since the 1970s and is substantially below the rate for white students. Given the poor quality of the educational resources available to African American and Latino children, it is unlikely that these differentials in attainment will be reduced any time soon. Even after decades of awareness of substantial inequalities in education, ethnic-minority students continue to be more likely to attend schools that are overcrowded, dangerous, and limited in the opportunities they offer for advanced course work with experienced teachers (Fuligni and Hardway 2004).

A central thesis of this volume is that persistent disparities in educational opportunities and achievement are often created and sustained by academic stereotypes that are ascribed to different social groups by the larger society and its institutions. In particular, groups in the minority and with limited socioeconomic standing become characterized as lacking in academic potential, motivation, and engagement with education.

The authors of the chapters in this volume, while not ignoring the role of traditional demographic and economic variations across social groups, highlight how the educational stereotypes associated with social categories have a life of their own and can powerfully shape the educational opportunities and experiences of children and adolescents. As the authors describe, the effects of these stereotypes can be as obvious as the blatant segregation of minority students away from quality schools or as subtle as a teacher expressing surprise at the appearance of African American students in a college prep class during high school. At the same time, the authors demonstrate how students and their families challenge these stereotypes by redefining and employing their own social identities as they try to progress through the educational pipeline. The authors report that contrary to popular belief, most minority students go to great lengths to create identities in ways that both embrace their ethnic and cultural heritage and foster an endorsement of educational participation and success. These efforts to challenge society's view of their educational commitment, however, can be taxing; the authors describe how many students cannot help but be negatively impacted by the diminished expectations institutions have for them.

The educational experience of many students from minority and socially disadvantaged groups, therefore, includes the task of contesting stereotypes and developing social identities that provide them with the confidence, motivation, and ability to participate fully in the educational system. In order to more effectively address long-standing educational inequalities, researchers and practitioners need to obtain a better understanding of the role played by stereotypes, social categories, and social identities in educational participation. The Russell Sage Foundation Working Group on Social Identity and Institutional Engagement was formed to work toward a better understanding of these issues, and the present volume is a product of the efforts of this group of social and developmental psychologists with expertise in stereotyping, social identity, and educational achievement. The chapters of the volume are grouped according to three key questions that need to be addressed in order to better reduce educational disparities:

1. How do social categories and their meanings shape educational opportunities and barriers?
2. How do social identities facilitate or challenge achievement and engagement in school?
3. How do social relationships mediate the effects of social categories and identities?

In order to answer these questions, the authors employ a wide range of methods (for instance, experiments, ethnographies, historical and literary analyses) to examine these dynamics at multiple levels (for instance, cultural narratives, school practices, and interpersonal relationships), resulting in a rich compendium of scholarship on the role of social categories, social identities, and their social meanings in educational participation. The individual chapters and the answers that they provide for the three key questions are described below.

Part I focuses on how societies and educational institutions use social categories and their social meanings to create and sustain inequalities in educational resources and opportunities. The three chapters in this section are diverse in their focus and level of analysis, and collectively provide vivid examples of how social categories can shape the educational experiences of students at many different levels. Three key themes emerge from the work presented in this section. First, longstanding cultural myths about the educational abilities and potential of marginalized groups, such as the purported impact of the legacy of slavery on contemporary African Americans, are commonly used to explain and justify the great difficulties students from these groups have in finding educational success. Second, these myths have tremendous staying power because they act to essentialize the group. That is, cultural myths and stereotypes about marginalized groups serve to identify the "true" or "essential" character of the group in the social imagination, such as the view in India that the Dalit, or "untouchable," class is inherently inferior to other castes. By nature, the "essential" character of a group is impermeable to change or improvement, thereby justifying the marginalized position of the group. Third, individuals and societies are predisposed to divide up the social world into social categories, and the tendency to characterize, judge, and rank different groups according to factors such as academic motivation and potential is virtually an automatic cognitive process. Therefore, the most subtle and seemingly innocuous ways that teachers and schools draw attention to groups can create an environment in which some groups are viewed as more superior and valuable than others. And, in a more concrete manner, even well-intentioned efforts to desegregate schools and academic tracks can backfire and actually reify inequalities.

In the first chapter, Anne Galletta and William E. Cross use a variety of sources and methods to demonstrate how the educational motivation of African American students and families has been historically misrepresented. In contrast to the views of many observers, African Americans emerged from slavery with an extremely strong and optimistic view of the importance of education. As the authors put it, the ex-slaves demanded educational opportunities for themselves and their children. Galletta and Cross argue that the historical record demonstrates a remarkably high level of academic motivation among African Americans. Contrary to the argument of some theorists, most notably John Ogbu (1987), the current difficulty of some segments of the African American population, therefore, cannot be attributable to the historical legacy of slavery. Rather, more contemporary factors come into play. In the second half of their chapter, the authors provide an in-depth ethnography of how one school district has dealt with achievement gaps and issues of educational inequality over the past forty years. The authors show how even within efforts to ostensibly promote equality, social meanings and stereotypes can shape the opportunities afforded to African American students within the same school and even within the same classroom. These have important implications for the self-concept of these students, which the authors vividly describe through a series of case studies of individual students.

Stepping outside the United States in the second chapter, Ramaswami Mahalingam describes the case of the Dalits, the so-called untouchable caste groups of India. Mahalingam takes a social-marginality perspective, looking at the multiple ways in which certain social groups are ostracized, oppressed, and marginalized by the larger society. One of the most powerful ways social marginalization can take place is through essentializing the stereotypes and traits of oppressed groups. That is, social groups in power and the larger society attempt to define the "true" and "natural" qualities of marginalized groups in ways that serve to justify the existing social hierarchy. In the case of the Dalits, these purported true and natural qualities include their inherent inferiority in ability, intelligence, and potential. A powerful way in which this process of essentializing marginalized groups takes place is through cultural narratives, commonly known tales and myths, that carry messages of group difference and hierarchy. Mahalingam presents the story of Ekalaivy, a part of the Indian epic, the *Mahabharata* which describes a Dalit who ended up forgoing his education out of respect and honor for his superior, a Brahmin of the highest caste. The differing interpretations of this tale by members of higher and lower castes nicely demonstrate the role of cultural narratives in shaping the educational opportunities afforded to social groups, as well as the extent to which marginalized groups create their own social meanings in their efforts to resist the oppression that they face.

Finally, Meagan M. Patterson and Rebecca S. Bigler present a program of research that has examined the specific intragroup and intergroup dynamics that are involved in how social categories and social identities shape students' educational experiences at school. Using a paradigm that experimentally creates novel social groups, the authors are able to manipulate the types of practices that exist within real school settings among real social groups in order to better understand how these conditions create group differences in academic opportunities and attitudes. Patterson and Bigler show how common school practices such as teachers' labeling and use of social groups and segregation stimulate the tendencies of children to categorize, label, stereotype, and rank other students on a number of attributes, including academic ability and potential. Group dynamics also affect how children interpret both explicit and implicit curricular messages about social groups. This chapter is particularly valuable in showing how the larger social and institutional dynamics described in the other two chapters of this section can ultimately influence the educational meanings that students ascribed to their own and other social groups and categories in the school.

The chapters intersect nicely to provide a compelling picture of how social categories shape educational experiences through the meanings and stereotypes accorded to the educational potential of social groups. Mahalingam's description of the use of cultural stories to essentialize marginalized groups provides a good explanation for why the historical experience of slavery continues to be used to explain and perhaps even justify the inequalities in educational opportunities and attainment of contemporary African American students described by Galletta and Cross. Patterson and Bigler then effectively demonstrate the power of the most microlevel interactions in the classroom to further divide social groups and create stereotypes about ability and potential, which is what appears to have happened in the attempts to desegregate the schools described by Galletta and Cross. Patterson and Bigler's developmental intergroup theory offers concrete suggestions for avoiding these outcomes in the future by acknowledging that the powerful tendency for students to draw their own conclusions about social groups and social hierarchies render "color-blind" approaches ineffective, and that an open and focused discussion of the structural reasons for such inequalities could result in a learning environment that is truly open for students from minority and socially marginalized groups.

Part II moves to a focus on the students' own social identities and on how these facilitate or challenge engagement in school, with four chapters that address how the children and their families accept, challenge, or redefine the social meanings ascribed to their social groups through the processes described in the first section. Experiencing the process of identity development at the same time that they are moving through school, children and adolescents are faced with the task of integrating their educational experiences into their more general identity development. As students attempt to figure out how they fit into society's existing array of social categories and groups, they soon discover the social meanings and stereotypes regarding education that are associated with group membership. This discovery is particularly challenging and threatening for students from minority and marginalized groups, who encounter cultural stereotypes and institutional practices that characterize or even "essentialize" their groups as lacking in academic desire and potential. How do students from these groups identify with their derogated social group, yet still retain the aspirations and motivation needed to confront the educational challenges that they face? According to some previous observers, they don't. Most notably, John Ogbu (1987) argued that many African American students are unable to both identify with their ethnic background and remain engaged in school, and therefore an attachment to their ethnic background leads to a de-identification from school.

Chapter 4, by Daphna Oyserman, Daniel Brickman, and Marjorie Rhodes, and chapter 6, by Jason S. Lawrence, Meredith Bachman, and Diane N. Ruble, convincingly demonstrate that the simple form of the Ogbu hypothesis is not true, and that stronger ethnic identification among African American and Latino students actually is associated with higher levels of academic effort and desire. In fact, rather than caring too little about academic achievement, many members of minority and marginalized groups may actually care too much. Chapters by Julie A. Garcia and Jennifer Crocker and by Catherine Good, Carol S. Dweck, and Joshua Aronson describe how students who closely identify with their ethnicity or gender and want to achieve in school may care so much about disproving negative stereotypes about their potential that their performance in stressful achievement situations can become compromised. The effort required to combat the threat of these stereotypes creates anxiety and pressure that prevents the students from performing up to their potential.

Collectively, then, the chapters in this section show that the association between ethnic identity and achievement is much more complicated than originally envisioned by Ogbu and others. Ethnic minority students go to great efforts to develop an identity that includes a desire to do well in school, but these efforts to refute the stereotypes they encounter can make it difficult for them to perform well in achievement settings. Several of the authors in this section propose strategies for assisting these students with their difficulties. Most notably, none of these strategies involved minimizing the students' identification with their ethnic background. Rather, the strategies focus on providing a better understanding for the sources of group differences in achievement to both the students and their peers, as well as emphasizing the malleability and incremental nature of intelligence.

In chapter 4, Oyserman, Brickman, and Rhodes present a theoretical model that links African American and Latino students' racial and ethnic identity with their educational achievement. They then describe a series of students that indicate that having a strong sense of connectedness with one's ethnic and racial group as well as an awareness of racism and social obstacles is associated with a higher level of engagement and motivation at school. In addition, having a sense of oneself as being a member of both one's ethnic group and the larger society is associated with better psychological health. The studies demonstrate how holding positive views of one's ethnic and racial group is important for the educational adjustment of ethnic-minority students, but that students still need to be aware of and deal with the threats to their identity by social institutions and the larger society.

The ways in which many ethnic-minority students in American society must deal with threats to their identity is the focus of chapter 5, by Good, Dweck, and Aronson. The authors describe how the phenomenon of "stereotype threat" can influence the achievement activities of students who are in social groups devalued by the larger society. Through a fascinating set of experimental studies, the authors show how the fear of confirming the stereotypes of underachievement and lack of intelligence associated with their social groups can impede the performance of students in immediate achievement situations such as taking a test. These studies are critical in these days of high-stakes testing in the United States, where performance on standardized tests has a powerful impact upon the educational prospects of students. The authors then proceed to describe how social identities interact with the experiences of stereotype threat, either by exacerbating or by ameliorating the effects of threat according to the specific social identity that becomes involved. Finally, the authors show how the negative effects of stereotype threat can be minimized by emphasizing the malleable nature of intelligence to students, thereby giving students an important tool to fight back efforts of the larger society to, as described by Mahalingam in a previous chapter, "essentialize" their social groups in terms of innate intelligence.

In chapter 6, Lawrence, Bachman, and Ruble expand the social groups being studied by focusing on young children from immigrant Chinese, Dominican, and Russian families. The authors focus on the connections between ethnic identification, awareness of discrimination, and school valuing among groups that have spent relatively less time in the United States. They also explore the students' knowledge of social norms by asking whether their peers sanction academic motivation and effort, and include students from American-born families with African American and European American backgrounds. Their results show that despite having a higher level of anxiety about school, the students from immigrant and African American families valued school just as much as their counterparts from European American families. The students believed that their peers also valued schooling. Finally, a more positive identification with one's ethnic background generally was associated with more positive attitudes toward groups. There was no evidence that a stronger identification with one's ethnic or racial group was associated with oppositional attitudes toward school (also described by Oyserman, Brickman, and Rhodes among adolescents in chapter 4). In fact, just the opposite appears to the case.

In the final chapter of part II, Garcia and Crocker focus on women of color who attend four-year colleges and universities. Given that these students face dual stigmas about their academic capabilities because of the ethnicity and gender, the authors argue that it is important to focus on the students' psychological experiences as they progress through the different settings that constitute the American college experience. Garcia and Crocker employ an exciting method to naturalistically sample the daily experiences and settings of these students, and focus on the extent to which the students maintain their academic self-worth when faced with challenges to their academic abilities and self-concept. Their unique method shows how different academic settings at college can make the negative stereotypes of the women's social groups more salient to them, which can make them feel that their abilities are suspect. The women respond to this threat by emphasizing their self-concepts in their academic abilities. Although this can help the students deal with the immediate situation, the continuous experience of threat and the need to shore up one's self-concept and self-esteem can lead to less advantageous academic behaviors and outcomes over the long term. Garcia and Crocker close by proposing strategies for easing the pressure experience by these women, ranging from the institutional to the personal, that include several of the ideas expressed by in earlier chapters by Patterson and Bigler and by Good, Dweck, and Aronson.

Part III looks at how social relationships mediate the effects of social categories and identities. The association of students' ethnic identification with their academic motivation and performance raises the question of what might account for this link. Three chapters argue that the dynamics of social categories and social identities that were discussed in the first two sections of the book play themselves out in students' relationships with their peers and their families. Social identities, by definition, are based on individuals' interactions with their social environments. For children and adolescents, peers and families are the primary social relationships of their daily lives. These two social groups serve as key reference groups for students as they engage in the process of identity development, and it is likely that the messages children receive about the stereotypes regarding their social groups and their educational potential are learned through their interactions with peers and families. Likewise, the strategies that the students develop to combat those stereotypes and redefine their identities are learned and employed within these social groups. Consequently, any attempt to improve the educational participation of minority and marginalized groups must proceed from an understanding of how the dynamics of stereotyping, social identity, and academic achievement play themselves out in peer and family relationships.

Two key themes emerge from the chapters presented in this section.

First, students learn about the expectations that society and educational institutions have for them through their interactions with peers in the school setting. In particular, minority and disadvantaged students quickly learn about the social boundaries that delimit their participation, such as unofficial ethnically defined locations in the school that determine where students from different racial and ethnic groups enter the school, eat their lunch, and spend time with one another. Second, despite these challenges, students possess several strengths and strategies that they can employ to traverse these boundaries. These skills, or "tool kits," include the ability to employ multiple identities in different settings as well as a sense of purpose and obligation to succeed in school in order to repay their parents and fulfill their families' goals for a better life. As might be expected, some segments of the population continue to have difficulty when these unique skills and tools are not supported and conflict with the expectations of the society and its educational institutions. A primary goal of these chapters is to clearly identify the unique strengths of students from these groups so that they may be better appreciated and built upon when policies and programs to minimize educational inequalities are designed.

The first two chapters offer rich ethnographies that present compelling portraits of the complex and nuanced ways that adolescents from African American and Mexican backgrounds explore and negotiate the meanings of their ethnic identities with their families and friends. Carla O'Connor, Sonia DeLuca Fernández, and Brian Girard examine how social relationships, social spaces, and academic achievement become "racialized" in educational institutions with varying practices and varying demographic makeups of their student bodies. The authors follow four African American and black students as they move from a large, predominantly white high school to historically black colleges and universities. The organization of the high school into instructional wings resulted in the clustering of classrooms in which courses on different levels of the academic track were being taught in distinctly different parts of the school. The differential enrollment of students according to ethnicity resulted in the creation of very different social spaces of the school in which students congregated. The African American and other students gathered together in separate areas of school, serving to reify the association between ethnicity, race, and achievement and creating larger barriers for the African American students to cross in order to enroll in the more-advanced courses offered by the school. In their interviews, the four students discuss how academic success and being white became aligned with one another at Hillsdale, as a result of the social distribution and the social barriers of the students from different ethnic backgrounds. Much of this changed when the students entered the historically black colleges and universities, at which there was no longer a connection made between race and academic achievement and intelligence.

In chapter 9, Elizabeth Birr Moje and Magdalena Martinez emphasize how social-identity development is inherently relational, occurring within the context of meaningful social relationships. This is particularly true during the years of adolescence, a time of important changes in family and peer relationships, within which identities are tried on, explored, and either accepted or discarded. The description of these identity "enactments," as the authors call them, provide a nice complement to the largely psychological and phenomenological explorations of identity described in the second part of this book. Moje and Martinez effectively describe how the culturally and ethnically relevant "tool kits" such as language, traditions, and values that the adolescents acquire from their families eventually come into conflict with some of the norms and stereotypes of American society. As a result, many youths develop multiple identities that allow them to traverse the social boundaries that they increasingly face as they progress through the teenage years. These multiple, or hybrid, identities prove to be critical to the ways in which the students, many from immigrant families with parents who have had little formal education, negotiate and try to succeed in the American educational system.

In the final chapter, Andrew J. Fuligni, Gwendelyn J. Rivera, and April Leininger examine how the links between ethnic identity and educational engagement that have been highlighted in previous chapters of this volume may be due in part to the links between ethnic identity and students' connections with their families. The authors argue that family membership serves as an important social identity for many students from ethnic-minority and immigrant families, and they specifically focus on the sense of obligation to support, assist, and respect the family among children and adolescents from Asian and Latin American backgrounds. Fuligni, Rivera, and Leininger summarize a series of studies and present four case studies that highlight how a sense of obligation to the family, which is linked to the students' ethnic and cultural identification, is an important source of their belief in the importance of schooling. In particular, it is one reason for the high levels of academic motivation reported by many students from Asian and Latin American backgrounds. A sense of obligation is also associated with the very real need to help the family on the part of students whose families are in difficult economic circumstances, and high levels of family assistance can make it difficult for poorer students from Asian and Latin American backgrounds to continue their education after high school.

Thus, through the use of diverse perspectives and methods to look at diverse populations, the chapters in this volume collectively provide a rich portrait of how factors such as race, ethnicity, gender, and socio-economic status are more than just cold demographic characteristics that categorize members of a society. Rather, these are social categories that have powerful social meanings and stereotypes that are employed by social institutions and their members to differentially distribute educational opportunities and resources, either intentionally or unintentionally. Even the best-intentioned efforts to address educational inequalities may unwittingly feed into existing stereotypes or trigger the tendency of students and school personnel to categorize and rank groups according to their educational potential. Students on the losing end of the distribution of educational resources and attainment find powerful and creative ways to battle against such stereotypes. Yet these efforts are not without their own costs, especially if they are not recognized and supported by the educational institutions that serve these students. Several of the authors suggest concrete ways to build upon the existing strengths of these students, ways that enable the students to maintain a positive identification with their social group as they participate more fully in the educational system.

References

Buchmann, Claudia, and Emily Hannum. 2001. "Education and Stratification in Development Countries: A Review of Theories and Research." *Annual Review of Sociology* 27: 77

Fuligni, Andrew J., and Christina Hardway. 2004. "Preparing Diverse Adolescents for the Transition to Adulthood." The Future of Children 14(2): 99–119.

Laird, Jennifer, Stephen Lew, Matthew DeBell, and Chris Chapman. 2006. Dropout Rates in the United States: *2002* and *2003*. NCES publication no. 2006-062. Washington: U.S. Department of Education, National Center for Education Statistics.

Ogbu, John U. 1987. "Variability in Minority School Performance: A Problem in Search of an Explanation." *Anthropology and Education Quarterly* 18(4): 312–34.

Shavit, Yossi, and Hans-Peter Blossfeld. 1993. *Persistent Inequality: Changing Educational Attainment in Thirteen Countries*. Boulder, Colo.: Westview Press.

PART I

How Social Categories and Their Meanings Shape Educational Opportunities and Barriers

Chapter 1

Past as Present, Present as Past: Historicizing Black Education and Interrogating "Integration"

Anne Galletta and William E. Cross, Jr.

O ne of the objectives of the works included in this volume is to interrogate the so-called achievement gap between mainstream white and Asian American students as compared to minority students in general and black students in particular. The current chapter focuses on the latter, although our analysis has implications for the general discourse on the achievement gap. The intractability of the problem within the black community moved the late and renowned anthropologist, John Ogbu, to search beyond racism in his effort to pinpoint the origins of the gap, and instead to probe the dynamics of black culture and traditions (Ogbu 1987, 1998, 2003, 2004). Ogbu noted that blacks entered America on an involuntary basis, and during the nearly two hundred and fifty years that the institution of slavery lasted, captive Africans evolved various forms of psychological resistance to protect their humanity. In forging an "oppositional identity," the captive Africans, according to Ogbu's interpretation, achieved a modicum of self-definition, with a cost of cultural alienation from aspects of the dominant "white" culture. Ogbu believed that by anchoring blackness as the opposite of whiteness and by including schooling and education under the rubric of "whiteness," blacks initially developed a cynicism, estrangement, and resistance to achievement that stemmed from the slavery experience.

Since slavery was followed by years of legally sanctioned racial segregation, or the era of Jim Crow (circa 1890 to 1954), Ogbu concluded that historical circumstances never made possible an intervention, transformation, or corrective drift toward high achievement. Consequently, over time, what was originally a "healthy" response to slavery and the crude realities of life in the Deep South during the first half of the twentieth century "ossified" and became an anachronistic aspect of black culture. According to this perspective, blacks continue to "resist" and be "oppositional" even when they are nested in educational environments characterized by opportunity, equality, fairness, and choice rather than exclusion, stigma, inequality, and racism.

In his recent study of academic disengagement among black students in the Cleveland suburb of Shaker Heights, Ohio, Ogbu (2003, 2004) extends his theory of oppositional identity and black underachievement beyond poor and working-class black families to middle-class blacks in an affluent suburb. In locating oppositional identity and black underachievement among the black middle class, his theory gained greater credence, because in the face of the freedom and multiple "choices" afforded middle-class status, he could point to blacks who were conducting imaginary battles with racism, even when such vigilance seemed unnecessary and the resulting depressed achievement levels dysfunctional. Thus, Ogbu thought it critical to demonstrate the existence of academic oppositionalism among both poor and middle-class black students and its omnipresence or ubiquity became a pillar undergirding his theory that oppositionalism and underachievement were endemic to black culture and likely were the "legacy" of slavery and years of post-slavery oppression.

Historicizing Black Education: Black Achievement Motivation Following the Civil War

John Ogbu was not the first person to isolate, document, and theorize the existence of black educational oppositionalism, for in many ways his theory is an extension of observations made years earlier by Kenneth Clark in his ground-breaking text of the 1960s, *Dark Ghetto* (1965), or, reaching back still further, related themes can also be found in Carter G. Woodson's 1933 classic, *The Miseducation of the Negro* (Woodson 1933). Shortly we shall reveal the discovery of instances of academic oppositionalism and "planned" underachievement in our own research, but it is one thing to come to terms with the actual existence of academic oppositionalism in the behavior of today's black students and another to draw a straight line between the present and past by invoking the legacy-of-slavery thesis. We contest the legacy argument and show that contemporary displays of oppositionalism and muted achievement by black students are more readily traceable to structural elements and educational policies that define integrated schooling. But before deconstructing what is meant by "integrated schooling," let us step back in time to debunk the legacy-of-slavery myth.

In the late 1950s and early 1960s, there was considerable historical evidence that the ex-slaves became involved in educational activities almost immediately following the collapse of slavery (Bullock 1967; Butchart 1980; Du Bois 1935; Woodson 1919). At first, historians concluded, the ex-slaves' educational agenda had been suggested, imposed, or made possible by external influences such as key leaders in the Union Army and white teachers and benefactors who flooded the South to assist in helping the slaves transition to freedom. In this scenario, the ex-slaves had to be "shown" or convinced of the value of formal education. Whatever interest or enthusiasm they displayed toward schooling was thought to have been triggered by outsiders.

The image of the post–Civil War black community as neutral, passive, or at best naïve to the value of education extends into the history of black education in the 1930s, as evidenced by the fact that wealthy white northern philanthropists, such as Julius Rosenwald, the head of the Julius Rosenwald Fund, were depicted as having to prod the rural black communities of the 1920s and 1930s to build schools for their children. The Rosenwald Fund started a project to build schools in southern communities. Its agents would enter a rural black community, help the community organize itself for the purpose of building the first schools to service blacks in the county in question, and put up funds, which the community had to "match" as a demonstration that it agreed with the educational thrust being pressed by the foundation. This theme of black attitudinal underdevelopment drives the historical record on the evolution of black education up to the late 1960s, and is central to the standard text on the topic, *A History of Negro Education in the South, 1619 to the Present*, by Henry Allen Bullock (1967). It should be noted that although Bullock and others did not speak explicitly of a legacy of slavery, their depiction of ex-slaves as passive, crude, and naïve and their description of rural blacks of the 1920s and 1930s as being in need of conversion to the value of education comes very close to saying that from the end of slavery into the twentieth century the value of education was not organic to black culture.

In 1935, W. E. B. Du Bois, one of the leading intellects of the twentieth century, published a radical critique of the then-current mainstream perspectives on America's failed attempt to proactively transition blacks from the status of slave to citizen. In his controversial text *Black Reconstruction*, Du Bois accords greater agency to blacks themselves. He paints a picture of the average ex-slave "demanding" education for black children; however, because Du Bois was at the time an avowed Communist, his depiction of the ex-slaves as agentic, focused, and self-motivated toward education was considered "radical" history. *Black Reconstruction* was a masterfully written history of the Reconstruction period that reflected the application of state-of-the-art historiography, so it could not be summarily dismissed. However, by depicting blacks as the social equal of others, it became a thorn in the side of mainstream historians, never fully dismissed but never fully accepted, either.

Observers of the black experience would have to wait until 1988 and the publication of *The Education of Black Americans in the South, 1860–1935*, a ground breaking work by James D. Anderson, before they could fully comprehend that the adult ex-slaves and their children transitioned from slavery to freedom holding attitudes toward the value and importance of education that not only were positive and reflective of high achievement motivation but also matched the positive attitudes toward education once associated only with ethnic white immigrants who would not hit America's shores for another twenty to forty years. Anderson traces the origins of high black achievement motivation (BAM) to the worldview developed by blacks within the context of slavery. Even without the benefit of literacy, the slave community was able to decipher how formal education helped explain the social hierarchy found among whites, in that landless, poor, and politically vulnerable whites were typically those who had little or no education, whereas the plantation owners, schoolteachers for the owners' children, and key figures in the larger white society evidenced the benefits of formal education. Though they were but a tiny fraction of the slaves' ecology, there were often pockets of free blacks near the plantation and the free black community teemed with educational activities. It was not uncommon for educated free blacks to assist in the formal education of the slave owner's children, and clearly this made an impression on the average slave. From time to time, a literate black would fashion a pamphlet urging blacks to rise up and overthrow the owners, and near the end of slavery, the abolitionist movement provided written as well as living icons, such as Frederick Douglass, that clearly guided the average slave toward a nuanced understanding of the "power" of literacy and formal education.

Anderson shows how such experiences and observations helped shape the educational attitudes of the slaves such that when they left slavery, one of their most potent assets was a positive attitude toward education. From Anderson's research we see the ex-slaves beginning the education of their children before friends from the Union Army and teachers and supporters of black freedom from the North even came into contact with the ex-slaves. However, when the ex-slaves and white sympathizers did eventually make contact, the fusion of the ex-slaves' desire for formal education and the immense resources of the northern Army in conjunction with the aid of northern sympathizers, including many black teachers willing to return to the South at the risk of their lives and futures, exploded into a social movement for black education

(Cross 2003). William E. Cross, Jr., has shown that had the drive for education and meaningful freedom been allowed to run its natural course, by the beginning of the twentieth century, some forty years after the end of the Civil War, blacks would have been disproportionately represented across all levels of the public education establishment in the South, including in higher education.

Finally, Anderson was able to link BAM to black educational activities in the South up to the beginning of the Great Depression in the 1930s. Black tenant farmers were the poorest of the poor, yet so motivated were they to educate their children that they in effect double- and in some case triple-taxed themselves to make it happen. Anderson points out that during the Jim Crow era, southern rural blacks seldom saw a fair share of their tax dollars spent on the education of their children. So blacks would impose on themselves a second tax by holding a festival where people volunteered their labor, bartered goods, and gave money to build rural schoolhouses. The schools were built on land given to the black community by one of its land-owning members. Yet another festival might be scheduled to raise funds to pay the teachers' salaries and buy books. Anderson also uncovered historical documents showing that when, in the 1920s and 1930s, the Julius Rosenwald Fund injected its presence into a black community, there was no evidence of the community's having to be prodded to embrace the education of their children. If anything, Anderson showed that the fund's importance has tended to be exaggerated, for in looking at the projects supported by it, time and again the black community itself provided the larger sum of funds and material support in the building of a "Rosenwald school." With equal force and clarity, he also documents the way in which the larger white-controlled society systematically turned its back on the black community by segregating it and, where possible, radically underfunding black education. "Separate" never approached "equal."

In summary, there is no legacy of slavery that explains the educational attitudes found among contemporary blacks, whether they be the children of the poor or of the middle class. Given that Anderson's work and the follow-up research that gave it even greater credibility did not appear until 1988 and later, it is understandable how Ogbu and others might have entertained the legacy-of-slavery thesis. More difficult to comprehend is why Ogbu held on to this discredited thesis long after the historical studies that disprove it were readily available. There simply is no straight line between the educational attitudes slaves embraced when they exited slavery and the evolution of oppositional attitudes held by a significant portion of black youths in the present. The origin of such attitudes is much more recent than Ogbu and others have been able to comprehend.

Interrogating "Integration": Attending to Policy and Student Experience of Systemic Factors

Fast-forwarding to the present, the second part of this chapter draws on new work (Galletta 2003) that focuses on the history of school integration within the Shaker Heights, Ohio, school district (referred to henceforth referenced as the Galletta study). This study synthesizes archival materials, original school documents, newspaper reports, interviews with key teachers and administrators, and interviews with different cohorts of both white and black parents as well as with youths and alumni who attended the Shaker Heights schools between 1965 and 2003. The Galletta study offers a fine-grained discussion of the policies, practices, strategies, and narratives linked to the Shaker Heights integration experience.[1]

The Galletta study was never meant to be a counterpoint to the late John Ogbu's important work on the Shaker Heights schools, as Anne Galletta's original motivations for undertaking the dissertation were grounded in her own personal history as a resident of Shaker Heights and mother of children who continue to attend the district schools. In fact, she made the Shaker Heights–John Ogbu connection after much of her own data collection was completed. Reflecting a desire to capture the frames of reference of informants on their own terms, and guided by an interdisciplinary base of desegregation history, educational policy, and social psychological theory, the Galletta study engaged grounded data and extant theory in the analysis of the data (Lather 1986; Weis and Fine 2004). Nevertheless, the Galletta study now stands as an important counterpoint in that it complicates, rather than negates, the Ogbu thesis by showing that it underestimates the power of certain integration polices and practices and exaggerates the role of black culture in explaining the origins of black student oppositional attitudes. In light of John Ogbu's recent and premature passing, we regret not being able to engage him directly, but we hope our discourse reflects the high esteem with which we approach his scholarship.

Brown and the Shaker Heights Integration Experience: 1965 to the Present

America's response to the 1954 Brown v. Board of Education Supreme Court decision—with its mandate to provide an "equal" and integrated education—varied by state, region, and school district. Virginia simply shut down those schools in which black and white children would attend classes together (Irons 2002), and other southern states came close to instituting the same strategy of resistance. As noted by Orfield (1978), white students in the South were serviced by top-quality "alternate" systems, while the public schools, now the province of mostly black students, were grossly underfunded, understaffed, and cut off from key components of the larger society. Northern as well as southern urban centers saw whites simply abandon urban districts and move to distant suburbs, creating a form of American apartheid (Massey and Denton 1993). Many whites did not change their place of residence but simply pulled their children out of the public schools and enrolled them in private schools.

Other school systems—such as Hyde Park in Chicago; Evanston, Illinois; Montclair, New Jersey; and Shaker Heights, Ohio—struggled to define proactive strategies that let integration happen by positive design, courage, and good planning. In Shaker Heights, there was a powerful drive among educators to carry out the mandate of Brown. On the other hand, the school district sought to sustain itself financially and preserve its stellar reputation. These dual needs in effect translated into not only stemming white flight but also building white confidence in the district's capacity to sustain quality in the face of integration. The double institutional prerogative also reflected the views of the students, parents, and educators in this city. While some white residents on the school board and in neighborhood meetings supported and even brokered desegregation efforts, others opposed them outright or accepted desegregation conditionally. In this situation, the social and material capital of this historically affluent community has been a powerful lever in supporting the district's commitment to racial diversity and good schools, but it has also served as a drag on the extent to which educational policies designed to facilitate racial and economic equality are actually carried out.

In this sense, education is truly a "property of power" (Ng 1982) and as a source of social advantage its distribution is frequently contested. This is key to our deconstruction: that desegregation has meant access to a privilege once enjoyed only by whites. In this sense, privilege is intimately tied up with exclusion, since what has historically contributed to the school system's privileged status is the exclusion of others by race and class. While notions of "equality" were explored and debated, terms like "standards" and "excellence" remained impervious to scrutiny, creating a firewall around those policies and practices presumed to sustain "quality," while simultaneously replicating race and class inequalities.

The Galletta study of the integration history in Shaker Heights explored four principal areas:

1. *Racial balance or literal integration.* These are efforts to make it possible for black and white children to attend the same schools, regardless of the racial composition of the immediate neighborhoods where their individual households are located.

2. *Enactments of quality and excellence.* These are the policies and practices, such as the levels system and various enrichment and remedial programs, meant to sustain the district's pre-integration historical reputation for educational excellence.

3. *Adjustments, interventions, and "fixes."* Actions taken when some aspect of the original integration policy or strategy causes unintended, negative consequences.

4. *Narratives.* Stories told by students in their narration of the integration experience.

Racial Balance or Literal Integration

Shaker Heights, an upscale, and newly developed affluent suburb of Cleveland, was incorporated in 1912. Until 1955, the city and its school system were segregated. Shaker Heights used restrictive racial and religious covenants in its property sales, until the Supreme Court ruled these practices unconstitutional in 1948 in Shelly v. Kraemer.[2] Still, realtors encouraged or pressured their clients to abide by these now-illegal covenants through the 1960s.[3] The first neighborhood within Shaker Heights to desegregate was Ludlow, bordering on Cleveland; it drew middle-class and professional African Americans in the late 1950s from the Cleveland area. This neighborhood, through the work of its community association, engaged financial institutions and realty firms in crafting policies that stemmed white flight. However, in the nearby Moreland neighborhood, working-class white families abandoned the area upon the arrival of middle- and working-class African American families, and Moreland resegregated. Other Shaker Heights neighborhoods to the east remained predominantly white and middle class, with very affluent families located along the wooded northern boundaries of the city in the Boulevard and Malvern areas. Moreland and Ludlow, the neighborhoods reflecting significant demographic change, were often referred to as "the other side of the tracks," whereas the areas to the north and east were viewed as "deep Shaker,"all-white and impenetrable to blacks.

These distinctions are both historical and contemporary, and they carry race and class signifiers evident in the narratives of students, parents, and educators. Also evident in the data is the classification as "pioneers" of the black families who first desegregated Ludlow. Implicit in the story of the "pioneers," however, is the story of the "trespassers," black families that stretch beyond their working-class means to move their children into middle-class status. This group in particular has experienced the greatest struggle in fully realizing the educational opportunities available in the Shaker Heights City School District. Nevertheless, even the pioneers' educational and economic standing did not fully ensure access to the same sites of educational privilege as it did for white students.

From 1965 to the present, the school district has struggled to make racial balance or "literal integration" a reality in all the elementary and middle schools, regardless of whether the neighborhood site of the school was "deep Shaker" or "the other side of the tracks." Integration took place fairly quickly at the high school, because there was and continues to be only one high school servicing the entire district. However, at the elementary and junior high schools, racial balance would be a new venture. The school district has reconfigured its racial-balance strategy to stay ahead of demographic shifts through mandatory and voluntary policies as well as a district-wide reorganization in 1987. Currently, nearly all elementary schools are racially balanced, while the upper elementary school, middle school and high school serve the entire district. To a certain extent, the fact that Shaker Heights continuously struggled to make "literal integration" a reality was a victory for the black community and progressive and moderate whites. Being admitted to the same schools and entering the same buildings meant to many that black and white children would experience the same classes, the same teachers, the same curriculum, and the same overall quality education.

Quality Education and Excellence: Sustaining the Shaker Heights Tradition for Educational Excellence

Not only was the Shaker Heights educational establishment victorious in the promotion of an aggressive racial-balance program at the level of practically every school building, even in the face of objections from segments of the "deep Shaker" population, but it also was prohibited from equivocating on how quality and excellence would be sustained within each building and across the system as a whole. The strategy for programmatic quality also involved change. Before 1964, the district offered a few advanced-placement classes and provided a rigorous college preparatory program for most of its students. Then, at the very same time the district was experiencing high migration of black students into the district, the high school introduced a new five-category "levels system."[4] Subsequently, the junior highs, particularly the more economically and racially diverse Woodbury, instituted "individual pupil scheduling."[5]

The district introduced the levels system as an educationally sound practice and an indicator of excellence.[6] It distinguished course levels from academic tracks and tracking in the following manner: "The system is unique in Shaker Heights, though many schools have instructional tracks, a closely allied method of ability grouping. Students . . . are not frozen at any level in any subject, but may choose in time to move to another level."[7] In a manner of speaking, the upper tracks would service gifted and advanced children and the middle and lower tracks the less-gifted and regular students. In this light, the new system would provide quality and continuity to satisfy white and black middle-class families, and theoretically, at least, provide access to other students who might start out at one level and progress over time to a higher level. A full-fledged levels system did not make educational sense in elementary schools, but what evolved were special enrichment programs for the gifted that had the effect of being precursors or feeder programs designed to funnel students into upper levels in junior high (later, the middle school) and high school.

Early on, placement into programs and levels in the junior high and high school relied heavily on some combination of testing and teacher recommendation. Use of tests was considered part of a fair and color-blind way of administering quality and excellence. Over time and with increased scrutiny, enrollment at the higher levels became increasingly "open" and did not require testing or teacher recommendation. However, participation in enrichment programs at the upper elementary school (now Woodbury School) requires students to achieve a designated high score on standardized tests.

The program of testing and placement in the early grades and the district's policy of "open" levels at the middle and high school exemplify quality control strategies common in desegregated school systems such as Shaker Heights. The racial-balance strategy made literal integration a reality within each school building, while the combination of enrichment programs and the high school levels system met or exceeded the demands of "deep Shaker" that the district as a whole continue its legacy of excellence for all children (Bell 1995, 2004). The many white and small number of black parents saw in these educational programs a clear pathway for their children to socially and educationally reproduce their privileged status. They also took for granted that for those "trespassers" with the right stuff, the system also made possible social mobility to the extent that black working-class students took advantage of the various programs and levels classes.

Program Adjustments, Fixes, and Interventions: Addressing the Achievement Gap

Early in the district's experience with integrated education, officials publicly and privately expressed concern about the gap between standardized test scores of black students and white students. Differences in test scores translated into differential participation in programs for gifted children at the elementary level, and in the higher-level courses in the upper grades. Black and white students were entering the same buildings, but once in school, they separated and headed for classes that were racially identifiable (Mickelson 2001; O'Connor, DeLuca Fernández, and Girard, chapter 8, this volume). At the elementary and middle school level, white students dominated the enrichment programs, save for a few black children of the middle class. At the high school, black students predominated in the lower and middle levels and the higher levels were largely white.

Archival materials from the period 1965 to 1980 reveal little debate among officials and the general public concerning the relationship between racially identifiable course levels and the gap in test scores by race and class. The gap was discussed in isolation from the levels system. Beginning in 1980, questions about the levels system and racial isolation in the system came into focus, particularly at the initiative of African American parents, but so far the system remains in place. Enrichment programs and the levels system continue to be seen as race-neutral, and even the standardized tests are viewed as color-blind (Peller 1995; Schofield 1982). Race-neutrality emerges in the narrative data as well. A white educator, who reflected on how her style of teaching may once have excluded black students, noted that she and many of her colleagues often equated color-blindness with equality. From this perspective, race "differences" pointed not to problems in teaching methods, curriculum, access, or the school system but to problems within the students themselves. She noted it was not uncommon for teachers to affirm (perhaps not out loud), "I'm treating everyone equally; I don't see what their problem is."

In 1997, the achievement gap between black and white students at the high school took on added significance through the publication of a report in *Shakerite*, the student newspaper, dramatically presenting the "races" as distributed by tracks, with blacks at the middle and bottom and seldom represented at the top levels, which were occupied mostly by whites. The event reveals the high degree of contestation of beliefs concerning the causal factors for the gap. While some teachers and parents felt the urgency of the issue justified the article's publication, others, particularly African American parents and students, were angered by the one-sided portrayal of all black students as underperforming (Patterson and Bigler, chapter 3, this volume).[8] The article appeared during Black History Month, and many resented that as well. The lack of representation of black students on the *Shakerite* staff also contributed to black students' and parents' suspicions about the intentions underlying the article. Additionally, the power of such unnuanced reports served to reinforce racial stereotypes concerning achievement and motivation, as evident in the comments of one white student's reflections on the data provided in the article:

> It [the article] was factual information that they were presenting, it was not an opinionated article. It was these are the scores, there is a problem that there is this racial difference in test scores, and these kids are coming from the same elementary schools, and the same middle schools, the same high schools, there shouldn't be—such a discrepancy in who's in the AP classes and who's in the general classes and who's scoring this and who's scoring that, um, so I think it was a very eye-opening article that sort of got started this initiative of trying to—bring up the scores and bring up the level of achievement of African American students, and I think that one of the things that was focused on there was that family involvement, that if the education is not supported in the home, then it's not gonna go very far.

Many black parents voiced a different point of view. They longed for a "report" that interrogated the system, which in their eyes made it nearly impossible for their children to perform at their best. A black middle-class father noted that he encountered teachers who questioned the academic competence of his child on the basis not of his child's performance but of the teachers' acceptance of racial stereotypes. Although his children attended school in the 1970s, his frustration reflected similar experiences narrated by black parents in more recent years. He summarized the teachers' attitudes toward black students as follows: "I don't believe you read this book, I don't believe you are supposed to be in this class. I don't believe [this or that]. [Now] prove yourself!" This parent noted that after repeated encounters with such enactments of exclusion, it became increasingly difficult for him to support the authority of the school system. Although his son was eligible for the advanced classes, he experienced racial isolation within these classes. Ultimately this parent chose to transfer his son to a private school, noting:

> I believe teachers should be respected and trusted, and once you say that teachers are going to make decisions that you believe are unjust, it's hard to trust [them], [and] I had to come out [take my child out of the public schools]. . . . If the school system is elevating some [kids] . . . because of one variable or another, then it's very hard for a parent to avoid buying into the same system, okay, because you're gonna be suggesting to your kids that somehow they're [other kids] not as bright, or they're not as fast. . . . [So taking your kid out is] a matter of self-defense.

One black mother whose children were also in the high-level classes in the 1970s recalled the distraught nature of a black father's response to the school system, when he declared, "They're killing our students!" and described his children's experience as "murder in the classroom!" This parent continued:

And I thought, "Gee, this man is crazy!" That was before our kids went to school. . . . He had had some experiences [and] . . . it was trauma for him. I mean, and so, people just sort of looked at him, like he was not with it. Until you *really* found out that there were some of these attitudes [about our kids in the schools].

Another mother who was African American and whose child graduated from high school in the 1990s told the story of her child coming home and saying of some other black boys, "Those kind of kids are always bad—they always have to sit in the corner." She visited her child's classroom and observed various forms of inappropriate behavior on the part of a number of the boys in general but she noticed it was the "very kinetic black boys" who were singled out for punishment. She noted that the teacher depicted the black but not the white boys as being "out of control." The same parent said that later, in high school, it was this group of boys who were enrolled in alternative classes, often located in the basement of the high school, or taking "CP" class—that is, class for "colored people."[9] She felt these students had lost interest over the years and did not want to learn.

The concerns of the black parents, particularly the activism, in the 1970s of the group Concerned Parents and of Caring Communities Organized for Education in the 1990s and continuing to the present, coupled with the targeted efforts of a number of black and white educators, resulted in the implementation of new programs focused on student support, intense skill building, and the development of study skills. The first example of this occurred in 1979 with the establishment of the tutoring center for junior high and high school students, providing free tutoring by certified teachers after school in the afternoon and the evening four days a week.[10]

More recently, there was a coming together of teachers in the high school to respond to their concerns about the differentials between white and black students in accessing educational opportunities and producing academic outcomes. The faculty achievement committee at the high school was formed around 1983, and their study of the gap, which included the participation of a number of high-achieving black male students, led to the formation of the Minority Achievement Committee (MAC) scholars, beginning in 1991, the establishment of the MAC Sisters several years later, and then the establishment of both programs reaching down to fifth grade in the 2000–2001 school year. In the late 1990s, through the work of a white educator, study circles were established, based on research conducted by Urie Triesman at the University of Texas at Austin on engaging students of color in math and science education. This program, designed to provide support for students enrolled in the advanced classes, particularly African American students, expanded to include the middle and upper elementary school in the 2002–2003 school year. In 1999, with fourteen other urban and suburban school districts, the school system also formed a consortium called the Minority Student Achievement Network (MSAN) "to improve the academic achievement of students of color."[11]

Student Narratives: Integration as a Lived Experience

We now turn to narratives told by white and black students. To fully study the enigma of the "gap," the experience of both groups of young people must be analyzed. There is diversity within these narratives, but there also are disturbing patterns and trends by race and class. Here, we discover black students narrating how they maintained an academic sense of self in the face of school experiences that were ambiguously if not openly racist. We also come to understand the narrations of white students who express either uncomplicated privilege or an uneasy awareness that notions of merit, choice, and an "open" levels system have effectively obscured their race and class advantage.

Jill   Jill, a white student who graduated from the high school in the late 1990s, began high school enrolled in all high-level classes. She felt she gained a lot from the school system's academic excellence and its racial diversity. At Lomond Elementary School and in the upper elementary Woodbury School, she participated in the gifted program, which she characterized as a strength of the Shaker Heights schools. She noted these were "great programs," and that they provided "a lot of creativity beyond just the basics" in math and language arts.

While Jill's experience reflects an experience central to sites of educational privilege, she did tell of a struggle in high school she had with a teacher in an advanced-placement class. She received an A in this class early on, but after she earned a B, Jill noted the teacher exhibited persistent antagonism toward her. She considered dropping down a level, but ultimately decided she did not want to leave the AP level nor sever her social ties with the cohort of students she had traveled with throughout her years in Shaker Heights. She stated, "Once you get into that [high] track, you're with the same people, for most of the same classes. . . . Those are the people that you're seeing and doing stuff with."

It is important to look at Jill's reasoning for remaining in her AP class and the factors that reinforced her sense that she belonged there. Jill narrated a compatible subjectivity as "student" that had been fostered over her many years of experiencing inclusion in sites of educational privilege. There was no previous experience of dissonance to compound this particular encounter with a teacher's negativity toward Jill. Toward this end, there were no racial stereotypes about achievement and motivation to threaten her position as an advanced-placement student in the high school. In fact, the stereotypes affirmed her position in the predominantly white class and helped her ward off this teacher's enactment of exclusion toward her (Good, Dweck, and Aronson, chapter 5, this volume). If the negative stereotypes about black students acted as a social psychological boundary for their movement upward to higher tracks, the positive stereotypes concerning whites meant that these students were far less likely to exit the higher tracks. In Jill's case, the social and structural factors support her implicit assignment to the high levels in the district's "open" levels system. In a manner of speaking, Jill was "stuck" within the higher track.

Mark   Mark, a white student during the early 2000s, entered the system as a transfer student, coming from a nearby suburban district. Early on he had trouble keeping up in his higher-level courses, but his parents were in contact with his teachers, who provided support. In his own struggle to "belong" in the higher-level classes, Mark narrated an understanding of the racial stereotypes about achievement and motivation that white and black students absorb. He indicated that for a white student, the assumption was that the student took honors or advanced placement. And if a student was enrolled in advanced-placement classes, others assumed that student to be a good student. Hence, white students were good students, "even if you haven't proved yourself to be." When asked about the assumptions attached to students who take college preparatory classes, he noted that students' views of another student's enrollment in these classes depended on the student's race. Here he most clearly articulated the difficulty of resisting a racial stereotype that was reinforced in the enrollment patterns by race evident in an "open" enrollment system. Calling it a "battle," he noted that many students were unwilling to fully explore the complex factors at work in the school system such that fewer black students accessed educational opportunities such as the higher-level courses:

> I think the general judgment is, if you're in, if you're a white kid in CP classes, you're lazy, and if you're a black kid in CP classes—it's expected . . . I guess that's it, if you're a white kid in CP classes, they assume you're lazy or you don't, you don't want to try hard. But if you're a black kid, they won't really judge you because they don't, you know, people really don't—they don't want to get in that battle or whatever it is.

Mark's father, Matt, also attended Shaker Heights schools and participated in one of the early integration programs. Matt talked about his interactions with teachers in making them aware of Mark's struggle to complete assignments under very short deadlines. Matt reported that teachers responded positively and were supportive of his son. However, he also discussed how he felt racial stereotypes were operating within parent-teacher interactions, and these stereotypes made it more likely that teachers would perceive Mark's difficulty as a learning problem, a solution to which the teacher and parent could support. Matt noted that he felt African American parents presenting a similar case were more likely to have their child's difficulty interpreted as a motivational problem.

Stephen Black students sometimes narrated what can be called the "zigzag" story line in that they bounced from one academic frame to another and sometimes back again. Stephen, an African American student, grew up in the predominantly black Moreland area and graduated from high school in the early 1990s. He spoke very fondly of the Moreland School, and told me he was "proud to be from Moreland," because they were "doing big things there"—the school had won an award for its academic excellence and educational activities. It was "the black school in the district,"[12] and its principal was an African American man. Stephen recalled that at the close of the school day, the principal, who knew his students well, would say good-bye to the students by name. Stephen's academic performance was above his grade level, so he took some subjects in classes with students in the older grades. He was also one of the very small number of African American students who participated in "Moreland's Math Projects" class, an advanced math class offered as part of the school's magnet program.

When Stephen reached the upper elementary grades, his father thought there might be more opportunities in a predominantly white school, and his parents transferred Stephen from Moreland to a predominantly white school through the Shaker Schools Plan for voluntary school transfer.[13] He said he "hated" his experience at this school. "I felt alienated, being [a] new kid, but also being [from] Moreland." He stated that his teacher had a negative attitude toward him. It seemed to him that his teacher, also African American, "disciplined black kids differently," and was more lenient with white children. Like several other African American students interviewed, Stephen wondered aloud whether he could be imagining this. There was a noticeable drop in his school performance.

He described a split in a formerly coherent view of himself as a "student." At the middle school and in his early years in high school he did not enroll in higher-level courses. He was not focused on classes and grades, although he was active in the high school band, which he en-joyed very much. He said, "I saw how much attention I was getting and that was my focus. [My] focus [was more] being popular than being smart." He noted that a lot of this solidified for him while he was in the predominantly white school, saying, "To be black was to be—you had [to] be more cool than smart, you had to know how to fight." He stated that if you "succumbed to academia, you were an Oreo," and, "I had been alienated at [name of predominantly white school]; [I] didn't want to be alienated again."

Stephen's trajectory from within sites of educational privilege to out-side them was dramatically halted the year he learned he would be held back a grade and would not enter high school. "That was the day the world stood still." Several educators became closely involved with his academic progress and made strong connections with him during the year he repeated, and he was able to make further connections with more educators during the years that followed. These individuals de-flected the enactments of exclusion and competing subjectivities that he continued to encounter as a black student, particularly a black male student reentering sites of academic privilege. Stephen stated that in the one advanced-placement course he eventually elected to take in high school, he experienced inclusion and a compatible subjectivity as "student." He described the teacher of this AP class as someone who valued his opinion and in whose class, where he was the only African American male student, he felt fully supported and included. Addi-tionally, Stephen told me the principal of the high school was "very in-fluential, very powerful" in engaging him in academics. At the same time, Stephen dreaded meeting with his high school counselor. His counselor did not discuss opportunities at the different course levels and was "rather reluctant" to let him take an advanced-placement course. Stephen "blew the counselor out of the water" when the coun-selor saw how well Stephen performed in the advanced-placement course. In the end the counselor wrote him a recommendation for col-lege, but only, in a sense, after Stephen "proved" himself by scoring high on tests.

Diana   The "zigzag" pattern narrated by Stephen is echoed in Diana's narrative but the outcome is a downward trajectory. Diana is an African American student who graduated from high school in the early 2000s. Her experience with schooling had been an uneasy one. She loved her elementary school but she had "conflicts" with all her teachers. In her interview, she noted that she did not think the teachers accepted what she said as truthful, but then, like Stephen at a predominantly white school, she wandered into a less defensive stance, concluding, "I don't know, maybe it was just me." In middle school, however, she had a class with a teacher whom she described as having "just completely opened my mind to something completely new." She noted that she felt very comfortable with this teacher, who was also African American, a person for whom she had "great respect and admiration." She invested a lot of effort in his class, saying "I came to his class every day, I did my work to the best of my ability."

When Diana entered Shaker Heights High School, she was enrolled in the Humanities Program, a less demanding program, even though she had passed the state mandated proficiency tests in eighth grade and thus qualified for higher placement.[14] Predominantly black students are enrolled in this program. Diana loved her teachers, who supported and encouraged her, and ironically, she was reluctant to move up from the Humanities Program to the "regular" program, because "I got decent grades, and I was, I had a sense of belonging, I had a relationship with the teachers." Here, her strong connections with teachers in the Humanities Program evolved into a rationale as to why she should not move up to a higher track. In addition, she did not see herself as "honors material" or "book-smart." When asked for a definition of "honors material," she said that it meant dedicating time outside of school to studying and doing homework. She was quite adamant about her unwillingness to do this, but she noted that she might make an exception for a teacher she had in the middle school, noting that her attitude in his class was "I'm gonna do it because I, I don't want to let him down." Though Diana was comfortable in what can be called sites of educational exclusion, characterized by strong student-educator relationships within less academically rigorous settings, she also knew them to be inferior to the sites in which most white students participated. Therefore she did not view education as equally available to black and white students within the school system.

Nika   Nika, an African American female student who graduated from high school in the middle 1990s, was in the gifted track, beginning with the Ludlow Elementary School Special Program for the gifted, followed by advanced classes in the fifth through eighth grades and advanced placement in the Shaker Heights High School. Although she was the product of educational privilege, she narrated what it was like to be caught between black and mainstream white experiences, located within sites of educational privilege but on the periphery.

Originally, Nika was not bothered by the negative vibes she felt coming from the African American children who remained in the regular as compared to gifted classes, noting, "It was the black girls . . . maybe they were jealous . . . they would like call me an Oreo, stuff like that, just because I was in those classes." She stated that she ignored the harassment, saying she did not care, and "I'm gonna interact with the people

I spend the whole day with." In high school, Nika noted differences between herself and many of the other black girls, particularly in what she saw as their undue attention to clothing and appearance. Nika reported that she felt no such distance from or dislike of African American boys her age. Her friendships with white students also continued through the middle and high school.

Nika's somewhat naïve attitudes about race and the role played by the system in discouraging the black students who were sometimes her harshest critics, changed in the vortex of an experience—an encounter, if you will—that took place in middle school:

> [The teacher] called all the black students' names and told us—in front of the whole class—that we were in the wrong class, that we were supposed to be in the other teacher's and [the teacher] said [the other teacher's] name, and the other kids in the class knew that wasn't the enriched class, and I'm, and I'm thinking to myself, this is wrong, this is not—how could that be? And we were all kind of like embarrassed, you know, because why are you like singling—you're singling us out, number one, and then, you don't have to say, you can just say, "Oh, I need to see these students," you don't have to say, "You're in the wrong class"… and all of us were like, "What?!" Like [hands come down lightly on desk] and that doesn't make any sense, and I was—*mad*, I mean I was like *livid*.

Nika knew the information was incorrect. She noted that the other black students in the class likely did too, because many had taken advanced classes together. She quickly surmised that the error was tied to the racial stereotype that claims African American students are academically inferior—"I knew it was racial the moment every single black student in that class, no one else's name, only—not—and it wasn't like they called all but one black student, it was every single one." According to Nika, most of the black students who were removed from the class did not return, even those who rightfully belonged in the class. She recounted the academic repercussions for these students: "When I got to ninth grade, they weren't even, they weren't in my AP classes, it's like they were, like de-tracked."

That night she discussed the incident with her parents. In a separate interview, Nika's mother, Lynne, revealed she, too, had experienced acts of exclusion when she was a student in the Shaker Heights schools. Lynne's ability to handle the demands of advanced classes had also been called into question when she was a Shaker Heights student, so her daughter's story hit close to home. Lynne and her husband immediately responded by calling the school and a correction was made. The next day Nika and only one other black student returned to the class. None of the other black students ever attempted to rejoin the class. The experience of reentering the classroom for the first time felt odd, surreal to Nika. It was the first time she understood how a black person can achieve "token" status in the perceptions of white teachers and students alike. The experienced shattered Nika's sense of comfort with the system:

> That's when I saw like the light, I saw really what was going on in that whole school system, it's like, they showed their face pretty much, and, I mean, if you don't really, if you don't get hit like that, then you're naïve, you don't even know, and you just let it go, you don't do anything because you think there's nothing to do, you think you're in the right place and you're not.

The experience opened Nika's eyes to the way academic levels and enactments of exclusion reinforce each other to create a powerful deterrent for African American students accessing sites of educational privilege in an "open" enrollment system. Nika continued, "They tried to *suck* the black males out . . . in the middle school, so that you can't even get in, like I said, it's like either you're in or you're out, so they want them out, before they even get to the high school." There also was a lack of clarity as to when prerequisite courses were necessary and when they could be waived. She noted, "Some students that I knew—could do that work but they were in CP because no one ever sat there and told them that they *could* take that class, they made you think that if you didn't start with AP in the ninth grade, or if you weren't in enriched in the eighth grade, you couldn't get in, kind of like, it's this exclusive club membership—you know if you're not a member by this time, then you just can't be at all."

Nika remarked that the group of mostly white students in the AP track remained the same year after year: "A lot of those students that were in that twelve AP were the ones that were in AP chem, and those kids were the same ones that I went to Ludlow with in Special Projects, the same ones in my pull-out program for the advanced . . . [classes] at Woodbury . . . but it was interesting, I mean it's interesting because they all just stuck together."[15] Her perceptions are similar to Jill's, presented earlier. Moving beyond the outline of sites of privilege, Nika also noted the three major groups among African American students: black students in the honors classes and advanced-placement classes, those in the college preparatory classes, and "the Cru."[16] The latter she depicted as a group of about a hundred students across grades in the high school who hung out together in school and after school. Her description of the exclusive nature of this group sounded vaguely similar to her description of the exclusivity of the advanced-placement track: "It was kind of like, an *exclusive* club, like you couldn't get in—if you weren't already in from the beginning, you couldn't be pulled in by association or anything because they had already labeled you the way that you were."

As a "token" black among whites, and an Oreo in the eyes of fellow blacks, she felt estranged from both blacks and whites. As with other African American students interviewed who participated in one or all higher-level classes, the experience of access to the high-level classes did not guarantee encounters of inclusion but were likely to involve racial isolation. Things changed for Nika during her senior year, and black students reached out and expressed how proud they were of her accomplishments and success. She indicated that it did not make up for the more difficult times, but she was nonetheless appreciative of their newfound support. Her own experience had vividly inscribed in her mind the rigidity of social and structural boundaries for black students seeking access to sites of educational privilege. Looking back, Nika expressed the opinion that racial equality did not exist in the Shaker Heights schools or in the larger society.

Summary of Narratives

Black students tended to narrate various forms of self-concept "splitting." For students like Stephen, the split was along the fault lines of the Du Boisian (Du Bois 1903) double consciousness: there is the self-image I have constructed for myself, but what do I make of the image reflected back to me in the eyes of the "other"? Diana shared essentially the same dilemma. Nika's predicament took on a four-part structure: There was her personally constructed self-image; the "token" status in the eyes of the other; genuine acceptance in the hearts of some white friends; and the estrangement from other black students who sometimes pestered her with taunts of "Oreo."

As for their educational development, black students were subject to a "zigzag" pattern. At times they relied on one dimension of their split image and at other times shifted back to another image. Key shifts from one identity to another were sometimes elicited by at least one teacher—sometimes black, sometimes white—who challenged them to dig deeper into their sometimes self-neglected or self-repressed academic sense of self. The nature of the relationship with such a teacher took on the dynamics of an academic "intervention." Thus, whereas white students depicted fairly continuous support from a broad range of teachers across all grade levels, black students told of the discovery of their academic potential through only one or a limited number of teachers. Ironically, these few supportive teachers helped black students learn to negotiate interactions with less supportive teachers so that they could maintain high achievement motivation in the face of less than optimum conditions (Stanton-Salazar 1997).

In the grand scheme of things, Stephen and Nika were successful students, but at what cost? Are the test scores and grade point averages for black students who zigzag from kindergarten to twelfth grade as "high" as the scores recorded by white students whose student self-image has been consistently reinforced? Might their "depressed" scores and slightly subpar grade-point-averages be mistakenly understood as "self"- inflicted? In Diana's case, might her self-conscious decision not to participate in a higher educational track be interpreted as defiant oppositionalism? We saw that what appeared to be Diana's resistance to higher achievement was connected to the sense of belonging she experienced in the Humanities Program, something she did not want to risk losing by moving upward. What stories had she heard that made her think a black student's sense of belonging would be different in the higher tracks? The need to belong is, of course, not unique to black students: we saw in Jill's case that she, too, made decisions driven by her sense of belonging within the upper track; Mark struggled to "belong" in the higher-level courses, and parent and teacher support helped him maintain his placement. Finally, are test scores and GPA averages related to the total number of teachers who express support across K to twelve? Aside from the issue of conscious and unconscious racism, how does one measure the effect of going through a school system where students experience teacher support and educational structures that reinforce racial stereotypes about achievement and motivation?

At some points of entry into the narratives of Stephen, Nika, or Diana, one can find evidence in support of oppositional identity, but at other points, these same students are exemplars of high achievement motivation. The evidence that flows from the Galletta study can be used to negate or affirm notions of oppositional identity and oppositional "culture." However, taken as a whole, the Galletta study complicates and shows to be simplistic any explanation for the origin of the achievement gap that is not ultimately "ecological" and systemic, rather than personological, individualistic, and non-interactional. The Galletta study makes it possible to predict that over and above issues of gender, family structure, and socioeconomic status, variables such as splitting of the self, zigzag performance, and the existence and perception of everyday racism in the classroom should predict less than optimal academic performance for most black children. Such factors are explored in the empirical studies in this volume; like the Galletta study, they do not necessarily "reject" Ogbu's thesis, but it is most certainly *complicated* (in this volume, see Good, Dweck, and Aronson, chapter 5; Lawrence, Bachman, and Ruble, chapter 6; Moje and Martinez, chapter 9; O'Connor, DeLuca Fernández, and Girard, chapter 8).

Finally, Galletta reported that although most white students voiced almost unreserved appreciation, affection, belonging, and pride to be or once to have been students in the Shaker Heights school system, a cohort within this group also narrated dissonance toward the arrangement of educational opportunities and academic outcomes that they had come to understand as unfairly distributed by race and class. This knowledge did not, however, jeopardize the academic achievement of these students. Black students also shared a deep appreciation for the school system. Even among black students who recognized the inequality of the system and whose academic standing *was* jeopardized by this understanding, their pride in being Shaker Heights students was high. Galletta was caught off guard by this finding. When she dug deeper she found that the reference point the black students were using was not the white community and white students, but black students caught in the malaise of inferior educational settings in urban Cleveland. For all that they had endured in the Shaker Heights integration experience—that is, identity splitting, the acts of discrimination, the moments of estrangement from other blacks, or the sense of being a token to many whites—all of the students suggested with considerable certitude that they would be far "less" educated today, had they attended low-income predominantly black schools in nearby school districts.

Conclusion

Our efforts to historicize black education and interrogate "integration" situated the experience of African American students in general and black students in the Shaker Heights City School District in particular within a broad analysis of history, educational policies and practices, and individual student narratives of the educational experience. Our organization of the chapter itself shifts across time and contexts. We started with a historical analysis that revealed the high level of achievement motivation blacks embraced upon exiting slavery. We underscored how the social movement for education spearheaded by former slaves contests John Ogbu's interpretation of low-achievement attitudes found among many of today's black youth as being historically linked to whether a group entered the United States under voluntary or involuntary conditions. In the next section we fast-forwarded to the present and deconstructed the history of integration on the basis of Galletta's research conducted in the same school system studied by John Ogbu, where he collected data in support of his oppositional identity concept. After first casting doubt on the legacy-of-slavery thesis, we showed that Ogbu underestimated the role played by policies and practices associated with school integration in the social production of black youths' oppositional attitudes. In so doing we sought to illustrate the complexity of social identity development among youths in desegregated schools and its influence on the nature and extent of their educational participation.

Notes

1. A book-length version of Anne Galletta's dissertaion is in preparation (Personal communication from Anne Galletta to William E. Cross, Jr.).
2. Shelly v. Kraemer, 334 U.S. 1 [1948], followed by Jones v. Mayer [1968], according to Amy Stuart Wells and Robert L. Crain (1997). Also in 1968, following Dr. Martin Luther King's assassination, Congress enacted the Fair Housing Act. According to W. Dennis Keating (1994) there was little to no enforcement of the Fair Housing Act. In 1988 the act was amended to give the Department of Housing and Urban Development (HUD) "the power to initiate complaints" (Keating 1994, 196).
3. Kent M. Weeks and Karen Weeks (1968). Interviews with study participants also indicated these practices continued through the 1960s.
4. See Bristol (1958) and Randall (1958) concerning advanced-placement classes at the high school in the late 1950s. In terms of the high rate of transfer of African American students into the district in the mid-1960s, Susan C. Kaeser and Mark Freeman (1981, 1982) report that in the 1964–1965 school year, the first year enrollment by race was documented, the percentage of black students was 10.5 percent. This rose to 14.5 percent in the 1965–1966 school year—an enrollment increase of 42.3 percentage points.
5. See "Woodbury Inaugurates Individual Pupil-Scheduling" (1966, October). Some enrichment courses were established in the late 1950s in the junior highs in math and science, but it was not as extensive as the program Woodbury put in place in the 1966–1967 school year.
6. See "Levels of Instruction Inaugurated in Shaker" (1964, November).
7. "Levels of Instruction Inaugurated in Shaker" (1964, November). Level one was eliminated in the 1970–1971 school year (Lawson 1970).
8. Much of this event was captured in the film *Struggle for Integration* (Math 1999).
9. Current course levels include advanced placement, honors, college preparatory, general education.
10. A tutoring center in the high school library opened in 1979 and a tutoring center for elementary students was established in 1980 (Shaker Heights City School District 1997, 11).
11. See Ronald F. Ferguson (2002) for details on the MSAN, as well as a summary of data on the achievement gap from participating districts.
12. During the 1980–1981 school year, one of the several years Stephen was at Moreland, the elementary school was 72 percent African American. Because of the district's voluntary busing program, a percentage of black students elected to attend predominantly white schools elsewhere in the district, and a percentage of white students from predominantly white schools elected to attend Moreland. The percentage of enrollment of black students at Moreland without the busing plan was projected to be 96 per-

cent. See Jack P. Taylor (superintendent of schools) to Members of the Board of Education, memorandum and attachments, January 5, 1981, regarding: State Guidelines for Desegregation, Shaker Heights Public Library Local History Collection.

13. The Shaker Schools Plan began in 1970 as a voluntary two-way, or cross-enrollment, desegregation plan in the elementary schools, with transportation provided. It was later expanded to the district's two junior high schools. The Shaker Schools Plan was eliminated in the fall of 1987, the year the system reorganized and achieved racial balance.

14. State proficiency tests, in existence since 1990, comprise tests in math, reading, writing, citizenship, and science. In 1990 the overall passing rate was 51 percent of the 373 ninth-grade students, with the percentage of whites passing in the first year at 81 percent and for blacks, 22 percent (see B. Sims, "Proficiency Test Results Disappointing," *Shakerite*, February 7, 1991, 3). Diana took the test some years later, and passing rates for black students did show improvement. A study and preparation program for the proficiency tests, PROBE (Proficiency Review of Basic Essentials), was instituted in 1991 for students failing the test (Shaker Heights City School District 1997, 34).

15. In transcribing this statement, Galletta found that Nika used the word "they" instead of "we" as Galletta expected, revealing a level of distance on Nika's part toward the predominantly white, advanced-placement class with whom she spent most of her school years.

16. A review of yearbooks through the mid–1990s indicates students used various renditions of the social designation "the crew" to describe what may be different social groups of students.

References

Anderson, James D. 1988. *The Education of Black Americans in the South, 1860–1935*. Chapel Hill: University of North Carolina Press.

Bell, Derrick. 1995. "*Brown v. Board of Education* and the Interest Convergence Dilemma." In *Critical Race Theory*, edited by Kimberlé Crenshaw, Neil Gotanda, Gary Peller, and Kendall Thomas. New York: New Press.

———. 2004. *Silent Covenants: Brown v. Board of Education and the Unfulfilled Hopes for Racial Reform*. New York: Oxford.

Bristol, James. 1958. "Advanced Work in Mathematics Challenges Class." *School Review* (June): 3.

Bullock, Henry Allen. 1967. *A History of Negro Education in the South from 1619 to the Present*. Cambridge, Mass.: Harvard University Press.

Butchart, Ronald E. 1980. *Northern School, Southern Blacks, and Reconstruction, 1862–1875*. Westport, Conn.: Greenwood Press.

Clark, Kenneth B. 1965. *Dark Ghetto*. New York: Harper & Row.

Cross, William E., Jr. 2003. "Tracing the Historical Origins of Youth Delinquency and Violence: Myths and Realities About Black Culture." *Journal of Social Issues* 59(1): 67–82.

Du Bois, W. E. B. 1903. *The Souls of Black Folk*. New York: Dodd, Mead.

————. 1935. *Black Reconstruction in America.* New York: S. A. Russell.

Ferguson, Ronald F. 2002. "What Doesn't Meet the Eye: Understanding and Addressing Racial Disparities in High-Achieving Suburban Schools." Shaker Heights: North Central Regional Educational Library, available at http://www.ncreal.org/gap/ferg (accessed August 10, 2006).

Galletta, Anne. 2003. "Under One Roof, Through Many Doors: Understanding Racial Equality in an Unequal World." Ph.D. diss., City University of New York.

Irons, Peter. 2002. *Jim Crow's Children: The Broken Promise of the Brown Decision.* New York: Viking.

Kaeser, Susan C., and Mark Freeman. 1981. *A Review of School and Housing Integration Data in Shaker Heights and Strategies to Improve School Integration through Housing Policy.* Shaker Heights, Ohio: Shaker Heights City School District.

————. 1982. *A Special Report on Data and Data Needs Related to School and Housing Integration.* Shaker Heights, Ohio: Shaker Heights City School District.

Keating, W. Dennis. 1994. *The Suburban Racial Dilemma: Housing and Neighborhoods.* Philadelphia: Temple University Press.

Lather, Patti. 1986. "Research as Praxis." *Harvard Educational Review* 56(3): 257–77.

Lawson, John. 1970. "For Answers to Questions on Balance, Ballots, and Levels." *School Review* (October): 3.

Massey, Douglas S., and Nancy A. Denton. 1993. *American Apartheid: Segregation and the Making of the Underclass.* Cambridge, Mass.: Harvard University Press.

Math, Stuart, producer and director. 1999. *Struggle for Integration.* Documentary film. Available from Transit Media, 22-D Hollywood Avenue, Hohokus, New Jersey 07423.

Mickelson, Roslyn Arlin. 2001. "Subverting Swann: First and Second Generation Segregation in the Charlotte-Mecklenburg Schools." *American Educational Research Journal* 38(2): 215–52.

Ng, Sik Hung. 1982. "Power and Intergroup Discrimination." In *Social Identity in Intergroup Relations,* edited by Henri Tajfel. Cambridge: Cambridge University Press.

Ogbu, John U. 1987. "Variability in Minority School Performance: A Problem in Search of an Explanation." *Anthropology and Education Quarterly* 18(4): 312–34.

————. 1998. "Voluntary and Involuntary Minorities: A Cultural-Ecological Theory of School Performance with Some Implications for Education." *Anthropology and Education Quarterly* 29(2): 155–88.

————. 2003. *Black American Students in an Affluent Suburb: A Study of Academic Disengagement.* Mahwah, N.J.: Lawrence Erlbaum Associates.

————. 2004. "Collective Identity and the Burden of 'Acting White' in Black History, Community, and Education." *The Urban Review* 36(1): 1–35.

Orfield, Gary. 1978. *Must We Bus? Segregated Schools and National Policy.* Washington, D.C.: The Brookings Institution.

Peller, Gary. 1995. "Race-Consciousness." In *Critical Race Theory,* edited by Kimberly Crenshaw, Neil Gotanda, Gary Peller, and Kendall Thomas. New York: New Press.

Randall, Burton. 1958. "Teacher Tells of First Year's Work in English Advanced Placement." *School Review* (June): 3.

Schofield, Janet W. 1982. *Black and White in School: Trust, Tension, or Tolerance?* Westport, Conn.: Praeger.

Shaker Heights City School District. 1964. "Levels of Instruction Inaugurated in Shaker." *School Review* (November): 3.

———. 1966. "Woodbury Inaugurates Individual Pupil-Scheduling." *School Review* (October): 3.

———. 1997. *Selected Initiatives to Improve Student Achievement in the Shaker Heights City Schools.*

Stanton-Salazar, Ricardo D. 1997. "A Social Capital Framework for Understanding the Socialization of Racial Minority Children and Youths." *Harvard Educational Review* 67(1): 1–40.

Weeks, Kent M., and Karen Weeks. 1968. "A Suburb Faces the Future." Unpublished manuscript. Study prepared for the Shaker Public Library and the Shaker Housing Office, Shaker Heights, Ohio.

Weis, Lois, and Michelle Fine. 2004. *Working Method: Research and Social Justice.* New York: Routledge.

Wells, Amy Stuart, and Robert L. Crain. 1997. *Stepping over the Color Line: African-American Students in White Suburban Schools.* New Haven, Conn.: Yale University Press.

Woodson, Carter G. 1919. *The Education of the Negro Prior to 1861.* Washington, D.C.: Associated Press.

———. 1933. *The Miseducation of the Negro.* Washington, D.C.: Associated Press.

Chapter 2

Essentialism and Cultural Narratives: A Social-Marginality Perspective

Ramaswami Mahalingam

U sing an interdisciplinary perspective, I propose a life-span developmental framework to study social marginality. This framework will help further our understanding of the unique developmental changes in the lives of children and youths from marginalized communities. Social marginalization is experienced at multiple levels, often because of the minority status of a group or the low social status of a majority group. For instance, in India and South Africa, the dominant groups (Brahmins and whites) are numeric minorities, but they have a disproportionate stake in power, which is maintained through various institutional mechanisms (for example, the institutionalization of slavery in the United States and the practice of untouchability in India). Cultural and institutional practices also play a critical role in the social marginalization of various groups (O'Connor, De Luca Frenández, and Girard, chapter 8, this volume). In India, apart from the practice of untouchability, cultural preference for sons results in the social marginalization of girls and, in extreme cases, the extinction of female children in the form of female feticide and female infanticide (Miller 1981). Immigration also heightens individuals' awareness of their marginalized social status (Mahalingam 2006b). Irrespective of their status in their home country, for immigrants, displacement to a Western society creates a marginalized status and a self-awareness of the disparities in the cultural and economic resources of both their "home" and their host communities.

How does the experience of being marginalized mediate cognizance of self and others? How can we incorporate power into our theories of human development? How does social marginality affect identity development? How does it affect development of self? What is the role of cultural narratives in articulating the complexities of marginalized experience? What are the implications of a marginality perspective in cultural psychology for the study of minority children and youth? To answer these questions, we need a developmental perspective that is sensitive to power differences between social groups, in order to understand how marginalized experience produces certain embedded subjectivities at the intersections of race, class, gender, and caste.

In this chapter, after introducing the key concepts, I delineate a social-marginality perspective that integrates various strands of research on essentialism, critical theory, and social cognition. Marginalized social members essentialize their identity in four different ways to negate their marginalized social status: internalization, resistance, disidentification, and transcendence. Using my quantitative as well as qualitative research with Dalits in India, I discuss the usefulness of a social-marginality perspective to study ethnic minorities. Finally, I explore the implications of the social-marginality perspective to study the academic achievement of marginalized social groups.

Social Marginality

E. Robert Park's seminal work, "Human Migration and the Marginal Man" (Park 1928), has stimulated interest in the concept of social marginality for several decades (Antonovsky 1956; Green 1947; Mahalingam 2006b; Stonequist 1935; Weisberger 1992; Ziller, Stark, and Pruden 1969). Park argued that marginalized group members are "cultural hybrids" who creatively integrate the dominant and marginalized cultures. According to Park, African Americans and immigrants are two groups that exemplify the notion of cultural hybrids. Park proposed that by studying the minds of marginal people, "We can best study the process of civilization and progress." E. Everett Stonequist (1935) had tried to characterize hybrid personalities. According to Stonequist, ambivalence, a sense of inferiority, hypersensitiveness, and compensation reactions characterize hybrid personalities. Using German Jewry of the Wilhelmine era as an example, Adam Weisberger (1992) argued that marginalized group members cope with the pressures of cultural negotiations in four different ways: assimilation, return, poise, and transcendence. Assimilation refers to the integration of the dual cultural values, and return refers to the longing to go back to one's roots. Poise refers to simultaneous rejection and acceptance of the dominant and marginalized cultures. Transcendence refers to a fourth way to overcome the oppositions of the two cultures. Although most of the sociological research on social marginality has been rich in its theoretical articulation, very few studies have empirically tested the tenets of social marginality outlined by Park (1928) or Stonequist (1935).

By contrast, several psychologists have examined how social marginality influences various psychological processes. Using a projective task, C. Robert Ziller, B. J. Stark, and Henry O. Pruden (1969) found that those who viewed themselves as marginalized were less dogmatic and more creative in their ability to integrate conflicting demands at work. Ajay Mehra, Martin Gilduff, and J. Daniel Brass (1998) studied how social marginality influenced social networking in organizational contexts. Paul Atkinson and Sara Delamont (1990) investigated how women cope with marginalization in higher education. Other researchers, such as Jose Del Pilar and Jocelynda O. Udasco (2004), questioned the construct validity of marginality theory. On the basis of their research on East Asian immigrants, Sue Yeong Kim, Nancy A. Gonzales, Kunise Stroh, and Jenny Jiun-Ling Wang (2006) have argued that marginality is a valid construct because cultural marginalization is one of the significant predictors of depressive symptoms for East Asian immigrants.

One of the most influential works on marginalization and ethnic identity development was delineated by John U. Ogbu (2003). Ogbu argued that ethnic minorities challenge the dominant culture by adopting a subversive counterculture, and this could lead to academic disengagement of African American students. Ogbu's pioneering research on oppositional identity has been critiqued by several researchers for not sufficiently theorizing constructive and positive strategies deployed by African Americans to overcome social discrimination (see chapter 1, this volume). In addition, several researchers have demonstrated the positive influence of strong ethnic identity on psychological health and academic achievement (see chapter 4, this volume). Carola Suárez-Orozco and Marcelo M. Suárez-Orosco (2001) also found that positive self-identity could also buffer against negative societal views of one's ethnic group. Jason S. Lawrence, Meredith Bachman, and Diane N. Ruble (chapter 6, this volume) noted that positive ethnic identification was not associated with oppositional attitude toward academic engagement. In sum, these findings suggest that ethnic minorities cope with their marginalized social status in complex ways. However, much of the research on ethnic minority identity development does not adequately examine how intersections of various marginalized identities together affect identity negotiations.

Social Marginality and Intersectionality

Recently several researchers have called for the need to study ethnic identity at the intersections of other social identities (Stewart and McDermott 2004). Patricia Hill Collins's (1990) work on black feminism and W. Kimberly Crenshaw's (1995) critical theory of race and gender exemplify the growing interest in examining the complex relationship among race, class, and gender. Developing a research program that takes into account the intersection of race, class, and gender has been a challenge, since the dominant paradigms tend to focus on either race or class or gender, and race and class are often conflated (Stewart and Mc-Dermott 2004). I view intersectionality as the interplay between person and social location, with a particular emphasis on power relations among various social positions. A person's race, class, and gendered experience are embedded in a particular social and cultural matrix that influences the person's beliefs about various social categories and about the origins of social differences. Another key characteristic of this conceptualization is the issue of power. Power differentials among various social groups and their unequal access to resources affect representations of race, class, and gender. Intersectionality is the triangulation of a subject vis-à-vis her or his location and social positioning along class, gender, race, and or caste. This process is dynamic, multidimensional, and historically contingent. Power differentials and social stratification are integral to one's social and physical location. Ecological issues, such as living in a neighborhood where toxic waste is dumped, could be important factors in predicting a variety of social and psychological as well as physical outcomes. In the United States, housing and real estate are also tied to political economy, and the link between real estate and funding for schools becomes an important factor in one's social location.

An intersectionality perspective requires a deeper understanding of a person situated at multiple levels of historical, ecological, and material contexts. Michele Ferrari and Ramaswami Mahalingam (1998) elaborated a developmental perspective, *Personal Cognitive Development*, which is distinctly different from cognitive development. Personal Cognitive Development examines the development of the person across the life span as determined by participation in cultural practices and the learning of cultural narratives. By contrast, the cognitive development perspective generally refers to normative developmental changes in various aspects of cognition. Ferrari and Mahalingam argued that cultural participation shapes the development of the self. It reconstitutes a sense of personhood, raising a critical awareness of dominant narratives and a deeper understanding of context. Social status of a particular social identity shapes intragroup and intergroup interactions (Patterson and Bigler, chapter 5, this volume). For marginalized groups, these narratives offer a rich repertoire of metaphors to articulate various strategies to resist oppressive discriminatory representations and practices. A marginalized epistemology increases awareness of the social construction of a narrative and its strategic deployment, re-rendering, and various modes of articulations (Moje and Martinez, chapter 9, this volume; O'Connor, De Luca Fernández, and Girard, chapter 8, this volume). Issues concerning power, such as who is telling the story and whose power interests are served by a particular rendition of a narrative, become legitimate concerns of the marginalized epistemology.

Essentialism and Social Marginality

Essentialism refers to the psychological belief that there are essential and immutable differences between social groups, such as race, class, gender, and sexuality, and members of a group are believed to share the essential characteristics or traits of the social group they belong to (Gelman 2003). Even though essentialist views as they apply to race and ethnicity have been called into question by several social theorists (for a review, see Smedley and Smedley 2005), ethnic minorities face a unique predicament. On the one hand, members of marginalized groups have to contest essentialist beliefs about social identities because such beliefs often serve the ideological interests of dominant group members (Mahalingam 2003). At the same time, they also need to essentialize their group identity in order to construct a positive self-identity. Such strategic use of essentialism is shaped by the social and personal history of a person (Moje and Martinez, chapter 9, this volume). The lived, embodied experience between as well as within social loci could be hegemonic, marginal, or hybrid, depending on the hierarchical arrangement among a person's various social identities. Marginalized social experience mediates various psychological processes, such as conceptions of self, well-being, and emotion, and permeates identity politics, moral commitments, and our everyday understanding of social relations (Kim et al. 2006; Mahalingam 2006a) as well as the enactment of social identities (Moje and Martinez, chapter 9, this volume). Therefore, a developmental account of marginalization should examine the impact of social categories at their intersection, not in isolation from each other. An intersectionality focus is central to the developmental perspective on social marginality.

Recent research on power and representations of social categories suggests that power in the form of a privileged group membership influences beliefs about social categories (Fiske 1993; Mahalingam 2003). Mahalingam (2003) has distinguished between two modes of essentialism: cognitive and social. Cognitive essentialism refers our tendency to treat categories as if they have "true" essences—in other words, our cognitive bias is to essentialize social and natural kinds in order to make sense of the world (Gelman 2003). Social essentialism refers to strategic deployment of essentialism to justify as well as to resist existing social hierarchies. Privileged social location accentuates our tendency to essentialize social categories, and marginalized social location challenges such essentialist beliefs about social categories (Mahalingam 2003).

For historically marginalized communities, cultural narratives, in the form of life stories, folklore, or hagiography, play a critical role in articulating and affirming a positive self identity (Arnold and Blackburn 2004; Peacock and Holland 1993). Social marginalization prevents these communities from voicing their personal life stories and personal histories in "legitimized" sociocultural forums. Marginalized social experience embodies a lived experience resulting from active participation in cultural practices mediated by cultural narratives, family (Fuligni, Rivera, and Leininger, chapter 10, this volume) and community lore (Moje and Martinez, chapter 9, this volume). The residual effect of the marginalized experience permeates the collective memory for several generations. Cultural narratives have a dual purpose, serving both in the construction of self and in mitigating the severity of social domination and marginalization. Often, new forms of resistance are rearticulated over time. The intellectual lineage of rap music from the oral tradition of retorts is a prime example. Cultural narratives record and make creative links to the repository of the community memory. Cultural narratives are part of the repository of memory that archives forms of resistance in adverse conditions. They help people to cope with personal trauma (Scheper-Hughes 1992).

Social Marginality: A Life-Span Developmental Perspective

Cultural contexts, cultural narratives, and participation in cultural practices influence the various ways in which essentialism is invoked to interpret marginalized life experience. Early on, children invoke essentialism as a heuristic tool for social categorization. Later a critical awareness of the intersection of caste, gender, or race leads to a selective and strategic invocation of essentialism—social essentialism, which is distinct from cognitive essentialism when it is used merely as a cognitive bias (Mahalingam 1998). I have presented a developmental framework (figure 2.1) for social marginality to further our understanding of the unique developmental changes of children and youth from marginalized communities who experience social inequalities in three significant ways.

First, social marginality affects the emergence of a critical personal epistemology that enables a nuanced critical reading of cultural and personal narratives, challenging the interpretations of the dominant group (Moje and Martinez, chapter 9, this volume; O'Connor, De Luca

Figure 2.1   A Life-Span Developmental Perspective of Social Marginality

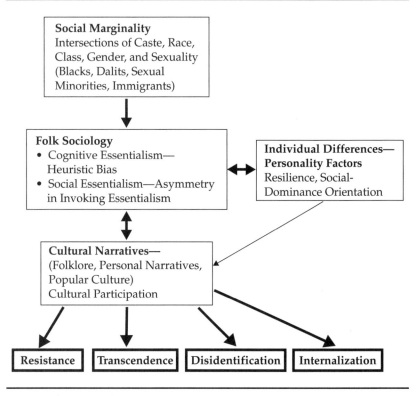

Source: Author's compilation.

Fernández, and Girard, chapter 8, this volume). Second, marginalized experience influences the development of a critical worldview to challenge stigmatizing essentialist representations. Third, marginalized experience also fosters a critical understanding of social context as a multilayered complex system. Thus, social marginality profoundly influences our emerging folk sociology, our naïve theories of social groups (Hirschfeld 1996; Mahalingam 2003)

The strategic deployment of essentialism—when to resist essentialist notions of identity and when to mobilize an essentialist but positive sense of identity—is largely shaped by the complex interaction between marginalized experience and identity development. The quantitative developmental research on children's understanding of caste, particularly Dalit children's notions of caste, shows these strategic shifts in endorsing essentialist notions of caste. Marginalized experience also results in the marginalized person's gaining a deeper sense of the interactive influence of contexts that shape human potentials in positive or negative ways. The understanding of self in relation to multiple identities also emerges through the participation in culturally valued activities.

Socially marginalized groups appropriate essentialism in four different ways: (1) resistance; (2) transcendence; (3) disidentification; (3) internalization. Like Dalit participants and activists who resisted biological essentialist representations of categories, youths from marginalized groups could embrace a non-biological essentialist account of group identity that recognizes the role of power in defining and constructing a social category in biological terms. Suárez-Orozco and Suárez-Orozco's (2001) research on social mirroring points out that when children of Latino immigrants realize that the societal perception of them is negative, they adopt social essentialist strategies to counter those essentialist perceptions. These young Latinos are resilient, have a high self-esteem, and counter negative essentialist representations of Latino youth by becoming the most successful members of the community and rejuvenating their communities.

Marginalized experience could also provide a unique standpoint that would enable youths to embrace a transcendental view of social categories. Transcendental essentialism provides a worldview tha´ unites human beings sharing the same essence and the same predicaments, regardless of the sociocultural context. By recognizing the interconnectedness of human beings as having relatable social experiences that are at the intersections of various social identities, transcendental essentialism could provide an alternate essentialist view to negate adverse demeaning stereotypes and discrimination.

Marginalized experience contributes to a greater awareness of context. Such heightened awareness of the context could lead in extreme cases to a total sense of helplessness resulting from an internalization of stigmatized essentialist representations. Suárez-Orozco and Suárez-Orozco (2001) found that such internalization of perceived stigmatized identity could also lead to resigned helplessness, self-defeating behavior, and depression. Claude Steele's (1997) work on stereotype threat and disidentification and Jennifer Crocker's (2002) contingencies of self-worth provide examples of the ways in which stigmatized group members can disconnect their self-worth from others' evaluative essentialist representations of the group. There may also be several unique mechanisms and contextual and individual-differences factors that lead one to disconnect one's group membership from his or her psychological representation of marginality (Good, Dweck, and Aronson, chapter 5, this volume). According to Mahalingam (2006b), cultural narratives play a critical role in "re-imagining" a positive self- identity for members of marginalized social groups in India (Bhatia and Ram 2001).

Cultural Narratives, Essentialism, and Social Marginality

According to the 2000 census, Dalits constitute about 18 percent of the Indian population. The term "Dalit" means "oppressed" and refers to caste groups that have historically been marginalized, dehumanized, and treated as "untouchables" (Jacob and Bandhu 2002; Thorat 2004; Zelliot 1992). After India obtained independence from the British colonial government in 1947, efforts were made by the federal government to constitutionally protect and promote the welfare of Dalits. Reservations (quotas) were introduced in the legislature, in educational institutions (including professional schools), and in government jobs. However, the reservation policy has not been uniformly implemented by various state governments. Although the educational opportunities that are available for Dalit children have improved since independence, Dalits are still oppressed and marginalized, especially in the villages, where they are economically dependent on upper-caste groups (Deliege 1999; Nambissan and Sedwal 2002; Thorat 2004). Varying degrees of social discrimination and systemic violence against Dalits have been documented by several activists and researchers (Deliege 1999; Franco, Macwan, and Ramanathan 2004; Jacob and Bandhu 2002; Thirumaavalavan 2003). All these researchers have noted that, despite this social discrimination, a renaissance is under way in Dalit literature and music (Franco, Macwan and Ramanathan 2004; Thirumaavalavan 2003).

Using quantitative and qualitative methods, I have been studying Dalits to understand the relationship between social marginality and various modes of essentialist beliefs about social identities. I was particularly interested in how Dalits appropriate essentialism to contest, negotiate, and challenge various dominant representations of Dalits. In my quantitative research, I used two paradigms to examine the relationship between social marginality and essentialism: an adoption, or switched-at-birth, paradigm; or a brain-transplant paradigm. In the adoption paradigm (Gelman 2003; Hirschfeld 1996), participants were presented a story of a child who was switched at birth by mistake and was raised by parents who are from a different ethnic or racial group (for instance, black infant raised by white parents). Participants were asked to make predictions about the social identity and personality characteristics, given the social and personality traits of the birth mother and the mother who raised the baby.

In a developmental study that examined the relationship between the role of social location and power, Dalit and a Brahmin children and adults were told a story about a Dalit and a Brahmin infant who were switched at birth by mistake (Mahalingam 1998). When asked about the caste of the child who was raised by a mother from a different caste group, most of Brahmin children believed that the caste of the child would be the child's biological mother's caste, whereas most of the adult Dalits believed that caste identity would be socially transmitted, and the caste of the child would be the adopted mother's caste.

Since Dalits thought that caste was acquired through parental socialization, I developed a caste transformation task to examine whether they also believed that someone could change his or her caste at will. I presented a vignette about a Dalit, a school-age child, who wants to become a Brahmin. Dalits believed that although caste was not determined at birth but through socialization, it could not be changed at will. According to Mahalingam (2003), Dalits believed in a caste identity that is socially transmitted but still retained an essence-like quality that could not be changed once acquired. By contrast, Brahmin participants believed in the biological determination of caste.

The brain-transplant paradigm used a vignette about a hypothetical brain transplant (BT) between two people who are from two different social groups (Mahalingam and Rodriguez 2003; Mahalingam and Rodriguez 2006; Mahalingam and Balan 2006) to examine whether a brain transplant would change the personal and social identity of the BT recipient. In the study, Brahmin and Dalit participants were told a story of a hypothetical brain transplant between a Brahmin and a Dalit (Mahalingam and Balan 2006). They were asked whether the recipient's personality would change after the brain transplant. Younger children (seven-to-eight-year-olds) in both caste groups believed that the brain transplant would change the recipient's personality only if the caste of the recipient of the transplant was not the same as their own. For the oldest age group, twelve to sixteen, however, there was a significant difference between Brahmins and Dalits. Brahmin participants believed that a brain transplant would not result in personality change, whereas a majority of the Dalits believed that the brain transplant would change the personality of the recipient.

In another study, I compared the Brahmin and Dalit adults' beliefs about personality change after a hypothetical brain transplant. Brahmins and Dalits believed that a brain transplant may not determine the social identity of the recipient. However, there was a significant difference by caste concerning the question about whether a brain transplant would change the caste of the recipient. Dalits were evenly split. Brahmins thought that a Brahmin who received a brain transplant from a Dalit would act like a Dalit, but a Dalit who received a brain transplant from a Brahmin would not act like a Dalit. In these studies, Brahmins either selectively essentialize or strongly essentialize social identity. Overall, Dalits resisted an essentialist view of social or personal identity.

Whereas quantitative studies were able to capture the relationship between privileged status and cognitive and social essentialism, I used cultural narratives to examine the complex ways in which Dalits resisted biological determinations of caste identity. Several researchers have pointed out the vital role of cultural narratives in challenging dominant accounts of caste. Robert Deliege (1999) has documented cultural narratives of Dalits about caste origins that are not part of canonical Indian mythological narratives about caste. These narratives "invert" and challenge dominant accounts of caste origin by providing an alternate and an egalitarian social essentialist account of caste (Mahalingam 2003). Lynn Vincentnathan (1993) has also found subtle but symbolically significant differences between Dalits' and upper-caste groups' rendering of a popular hagiography of a Dalit saint, Nandanar. Instead of scrutinizing marginalized cultural narratives for their veracity, researchers should view them as a "kind of objective knowledge themselves" (Franco, Macwan, and Ramanathan 2004) because they elucidate the complex layers of communal memory by synthesizing the lived experiences at the personal, social, and cultural levels.

A sense of a continuous remembered self (our rough and ready definition of identity from a psychological perspective) has both elements—the emotional and social, the internal and external. To locate identity in the external social world alone, where norms and practices reign supreme, is to ignore the private world of desire and feeling, a latent self as real as the role-playing, norm-observing one. Outer social world and inner felt world together make up identity (Franco, Macwan, and Ramanathan 2004, 2).

Since marginalized communities do not have the access or means to challenge stigmatizing dominant representations, cultural narratives in the forms of folklore, life stories, or hagiography are the only resources available to them to construct alternate conceptions of identity. In the following section, using the story of Ekalaivya, I will illustrate how Dalits appropriate a cultural narrative to construct a positive sense of Dalit identity based on my research conducted in Tamil Nadu, India.

The Story of Ekalaivya: The Power of Cultural Narratives

The story of Ekalaivya, part of Mahabharata (Narayan 2000), the great Indian folklore epic, exemplifies the interplay between power, social stratification, and the cultural construction of a person. Ekalaivya, a Nishad ("untouchable") who hailed from the lowest social stratum, wanted to learn archery. He approached Dhrona, the great Brahmin teacher of archery, who was teaching the young princes, the Pandavas ("Five Brothers") and the Kauravas ("One Hundred Brothers"). Because of his commitment to the 105 royal princes, Dhrona refused to take Ekalaivya as his disciple. He gave two reasons for the refusal. First, he believed that only Shatriyas, members of the ruling class, should be taught archery. Second, he had vowed to make a great warrior of Arjuna, his star pupil and a Pandava.

Years went by. One day Dhrona took his students to the forest to test their skills by assessing both their mastery of archery skills and their knowledge of the art of archery (*asthra sastra*), which includes learning how to give the arrow magical powers to spit fire or water or simultaneously attack several targets. He lined up the students before a banyan tree—a species that has long, wide leaves—told them that a student who has mastered archery should be skillful enough to make a hole on one side of the stem of all the leaves in the tree. All his students failed in the test, except Arjuna. Dhrona was quite pleased with Arjuna's progress and praised him for his mastery of archery. As the master and the disciples were walking back, they noticed several trees with leaves with a hole on either side of the stem—even trees with smaller leaves. Dhrona marveled at the mastery and the extraordinary skills of the archer who had accomplished this feat. He wanted to find the great archer to introduce him to his disciples. Dhrona was expecting to find a great teacher who might also serve as a resource for the princes. He traced the footpath in the forest and reached a small house. When he went inside and inquired about the archer, he found to his surprise that the archer was Ekalaivya.

Ekalaivya fell on his knees before Dhrona. He was so delighted to see Dhrona, who vaguely remembered his meeting with Ekalaivya. Dhrona was pleasantly surprised. He admired Ekalaivya's mastery of archery and asked him whether he could meet his guru, the teacher who had made him into a great archer. Ekalaivya bowed his head again and said he would take him to his guru. He took Dhrona to the back of his house and pointed to a statue of Dhrona himself, saying, "You are indeed my Guru. After you refused to take me as your student, I came back years ago and vowed to learn archery from none other than you. So I made a statue of you. I started practicing before your statue. I have been doing so with devotion for the past several years. All I learned came from your statue. Your presence and your spirit have guided me and made me what I am now. I owe you everything and I will give you anything you ask for. Whatever I mastered is because of you. Please do not hesitate to ask me anything as your guru *dakshina* (gift) from me." Dhrona was spellbound by Ekalaivya's devotion to him and to archery.

Delighted to see a disciple who was transformed into a great archer by virtue of the spiritual presence of his statue, Dhrona was also concerned about his promise to Arjuna that he would be his greatest disciple. Obviously, Ekalaivya was miles ahead of Arjuna in terms of skills and mastery. Dhrona thought for a while. He asked Ekalaivya to offer the thumb of his right hand as his guru *dakshina*. Without any hesitation Ekalaivya went inside and took a knife and cut off his thumb. He put it on a plate and offered it to his guru. Dhrona had asked for Ekalaivya's thumb so that he could never practice archery again, thereby leaving Arjuna as the greatest archer of all time. Dhrona, moved by Ekalaivya's devotion, declared that Ekalaivya was the paradigm of a disciple.

Ekalaivya was well aware of the consequences of his action. The ideological implication of the story is telling. While Ekalaivya proved that even a student from a marginalized group could excel, he was nevertheless denied the opportunity to live a life where he could demonstrate his mastery and gain social recognition. Instead, he became the paradigm of a great student, not for pursuing his interest to excel in archery but for *giving up* all of his learning. In the later part of the epic, Arjuna went on to become a great archer, while Ekalaivya vanished from the rest of the Mahabharata, but he is immortalized in the folklore and in the popular imagination. Ironically, for willingly giving up his mastery for his guru, Ekalaivya became a metaphor for an excellent student and a person of integrity who never goes back on his word. Today Ekalaivya is revered by both upper-caste Indians and Dalits.

Ekalaivya story has special meaning and significance for Dalits, who have been oppressed and marginalized for centuries. Hindus from the upper castes remain the major power holders in Indian society. Among Dalits, the literacy rate, especially for women, is very low, and the demographic indices as measured by life expectancy and infant mortality rates are far below those of the upper castes. Even after fifty years of independence and the legal erasure of their untouchable status, the efforts of Dalits to get respect and dignity in social interactions is far from successful (Thorat 2004). Recently, in a militantly segregated village, a Dalit youth was made to eat human excreta for committing the crime of trespassing (Kandasamy 2002). Aggressive affirmative action in the form of reservations—quotas—for Dalits has resulted in some progress. Given the social realities, it is not a surprise that Ekalaivya arouses emotions of pride and reverence because his story symbolizes the struggles of many talented Dalits in a caste-ridden society.

In fact, the story of Ekalaivya evokes different kinds of emotions and has different valence within various caste groups. After narrating the story of Ekalaivya to several Dalit and Brahmin graduate students from Tamil Nadu, in southern India. I asked for their interpretations of the story. There was a striking divide between Brahmins and Dalits in what they thought this story symbolized. The majority of the Brahmin participants viewed Ekalaivya as a paragon of the "ideal disciple" and saw that as the moral of the story. Their interpretations framed Dhrona as the moral center of the story. They discussed how hard it must be to be in Dhrona's place. They discussed the moral dilemma of Dhrona, the Brahmin teacher, who has given his word to Arjuna that he would make him a great archer but then meets Ekalaivya, who had attained a level superior to that of Arjuna. One Brahmin subject stated:

> I think Ekalaivya is a great disciple. It must be hard for Dhrona, who had really a hard time in deciding what to do with his promise to Arjuna. See . . . he was not aware of Ekalaivya. All of a sudden—out of the blue—he found out about Ekalaivya. He [Dhrona] had to keep his honor and promise. It must be hard to be a teacher in this context and make decisions like this. I am sure deep inside he [Dhrona] resented it.

The Dalits' interpretations of the story focused on Ekalaivya as the moral center of the story. They discussed why Ekalaivya made such a decision and how he stood by his words even though he knew Dhrona's intentions. Their interpretive framework anchors Ekalaivya as the oppressed protagonist who was robbed of an opportunity to show the world that, despite heavy odds, he could excel. One Dalit subject stated:

> This is typical. See . . . Ekalaivya became a great archer. His deference to Dhrona was amazing. See . . . Ekalaivya knew that his life as an archer would be over once he cut his thumb because, you see . . . there was no plastic surgery then. [Laughs]. But he still did it. It shows his strong will to achieve something on his own and his willingness to give up something so dear to him for a guru who did not actively participate and was not directly responsible for his learning. That shows what a great man he was! This is also in a way similar to the experience Dalits have been going through in this country. Ekalaivya is a man of his word, who had shown he can do it and also showed what an extraordinary human being he was.

The narrative of Ekalaivya clearly evoked different emotions among Dalits and Brahmins. The interpretive frame of reference chosen by the participants—Dhrona's versus Ekalaivya's—reflects the moral sentiments the participants identify with. Brahmin subjects focused on the contextual aspects behind the moral compulsions of Dhrona, which led to his strange and cruel request. The Dalits were in awe of Ekalaivya and they discussed Ekalaivya's accomplishments, as a student and as a person, with reverence. Ekalaivya is seen by them as a beacon to achieve and excel, while also being a stark reminder of social reality. His life is seen as a demonstration of the moral strength and courage of Dalits, virtues that are generally presumed to be the characteristic of the upper castes.

Ekalaivya and the Making of Self

Another revealing encounter occurred during my field study of Tamil children's concept of caste. I was interviewing Dalit children and I was about to meet a Dalit activist who was willing to help me contact schools in a nearby village. Since the activist was running an errand, I was waiting for him near the village council building. An elderly Dalit man in his fifties approached me. It seemed he was returning from the farm. He looked tired. He wanted to know what I was up to. The following is an approximate recollection and translation of the conversation between me (R) and the older Dalit man (S):

S: What do you do?

R: I am a psychologist.

S: You mean you work with mad, crazy people?

R: No. I am a child psychologist. I work with children. I try to understand how they think.

S: How do you do that?

R: I tell them a story and ask some questions.

S: Ah… You tell stories. I know many good stories. I have so many stories to tell. Even my life itself is a big story.

R: That will be interesting.

S: You want to hear?

R: [Realizing I did not have much choice.] Yes. I would like to.

S: My story . . . hmm where to start . . . You see. I was born just after independence from the British [1947]. I went to school in this village because they said all of us [Dalits] should go to school. We had to sit in the benches at the back of the class. We couldn't sit with the upper-caste kids.

R: Did you like going to school?

S: What school? My teacher would send us to work in his garden and farm. We had to pick the vegetables. We would bring them and give them to him. Then we had to run all the little errands in and around his house. I used to work very hard . . . He failed me in the examinations . . . I thought, "Okay. Despite my work he did not pass me. If I go to work with my parents, at least I will be paid. I don't have to work for free." So I left the school.

R: You started working in the farms.

S: I used to go with my father to the neighboring villages. There was lots of work available. I was also paid for it, unlike at my school, where the teacher did not pay me and also failed me. [Laughs]. Those were difficult times. I could not enter a tea shop.

R: Were there separate tea shops?

S: No. There were separate cups. They used to give us tea in a coconut shell, not in a metal cup. We could not sit inside the shop. I used to resent that we could pollute something like this you know. Same thing at the temple, too. We were not allowed to enter the temple. We had to wait outside. When they did the Pooja (a prayer and a ceremonial offering to God), I used to wait outside and close my eyes. That particular moment I forgot all the small and petty-mindedness of these people; I transcended and I became one with the Samy [God]. I had to remind myself of great accomplishments of our people, like our Ekalaivya. See, he did something extraordinary and Arjuna was scared. You know he [Ekalaivya] would have finished the war in a day (later in Mahabharata there is an eighteen-day long war between Pandavas and Kauravas, with lots of bloodshed). He had shown what dedication and hard work could do. He had shown that. They [the princes and Dhrona] were afraid of his success.

Ekalaivya's story is obviously seen as a triumph of will and sacrifice, characteristics that are normally associated with upper-caste groups. The elderly man's identity and sense of self as a Dalit are linked to his admiration and reverence for Ekalaivya. He identifies with Ekalaivya, who has transcended all the expectations and stigmatization to become the paragon of an ideal student, as he has done in his own life, like the few minutes of standing outside the temple in a transcendental union with his God.

The Dalit man's story informed me of everyday ignominies for his generation of untouchables and how these humiliations percolated through his everyday interaction with various social institutions (school, tea shop, and temple). In each instance, he tried his best to maintain his personal dignity, drawing on his personal resources. Schooling and education are typically seen as steps toward empowerment, but for him, the school context became merely a site for unpaid labor for an upper-caste teacher. To resist this, he left school. His experience is different from that of the current generation of Dalits, who, as a result of affirmative action in education, enjoy social mobility. However, in several parts of rural India, teachers still utilize Dalit students for their personal services (Nambissan and Sedwal 2002). The historical context of Dalits' experience plays a critical role in shaping their worldviews and attitudes toward social institutions like schools.

Social marginalization could lead to appropriation of essentialism in these four different ways, shaping the marginalized group members' pathways to academic success in unique ways. Individual-difference factors, the nature of cultural practices, and the resources of a community also play critical roles in determining in pathways to success. Personal narratives may play a crucial role in channeling these pathways. Dalits' use of the Ekalaivya story demonstrates the deployment of essentialism in all these four strategies. These strategies also illustrate how marginals can be *"cultural brokers"* (Weiss 1994) in their ability to operate in more than one cultural arena, and in their ability to appropriate and negotiate their identities in multiple contexts. However, individual-difference factors, such as lay theories of intelligence, contingencies of self-worth, and specific contextual affordances, mediate one's ability to be a successful cultural broker (Garcia and Crocker, chapter 7, this volume; Good, Dweck, and Aronson, chapter 5, this volume).

Dalits viewed the Ekalaivya story as an example of resistance, showing that Dalits were not biologically inferior groups but if they were given a chance they would excel and perform better than any privileged group member. Dalits considered Ekalaivya someone who transcended petty politics and became a role model for all communities in India. Ekalaivya, being an extreme example, could remind a Dalit both of the uniqueness of his success and the severe consequences of being a member of a marginalized group. Although Ekalaivya excelled as an individual, he was punished for being a Dalit. Perhaps such interpretation of a cultural exemplar could be a mechanism for disidentification. Some participants in the study viewed Ekalaivya's story as an overwhelming reminder of the harsh social realities and cruelties encountered by a Dalit who tried to challenge the status quo. Thus, extreme examples and role models could be viewed as illustrative of the futility of challenging essentialist representations.

While there is ample evidence that Dalits have challenged hegemonic representations of their caste identity, some researchers have found that Dalits also disidentify their Dalit identity to overcome subtle as well as blatant social discrimination. Some Dalits identify with the mores and customs of the upper-caste groups (Franco, Macwan, and Ramanathan 2004). Such emulation of upper-caste practices by the lower-caste groups as a result of social mobility is called Sanskritization (Srinivas 1962).

It is pertinent for us to recognize the significance of cultural and personal narratives in the emergence of personhood for those who experience social inequalities. We also need to identify the various modes of deployment of narratives and the manipulation of essentialist and fluid notions of identities. I have outlined at least four possible kinds of social essentialism that are shaped by marginalized social experience and participation in cultural practices and narratives. Perhaps the preference for the functional use of any of these construals would be influenced by personality factors, developmental changes, cultural participation, and salience of the narratives.

The qualitative and quantitative findings indicate that Dalits evoke all four kinds of social essentialist notions of identity. More empirical work is needed to identify the relationship between these four modes of essentialism and pathways to academic success. Specifically, we need to examine the interaction between these modes of essentialism, individual-differences factors, and social context in furthering our understanding of how these kinds of essentialist representations protect against perceived discrimination and perceived stress and affect academic achievement (Barry 2002; Barry and Grilo 2003; Mossakowski 2003; Suárez-Orozco and Suárez-Orozco 2001). There may be life-span developmental changes in the preferences and usefulness of a particular mode of cultural identity.

Implications of the Social-Marginality Perspective and the Academic Achievement of Dalits

The academic achievement gap between Dalits and non-Dalits persist. There are very few studies on Dalits' academic achievement (Nambissan and Sedwal 2002; Ravi Prasad 1997; Singhal 2004; Verma 2004). Dalit children continue to face discrimination (Nambissan and Sedwal 2002), and there is still a gap in the literacy rates of Dalits and non-Dalits (37 percent and 58 percent, respectively [Thorat 2004]). Various classroom practices reveal the deep-seated prejudicial attitudes toward Dalit children that underlie these practices (Nambissan and Sedwal 2002). In a review of the status of Dalit children, B. Geetha Nambissan and Mona Sedwal (2002, 81) list several discriminatory practices in schools:

(a) Teachers refusing to touch Dalit children[;] (b) children from particular caste groups being special targets of verbal abuse and physical punishments by the teachers[;] (c) low caste children frequently being beaten by higher caste classmates[;] (d) Dalit students being made to sit/eat separately, their copies/slates not being touched by higher caste teachers and children themselves not being touched.

It is important to recognize that the prevalence of such discriminatory practices varies widely across different parts of the country (Nambissan 2001).

Despite such discrimination, some studies have also found that Dalit adolescents' educational aspirations are as high as those of high-caste groups. D. M. Ravi Prasad (1997) found that 79.5 percent of Dalit youths he surveyed reported that upper-caste group members made sarcastic statements about them; 31 percent reported that they felt humiliated; and 41 percent reported that they got angry about how their aspirations were viewed by members of higher-caste groups. In a review of studies on the impact of academic stress on Dalit college students' lives, Sushila Singhal (2004) has noted that Dalit students are the most stressed group of students. They were more anxious and were found to have a significantly less positive academic self-concept than upper-caste students. Singhal (2004) also found a significant difference between Dalit men and women. Women showed higher stress, anxiety, depression, and psychological fatigue. Singhal (2004) has pointed to the "differential power of social category and gender" in the experience of stress and in the shaping of their academic self concept" (198). These findings indicate that Dalit children and adolescents are going through a complex process of negotiating the stigma associated with their caste identities.

Dalit literature is going through a historically significant phase. Collecting cultural narratives of Dalits has become a major area of research in India (Bama 2001; Franco, Macwan, and Ramanathan 2004; Racine and Racine 2004). Several autobiographical narratives document the struggles and sufferings of Dalits from various walks of life. These narratives reveal the myriad types of identity negotiation that elicit feelings of pride, joy, shame, and a sense of moral elation when Dalits resist violent forms of social discrimination. Considering the importance of cultural narratives for marginalized communities, it is critical to find venues to disseminate these narratives. Educational institutions need to incorporate them into school and college curriculums. These narratives are not yet widely available to Dalit children. Hence Dalits' community institutions need to be strengthened so that they can encourage the cultural production and circulation of these narratives. Since narratives function as cultural repositories of history and time-tested discursive strategies, the next step will be to identify when and how a cultural narrative gains salience and how such salience shapes the appropriation of essentialist construals of identity. Such an enterprise would help us understand the impact of social marginality on self-concept, academic achievement, and well-being.

Cultural narratives play an important role in the construction of an idealized positive sense of identity. Such idealized cultural identities can also become a source of stress because they set a high bar for personal evaluation, which can lead to shame and depression (Mahalingam 2006b). Future studies should examine the relationship between academic achievement, perceived discrimination, and different essentialist construals of identity with a specific focus on the positive and negative consequences of idealized cultural identities. Such studies will help us to identify the specific personality and contextual factors that allow individuals to appropriate cultural narratives to improve their psychological well-being.

Conclusions

Extending on earlier work on social marginality (Park 1928; Stonequist 1935), I delineated a life-span developmental perspective for social marginality that takes into account the myriad ways in which marginalized social groups navigate the complex demands of identity negotiations. Intersections of our social identities sensitize us to understanding the dynamic nature of the interaction between person and social context as researchers interpret such experiences. We can choose to emphasize various lenses of caste, race, class, and gender, but our research questions should emerge from a deeper understanding of our participants' social, historical, and cultural context. Integrating the notion of intersectionality, I proposed a developmental perspective for social marginality that would enable us to understand the complex dimensions of agency in our active invocation of multilayered identities at various social interactions. A social marginality perspective offers a possibility that we can meet the challenges of studying the complexities of social categories without isolating the significance of the power dimension of social location. Cultural narratives and practices mediate the complex process of making sense of marginalized social experience. Social marginality also heightens contextual awareness. It affects the ways in which essentialism is deployed to resist power and also to assert a positive identity that corresponds to the shift from cognitive to social essentialism.

Comparative perspectives on academic achievement have greatly enhanced our understanding of the powerful role of culture-specific curricular practices and parental beliefs in steering children's academic success (Stevenson, Lee, and Stigler 1986; Stigler, Lee, and Stevenson 1987). The social-marginality perspective highlights the central role of marginalized social experience in shaping various ways in which marginalized social groups negotiate, assert, and resist essentialist beliefs about social identities. Cultural narratives play a vital role in the production of idealized images of the community and self. We need to identify the cultural narratives that are salient to a marginalized social group in order to understand how and when such narratives become a personal resource to negotiate various forms of social discrimination. The modes of appropriation of cultural narratives may vary across one's life span and differ among minority groups. Identity negotiation is a complex process for minority children around the world (Boykin 1988). They have to juggle the demands of the dominant cultural identity with their awareness of their marginalized status, which is rooted in the unique aspects of their ethnic identity—what A. Wade Boykin calls a "triple quandary." The social-marginality perspective will help us understand how children and adolescents from marginalized social groups in different cultures appropriate essentialist beliefs about identity to deal with the culture-specific manifestations of the "triple quandary." It is critical to identify specific contextual and individual-difference factors as well as cultural narratives that enable members of marginalized social groups to successfully negotiate the stress as well as the strength associated with their social identities.

I would like to extend my sincere thanks to James Jones, Deborah Coates, Pamela Reid, Andrew Fuligni, and Oscar Barbarin for their thoughtful feedback on an earlier draft of this paper, which greatly improved its quality.

References

Antonovsky, Aaron. 1956. "Toward a Refinement of the 'Marginal Man' Concept." *Social Forces* 35(1): 57–62.

Arnold, David, and Stuart Blackburn. 2004. "Life Histories in India." Introduction. *Telling Lives in India: Biography, Autobiography, and Life History*, edited by David Arnold and Stuart Blackburn. Bloomington: Indiana University Press.

Atkinson, Paul, and Sara Delamont. 1990. "Professions and Powerlessness: Female Marginality in the Learned Professions." *Sociological Review* 38(1): 90–111.

Bama. 2001. *Karukku*. Chennai, India: Macmillan.

Barry, T. Declan. 2002. "An Ethnic Identity Scale for East Asian Immigrants." *Journal of Immigrant Health* 4(2): 87–94.

Barry, T. Declan, and Carlos M. Grilo. 2003. "Cultural, Self-Esteem, and Demographic Correlates of Perception of Personal and Group Discrimination Among East Asian Immigrants." *American Journal of Orthopsychiatry* 73(2): 223–29.

Bhatia, Sunil, and Anjali Ram. 2001. "Rethinking 'Acculturation' in Relation to Diasporic Cultures and Postcolonial Identities." *Human Development* 44(1): 1–18.

Boykin, A. Wade. 1988. "Triple Quandary and the Schooling of African American Children." In *The School Achievement of Minority Children*, edited by Ulrich Neisser. Hillsdale, N.J.: Lawrence Erlbaum.

Collins, H. Patricia. 1990. *Black Feminist Thought: Knowledge, Consciousness and the Politics of Empowerment*. Boston: Unwin Hyman.

Crenshaw, Kimberly W. 1995. "Mapping the Margins: Intersectionality, Identity Politics, and Violence Against Women of Color." In *Critical Race Theory: The Key Writings That Formed the Movement*, edited by Kimberly W. Crenshaw, Neil Gotanda, Gary Peller, and Kendall Thomas. New York: New Press.

Crocker, Jennifer. 2002. "The Costs of Seeking Self Esteem." *Journal of Social Issues* 58(3): 597–615.

Deliege, Robert. 1999. *The Untouchables of India*. Oxford: Berg Publications.

Del Pilar, Jose A., and Jocelynda O. Udasco. 2004. "Marginality Theory: The Lack of Construct Validity." *Hispanic Journal of Behavioral Sciences* 26(1): 3–15.

Ferrari, Michele, and Ramaswami Mahalingam. 1998. "Personal Cognitive Development and Its Implications for Teaching and Learning." *Educational Psychologist* 33(1): 35–44.

Fiske, T. Susan. 1993. "Controlling Other People: The Impact of Power on Stereotyping." *American Psychologist* 48(6): 621–28.

Franco, Fernando, Jyostna Macwan, and Suguna Ramanathan. 2004. *Journeys to Freedom: Dalit Narratives*. Kolkata, India: Samya.

Gelman, A. Susan. 2003. *The Essential Child: Origins of Essentialism in Everyday Thought.* New York: Oxford University Press.

Green, W. Arnold. 1947. "A Re-Examination of the Marginal Man Concept." *Social Forces* 26(2): 167–71.

Hirschfeld, A. Lawrence. 1996. *Race in the Making: Culture, Cognition and the Child's Construction of Human Kinds.* Cambridge, Mass.: Massachusetts Institute of Technology Press.

Jacob, T. G., and P. Bandhu. 2002. *Reflections on the Caste Question: The Dalit Situation in South India.* Bangalore, India: Nesa.

Kandasamy, Meena. 2002. "A National Shame." *Dalit*, May–June, 1.

Kim, Sue Yeong, Nancy A. Gonzales, Kunise Stroh, and Jenny Jiun-Ling Wang. 2006. "Parent-Child Cultural Marginalization and Depressive Symptoms in Asian American Family Members." *Journal of Community Psychology* 34(2): 167–82.

Mahalingam, Ramaswami. 1998. "Essentialism, Power and Theories of Caste: A Developmental Study." Ph.D. diss., University of Pittsburgh.

———. 2003. "Essentialism, Culture and Power: Rethinking Social Class." *Journal of Social Issues* 59(4): 733–49.

———. 2006a. "Culture, Ecology and Cultural Psychological Antecedents to Female Infanticide." Unpublished manuscript. University of Michigan, Ann Arbor.

———. 2006b. "Cultural Psychology of Immigrants: An Introduction." In *Cultural Psychology of Immigrants,* edited by Ramaswami Mahalingam. Mahwah, N.J.: Lawrence Erlbaum.

Mahalingam, Ramaswami, and Sundari Balan. 2006. "Caste, Brain, and Beliefs About Identity: A Developmental Study." Unpublished manuscript. University of Michigan, Ann Arbor.

Mahalingam, Ramaswami, and Joel Rodriguez. 2003. "Essentialism, Culture and Beliefs About Gender." *Journal of Culture and Cognition* 3(2): 157–74.

———. 2006. "Culture, Brain Transplants, and Implicit Theories of Identity." *Journal of Culture and Cognition* 6(3–4): 452–62.

Mehra, Ajay, Martin Kilduff, and J. Daniel Brass. 1998. "At the Margins: A Distinctiveness Approach to the Social Identity and Social Networks of Underrepresented Groups." *Academy of Management Journal* 41(4): 441–52.

Miller, D. Barbara. 1981 *The Endangered Sex: Neglect of Female Children in Rural North India.* Ithaca, N.Y.: Cornell University Press.

Mossakowski, N. Krisya. 2003. "Coping with Perceived Discrimination: Does Ethnic Identity Protect Mental Health?" *Journal of Health and Social Behavior* 44(3): 318–31.

Nambissan, B. Geetha. 2001. "Social Diversity and Regional Disparities in Schooling: A Study of Rural Rajasthan." In *Elementary Education in Rural India: A Grassroots View,* edited by A. Vaidyanathan and P. R. Gopinathan Nair. New Delhi: Sage.

Nambissan, B. Geetha, and Mona Sedwal. 2002. "Education for All: The Situation of Dalit children in India." In *India Education Report,* edited by R. Govinda. New Delhi: Oxford University Press.

Narayan, R. K. 2000. *The Mahabharata: A Shortened Modern Prose Version of the Indian Epic.* Chicago: University of Chicago Press.

Ogbu, John U. 2003. *"Black American Students in an Affluent Suburb: A Study of Academic Disengagement."* Mahwah, N.J.: Lawrence Erlbaum.

Park, E. Robert. 1928. "Human Migration and the Marginal Man." *American Journal of Sociology* 33(6): 881–93.

Peacock, L. James, and Dorothy C. Holland 1993. "The Narrated Self: Life Stories in Process." *Ethos* 21(4): 367–83.

Racine, Jociane, and Jean-Luc Racine. 2004. "Beyond Silence: A Dalit Life History in South India." In *Telling Lives in India: Biography, Autobiography, and Life History*, edited by David Arnold and Stuart Blackburn. Bloomington: Indiana University Press.

Ravi Prasad, D. M. 1997. *Dalit Youth: A Sociological Study*. New Delhi: A. P. H. Publishing Corporation.

Scheper-Hughes, Nancy. 1992. *Death Without Weeping: The Violence of Everyday Life in Brazil*. Berkeley: University of California Press.

Singhal, Sushila. 2004. *Stress in Education: Indian Experience*. Jaipur, India: Rawat Publications.

Smedley, Audrey, and Brian D. Smedley. 2005. "Race as Biology Is Fiction, Racism as a Problem Is Real: Anthropological and Historical Perspectives on the Social Construction of Race." *American Psychologist* 60(1): 16–26.

Srinivas, M. Narasimhachar. 1962. *Caste in Modern India and Other Essays*. Bombay: Asia Publishing House.

Steele, Claude. 1997. "A Threat in the Air: How Stereotypes Shape Intellectual Identity and Performance." *American Psychologist* 53(6): 613–29.

Stevenson, W. Harold, Shin-Ying Lee, and James W. Stigler. 1986. "Mathematics Achievement of Chinese, Japanese, and American Children." *Science* 231(4739): 693–99.

Stewart, J. Abigail, and Christa McDermott. 2004. "Gender in Psychology." *Annual Review Psychology* 55: 519–44.

Stigler, W. James, Shin-Ying Lee, and Harold W. Stevenson. 1987. "Mathematics Classrooms in Japan, Taiwan, and the United States." *Child Development* 58(5): 1272–85.

Stonequist, E. Everett. 1935. "The Problem of the Marginal Man." *American Journal of Sociology* 41(1): 1–12.

Suárez-Orozco, Carola, and Marcelo M. Suárez-Orozco. 2001. *Children of Immigrants*. Cambridge, Mass.: Harvard University Press.

Thirumaavalavan, Thol. 2003. *Talisman: Extreme Emotions of Dalit Liberation*. Kolkata, India: Samya.

Thorat, Sukhadeo. 2004. "Situation of Dalits Since Independence: Some Reflections." In *The Dalit Question: Reforms and Social Justice*, edited by Bibek Debroy and D. Shyaam Babu. New Delhi: Globus Books.

Verma, Anjuli. 2004. *Harijan Students in Modern India*. Jaipur, India: Sublime Publications.

Vincentnathan, Lynn. 1993. "Nandanar: Untouchable Saint and Caste Hindu Anomaly." *Ethos* 21(2): 154–79.

Weisberger, Adam. 1992. "Marginality and Its Directions." *Sociological Forum* 7(3): 425–46.

Weiss, S. Melford. 1994. "Marginality and Cultural Brokerage, and School Aides: A Success Story in Education." *Anthropology and Education Quarterly* 25(3): 336–46.

Zelliot, Eleanor. 1992. *From Untouchable to Dalit: Essays on the Ambedkar's Movement*. New Delhi: Manohar Publications.

Ziller, C. Robert, B. J. Stark, and Henry O. Pruden. 1969. "Marginality and Integrative Management Positions." *Academy of Management Journal* 12(4): 487–95.

Chapter 3

Relations Among Social Identities, Intergroup Attitudes, and Schooling: Perspectives from Intergroup Theory and Research

Meagan M. Patterson and Rebecca S. Bigler

One of the best-known manipulations of social identity and intergroup attitudes within the classroom is the blue-eye/brown-eye "experiment" performed by Jane Elliot, a third-grade teacher in Riceville, Iowa, in 1967. Following the assassination of Dr. Martin Luther King, Elliot felt compelled to teach her students about racial prejudice. She devised an exercise that would allow children to experience stereotyping, prejudice, and discrimination on the basis of their membership in a biologically based social group. On the first day of her exercise, Elliot informed her students that brown-eyed children were smarter, cleaner, and better behaved than blue-eyed children. As a result of their superiority, Elliot announced, brown-eyed children would receive better treatment in her classroom (for example, a longer recess period) than blue-eyed children. On the following day, Elliot announced that the roles would be reversed, with blue-eyed children occupying the superior position.

As documented in the book *A Class Divided* and the film *Eye of the Storm*, the exercise had startling effects on Elliot's students. Children with the low-status eye color reported feeling upset and sick, and said that they "just couldn't do anything right today" (Peters 1971, 77). Some children in the low-status group reported not wanting to return to school on the following day. The students' peer relations also suffered, with previously existing friendships between blue-eyed and brown-eyed children deteriorating. The children began to use the "inferior" eye color as an insult, leading to arguments and physical conflicts among some students.

The manipulation also appeared to affect children's academic performance. When Elliot led the children through a set of phonic flashcards, children in the "superior" group performed faster on both the blue-eyed and the brown-eyed days than children in the "inferior" group. Elliot noted that "both groups went through the pack much faster on the days they were supposedly 'superior' than they ever had before. And in everything else they did on those two days, it was clear that the children that had been labeled inferior were, in fact, behaving as if they were inferior, while the 'superior' children performed in a consistently superior manner" (Peters 1971, 86).

Elliot's exercise demonstrates that social identities and attitudes can affect children's schooling in powerful ways and, simultaneously, that experiences in school can powerfully affect children's social identities and attitudes. The exercise is especially compelling because eye color had never before been considered by the children to be an important aspect of the self, or a basis on which to discriminate against others. Further, it took only a few messages from Elliot to affect children's self-conceptions, attitudes toward peers, and academic performance. Elliot's exercise, and others like it, can tell us a great deal about the formation of social identities and stereotypes and their relation to schooling.

The purpose of this chapter is threefold. Our first goal is to outline the advantages of intergroup paradigms for understanding the reciprocal relations between social-group membership and schooling. Our second goal is to describe a theoretical model, and a body of related empirical work, that is useful for understanding the ways in which children's membership in social groups affects their intergroup attitudes (for example, stereotypes), peer relations, and academic outcomes. Our third goal is to provide a discussion of the implications of these studies for educational policies regarding the treatment of race and gender within educational environments. We begin by reviewing briefly some of the ways in which race and gender are linked to schooling.

Race, Gender, and Schooling

A large body of research indicates that social-group membership is linked to school outcomes. Links between school outcomes and gender, race, and ethnicity are especially well documented and are described in many chapters in this volume (see Galletta and Cross, chapter 1; Lawrence, Bachman, and Ruble, chapter 6). For example, African American, Latino, and Native American students are less likely than

Asian American and European American students to complete high school (Swanson 2004). Ethnic-group membership and ethnic identity are also related to course selection (Johnson and Viadero 2000), grades (Osborne 1997), achievement test scores (Kao and Thompson 2003; Kober 2001), and educational aspirations (Kao and Thompson 2003), with African American, Latino, and Native American students generally having poorer outcomes than Asian American and European American students.

Gender is also related to a variety of academic outcomes, including course selection (American Association of University Women 1998), grades (Bae et al. 2000), achievement test scores (Bae et al. 2000), and occupational aspirations (Wigfield et al. 2002). Girls typically have higher grades than boys and tend to perform better than boys on reading and writing achievement tests. Boys, in contrast, slightly outperform girls on math and science achievement tests (Bae et al. 2000) and are more likely than girls to take advanced math and science courses or science electives (American Association of University Women 1998). Furthermore, race and gender often interact in relation to schooling. Among minority students, for example, women are 25 percent more likely than men to pursue education beyond high school (Bae et al. 2000). Detailed discussions of intersecting social identities are also presented in several chapters in this volume (see Garcia and Crocker, chapter 7; Mahalingam, chapter 2).

Although race and gender affect schooling, it is also the case that school characteristics affect children's gender and racial identities (for example, how central a particular group membership is to one's sense of self) and attitudes (for example, stereotype endorsement). European American children attending segregated versus integrated schools have been found to hold different racial attitudes and show different academic outcomes (Goldstein, Koopman, and Goldstein 1979). Links have been found between students' gender and racial identities and attitudes and a number of school characteristics, including academic tracking (Kao and Thompson 2003), funding levels (Mayer 2002), student body diversity (Hanushek, Kain, and Rivkin 2002), and multicultural curricula (Borman, Stringfield, and Rachuba 2000). The chapter by Anne Galletta and William E. Cross provides rich insights into the ways in which adolescents' social identities are affected by their particular school contexts.

The importance of the links between race, gender, and schooling is illustrated by one of the most significant current educational debates in this country. Some individuals favor repealing aspects of Title IX, which prohibits gender discrimination in education, with the goal of spurring the creation of single-sex schools. Proponents of such schools argue that girls benefit from female-only classrooms, both academically and in their self-conceptions. There is, among some educators, a similar push for the creation of single-race schools. Should the government permit, or even promote, the creation of such schools? The answer to this question rests in part upon whether there is empirical evidence to support the notion that single-sex and single-race schools cause reliable, positive changes in children's social identities, social attitudes, self-esteem, and school achievement.

Unfortunately, it has been difficult to identify the causal mechanisms that produce links between (1) children's gender and racial attitudes, (2) school characteristics, and (3) academic outcomes. Students' gender, race, and ethnicity co-vary with an enormous number of variables. Individuals who differ in race are likely to differ in additional ways, including socioeconomic status, parental education levels, residential neighborhood characteristics, and reinforcement histories. It is often impossible to determine which of the numerous factors associated with any particular group membership are responsible for producing group differences in school-related outcomes.

Similarly, school characteristics that have been hypothesized to affect children's racial and gender identities occur in the context of many other variables. For example, racially segregated schools differ from integrated schools along many dimensions (students' socioeconomic status, neighborhood characteristics), obscuring our ability to determine whether, and if so, how, racial segregation per se works to affect children's social identities and intergroup attitudes. The same interpretive difficulty characterizes work on a host of other school variables (for example, funding levels, curricula, ability tracking, and teacher characteristics). Furthermore, the experimental manipulation of student and school characteristics is often practically impossible or unethical (for example, experimentally assigning children to segregated versus integrated classrooms). For these reasons, experimental studies that involve the creation and manipulation of *novel* social identities within school settings are useful for understanding the mechanisms that link gender, race, and ethnicity to children's school experiences and outcomes.

Intergroup Perspectives: Theoretical Frameworks and Methodological Paradigms

Intergroup research paradigms have been used within social psychology for several decades. In studies that resemble Elliot's eye-color exercise, social psychologists assign participants in their studies to novel social groups in order to examine the effects of group membership and environmental factors on a given outcome. The Robbers Cave study by

Muzafer Sherif and his colleagues (Sherif et al. 1961) is a classic inter-group study involving boys attending a summer camp. Sherif and his colleagues took a group of highly similar (white, Protestant, middle-class) boys and randomly assigned them to two groups, which the campers themselves labeled the Eagles and the Rattlers. The groups were segregated initially, and when they were brought together, com-petition between them was encouraged and facilitated by the experi-menters. Under these conditions, children developed strong biases favoring the in-group. In a later phase of this experiment, the experi-menters created situations requiring cooperation between the groups. This intervention led to significant reductions in the boys' levels of in-tergroup bias. Sherif and colleagues' work demonstrated children's readiness to form biases on the basis of arbitrary group memberships, as well as the effects of segregation and competition on intergroup atti-tudes.

In the decades after Sherif and colleagues' work, interest in inter-group theories grew and many intergroup studies were conducted, pri-marily with adolescents and adults (for reviews, see Brewer and Brown 1998; Messick and Mackie 1989). Many of these studies involved "min-imal groups," in which participants were assigned to groups randomly and told that group membership was either random or based on mean-ingless criteria (such as the tendency to over- or underestimate the number of dots projected on a screen). These studies indicated that, when categorized into social groups, individuals (1) favor in-group over out-group members in distribution of rewards (Billig and Tajfel 1973; Tajfel et al. 1971), (2) give more positive trait ratings to in-group than out-group members (Doise et al. 1972), (3) evaluate products cre-ated by the in-group more positively than products created by the out-group (Dustin and Davis 1970), and (4) perceive the in-group as more variable than the out-group (Simon and Brown 1987). In addition to documenting such biases, intergroup paradigms have been used to test theoretically derived hypotheses concerning the mechanisms that un-derlie the formation of social stereotyping and prejudice. Such para-digms have advantages over correlational approaches in that they al-low for a test of the causal role of various factors in the development of social identities and attitudes. So, for example, environmental mes-sages about groups can be tightly controlled (for example, presented to some individuals and not others), and the consequent effects on indi-viduals' social identities and attitudes observed.

Increasingly often, developmental psychologists have applied such paradigms to the study of children's social identities and attitudes (Bigler, Jones, and Lobliner 1997; Nesdale and Flesser 2001; Yee and Brown 1992). In a recent paper, Rebecca S. Bigler and Lynn S. Liben

(2006) drew on intergroup perspectives to propose a theoretical model of the formation of social stereotyping and prejudice among children. This account, titled Developmental Intergroup Theory (DIT), outlined four core processes believed to produce and maintain social stereotypes and prejudices, as well as some of the factors that shape those core processes. Although a full description of the theory is beyond the scope of this chapter, the model (depicted graphically in figure 3.1) provides a useful framework for understanding the effects of schooling on social identities and attitudes. Here, we discuss two of the component processes of this model: (a) the establishment of the psychological salience [EPS] of person attributes and (b) the development of stereotypes and prejudices [DSP] concerning salient social groups, highlighting the ways in which schooling might impact these processes.

Effects of Schooling on the Establishment of the Psychological Salience of Person Attributes

Most theorists agree that humans have a propensity to classify stimuli (including people) into groups and that classification plays a central role in the development of social identities and intergroup attitudes. Individuals can, however, be sorted into categories using a wide variety of possible characteristics (for example, eye color, hair type, height, language, attractiveness). How do children come to sort themselves and others into social groups on the basis of some characteristics but not others? Do school environments play a role in shaping children's attention to particular social categories?

On the basis of Bigler and Liben's (2006) model, we argue that three school-related factors affect the establishment of the psychological salience of person attributes: teachers' labeling and use of social groups, segregation, and minority status. A summary of these variables appears in table 3.1.

Teachers' Labeling and Use of Social Groups

In 1981, Sandra Bem argued that the explicit use of gender to label individuals and organize the environment plays an important role in the etiology of gender stereotyping. Furthermore, she noted that such practices are common in educational settings. Teachers, she pointed out, commonly address children with gender labels ("Good morning, boys and girls") and structure classrooms by gender (for example, seating pupils boy, girl, boy, girl). Such practices, she argued, led children to develop gender stereotypes and biases (Bem 1981).

Figure 3.1 The Processes Involved in the Formation of Social Stereotypes and Prejudice as Described by Developmental Intergroup Theory

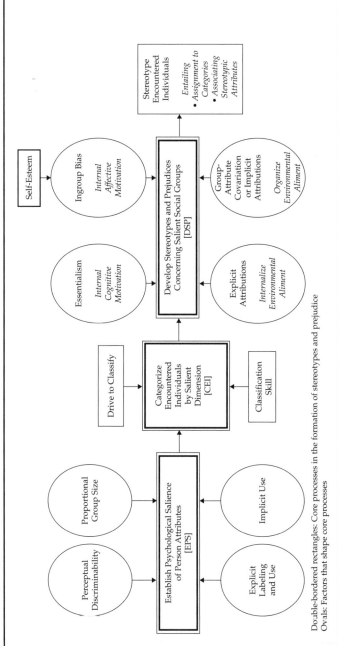

Double-bordered rectangles: Core processes in the formation of stereotypes and prejudice
Ovals: Factors that shape core processes

Source: Bigler and Liben (2006). Reproduced with permission from Elsevier.

Table 3.1   School Factors Affecting Children's Social-Group Identities and Intergroup Attitudes

Element of Developmental Intergroup Theory	Classroom Manifestation	Mechanism	Recommendations for Remediation
Explicit labeling and use	Teacher labeling and use of groups	Marks social groups as important; leads to essentialist thinking.	Avoid unnecessary labeling of social groups.
Implicit use	Segregation	Marks social groups as important; leads to assumption that groups show intergroup biases.	Avoid unnecessary segregation of social groups. Explain reasons for existing segregation.
Proportional group size	Minority status	Increases the salience of social-group identity; leads to stronger in-group preferences and biases.	Minimize numerical imbalances when possible. Be aware of greater salience of group for minorities.
Explicit attributions	Explicit curricular messages about group attributes	Creates stereotype content.	Avoid and counter explicit stereotyped messages.
Group-attribute covariation or implicit attributions	Implicit curricular messages about group attributes	Creates stereotype content.	Link roles and traits to diverse groups. Explain reasons for existing associations.

Source: Authors' compilation.

In 1995, Bigler conducted an experimental test of Bem's theory. In that study, elementary-school-age children attending a summer school program were assigned to classrooms in which teachers either refrained from using gender labels, or made extensive use of gender to label students and organize classrooms. After six weeks, children's gender attitudes were assessed. Results indicated that, for children with less-advanced classification skills (but not their more-advanced peers), personal endorsement of gender stereotypes was higher when teachers labeled and used gender groups than when teachers did not label gender. Although the study clearly demonstrated that teachers' labeling and use of gender could exacerbate stereotyping, it did not address the question of whether teachers' use of social groups to label and organize their classrooms might *cause* stereotypes to form, even in the absence of other cultural messages about a social group.

To examine whether labeling and use of social groups produces stereotyping and prejudice, Bigler and colleagues conducted a series of studies that involved the introduction of novel social groups. For example, Bigler, Jones, and Lobliner (1997) randomly assigned elementary-school-age children attending a summer school program to one of two novel social groups in their classrooms ("red" and "blue" groups). Because elementary-school-age children typically do not develop biases toward social groups that are visually undetectable (for example, Protestants and Republicans; see Bigler and Liben 2006), children wore colored T-shirts denoting group membership. Novel-group membership was assigned either on the basis of a biological attribute (light versus dark hair color) or randomly. Teachers were asked either to label and use the color groups in their classrooms or to ignore the existence of the two groups. After six weeks, children whose teachers made use of the color groups to label and organize their classrooms showed bias favoring their own color group in ratings of traits, particularly in ratings of positive traits. This was true whether group assignment was random or based on a biological attribute. Children whose teachers ignored the groups did not display intergroup biases. Several subsequent intergroup studies by Bigler and colleagues (Bigler, Brown, and Markell 2001; Brown and Bigler 2002) support the notion that authority figures' use of perceptually salient social categories to label individuals and organize educational environments facilitates the formation of intergroup bias among children.

With respect to educational policy and practice, intergroup research suggests that teachers should avoid routinely labeling social groups or using social-group memberships to organize the classroom. Although groups may be used for innocuous reasons or even in the interest of promoting equality (for example, requiring equal numbers of boys and girls to work math problems on the chalkboard), teachers' routine use of a social group in the classroom appears to encourage children to assign importance to, and endorse stereotypes of, that social group (see Bigler 1995; Leaper and Bigler 2004).

Segregation

The United States has seen a significant trend toward the resegregation of schools over the past fifteen years, with students increasingly attending schools composed primarily of students of their own racial group (Orfield 2001). Gary Orfield also notes that this resegregation has coincided with stagnation in the decrease of the achievement gap between European American students and students of color. Racial segregation is also associated with reduced numbers of cross-race friendships, which in turn is associated with higher levels of racial bias (Aberson, Shoemaker, and Tomolillo 2004; Aboud, Mendelson, and Purdy 2003). Even when students attend school with members of other racial groups, academic tracking or ability grouping may effectively resegregate them (Khmelkov and Hallinan 1999). As noted earlier, however, it is difficult to draw clear causal conclusions about the effects of segregation from studies that assess the attitudes and preferences of children sampled from across segregated and integrated schools.

According to developmental intergroup theory (Bigler and Liben 2006), segregation serves as an implicit form of authority figures' use of social groups to organize the environment and leads to the formation of intergroup bias among children in much the same way as does the explicit use of groups. Specifically, Bigler and Liben argue that segregation serves to make a particular social group salient and signals its importance. Children are then thought to develop hypotheses concerning the causes of the segregation and, in the absence of explicit information from adults, typically endorse the view that the members of the social groups differ from each other in important, unseen ways.

Bigler and colleagues studied the effects of segregation using an intergroup paradigm (Bigler, Patterson, and Brown, forthcoming). Colored T-shirts again provided a visually salient marker of group membership. In the first study, children were placed in either segregated (all blue or all red) or integrated (both blue and red) classrooms. Teachers did not mention color groups or make any explicit use of groups. After six weeks, children's intergroup attitudes and preferences were assessed. Results indicated that children in the segregated condition reported feeling significantly more similar to other members of their color group than did children in the integrated condition. Children in the segregated condition were more likely to prefer a segregated classroom and to predict that a child entering their school would choose a segregated classroom than children in the integrated condition. Contrary to expectations, children in both segregated and integrated conditions showed in-group bias on trait ratings. Bigler and colleagues hypothesized that the presence of segregated classrooms in the school might have led to the development of in-group bias among children who were not themselves in segregated classrooms.

To test their prediction that mere exposure to segregation can cause the development of intergroup bias, Bigler, Patterson, and Brown (forthcoming) created short films showing individuals wearing blue and red T-shirts and interacting in either integrated or segregated environments. Elementary- and middle-school-age children viewed either the integrated or segregated version of the film and reported their impressions of the people depicted. Results indicated that children who observed segregated environments formed distinctly different impressions of the groups than children who observed integrated environments. Relative to children who observed integrated environments, children who observed segregated environments were significantly more likely to endorse the belief that members of the two novel groups disliked each other, report that group membership and interaction patterns were consistent over time, and state that they would behave in an antisocial manner toward out-group members.

With respect to educational and social policy, these intergroup studies suggest that segregation increases the salience of social groups and leads to the development of intergroup bias, and thus should be avoided. A return to high rates of racial and ethnic segregation in American schools is, in our view, likely to produce increases in racial stereotyping and prejudice among children. Similarly, we expect children who attend single-sex schools to be more likely than children who attend coeducational schools to endorse gender stereotypes and exhibit gender biases. It is unwise, in our opinion, to promote such schools without a better understanding of their consequences for children's identities, self-conceptions, attitudes, and preferences.

Educators are unlikely to have control over the levels of segregation within their schools. They can, however, take steps to avoid segregation by social group within classrooms by promoting mixed-group activities and friendships. Children, especially those in high-status groups, have a tendency to select in-group members over out-group members as preferred friends and partners (Maccoby and Jacklin 1987; Patterson and Bigler 2006; Shrum, Cheek, and Hunter 1988). As a result, teachers should work to ensure that children have frequent, positive interactions with out-group members (as in the classic "jigsaw puzzle" interventions; see Aronson and Patnoe 1997). Nonetheless, all children are exposed to gender and racial segregation in their wider environments, and thus, it is also important for teachers to address the issue of segregation explicitly with children. Teachers might, for example, present some of the historical, social, economic, and psychological factors that produce segregation within and outside schools.

Minority Status

A child's status as a member of a numerical minority or majority group within a classroom or school can also affect social identity and school outcomes. For example, an African American child may develop a different sense of racial identity depending on whether she attends a predominantly European American or African American school. Similarly, girls may be especially vulnerable to the negative consequences of gender stereotyping if there are few other girls in their math classes.

Bigler and Liben (2006) review research on adults and hypothesize that proportionally smaller groups are more likely than proportionally larger groups to be salient to children and thus, more likely to be associated with stereotypes and prejudice. In a series of studies, Christia Spears Brown and Bigler (2002) evaluated the effects of relative group size on children's intergroup attitudes and relations. This study used their standard intergroup paradigm, but differed in that one color group represented approximately 70 percent or more of the children in each experimental classroom. In the first study, teachers labeled and used the color groups. Under these conditions, children in both majority and minority groups developed in-group bias in trait ratings and peer preferences. This is consistent with earlier studies on the importance of authority figures' use of groups.

In a second study, teachers did not make use of the color groups. Under these conditions, minority group members showed more in-group biased trait ratings and peer preferences than majority-group members. Brown and Bigler hypothesized that the conflicting pattern of findings across the two studies was caused by the differential salience of group membership in the two studies. They argued that when teachers label and use social groups, all children are highly aware of their group membership and develop in-group–biased attitudes; when teachers do not mention group memberships, however, members of the majority (but not minority) group find it relatively easy to ignore group membership and hence, show nonbiased attitudes.

This research suggests that the numerical balance of social groups within schools and classrooms has important effects on children's attitudes toward their groups and themselves and should be considered by administrators and policymakers. Educators should be aware that social identities are likely to be especially salient among members of numerical minority groups.

Effects of Schooling on the Development of Stereotypes and Prejudices Concerning Salient Social Groups

According to developmental intergroup theory, categorization of individuals along some salient dimension is hypothesized to trigger constructivist processes that serve to attach meaning to social groups in the form of beliefs (stereotypes) and affect (prejudice). DIT outlines the factors that guide children's acquisition of the content of their social stereotypes and the nature of their affective responses to social groups.

Minimal groups are, obviously, free from extant associations or meanings. Children's beliefs about "red" and "blue" group members are constructed (rather than learned or deduced from environmental sources) by cognitive processes characterized by essentialism and in-group bias (see figure 3.1, top ovals feeding DSP rectangle). In contrast, most of the social groups about which researchers and educators are concerned, including gender and race, are linked to specific traits and roles. Furthermore, the traits and roles associated with these social groups differ in status. African Americans are, for example, linked to lower-status traits and roles than European Americans, and women are associated with lower-status traits and roles than men (Bigler, Averhart, and Liben 2003; Liben, Bigler, and Krogh 2001).

Developmental intergroup theory posits that children come to learn the attributes that are associated with social groups via both the internalization of specific messages (for example, "Boys are good at math") and the detection of co-variation between social groups and attributes (for example, noting the number of male versus female mathematicians one has encountered; see figure 3.1, bottom ovals feeding DSP rectangle). We speculate that educational curricula often teach links between social groups and roles, sometimes explicitly, but more often implicitly (see table 3.1).

Explicit Curricular Messages about Groups

Developmental intergroup researchers have rarely given children messages about group status that are as explicit and strong as those used by Jane Elliot in her blue-eye versus brown-eye exercise because doing so would be unethical. Instead, researchers have typically given children messages (explicit or implicit) about their group's performance on a specific task or measure of ability, and then asked children to evaluate their in-group, out-groups, or themselves. Drew Nesdale and Debbie Flesser (2001) conducted one such study. They randomly placed children into high- or low-status groups ostensibly based on drawing ability. That is, they explicitly told children that, on the basis of their drawing ability, they were being placed within a group of "excellent drawers" or "good drawers." Social mobility was manipulated by telling children that the higher-status group would (high-mobility condition) or would not (low-mobility condition) accept more members at a later time.

Nesdale and Flesser (2001) reported that all children (regardless of condition) reported liking their in-group more than their out-group.

The in-group was favored more highly, however, when it had high status than when it had low status. Children in the low-status group were also more likely to want to change their group membership than children in the high-status group. This is consistent with findings on group cohesiveness with adults, in which desire to remain in a group is generally higher in groups that have previously succeeded or have reason to anticipate future success (Dion 1979; Lott and Lott 1965).

Nesdale and Flesser (2001) also reported that although children generally rated themselves as more similar to in-group members than to out-group members, the level of social mobility present in the experimental situation affected children's similarity ratings. Under conditions of high social mobility, children in the high-status group believed themselves to be more similar to other children (both in-group and out-group members) than did children in the low-status group. Under conditions of low social mobility, children in the *low*-status group believed themselves to be more similar to other children than children in the high-status group.

In a similar study, by Mia D. Yee and Rupert Brown (1992), children aged three to nine participated in a race and were then told that their time placed them in either a "fast" or a "slow" running group (in actuality, group membership was assigned randomly). Children were then asked to make assessments of their own running ability and satisfaction with their group. Children on fast and slow groups liked their own groups equally well. As in Nesdale and Flesser's (2001) experiment, however, children on the slow group were more likely than children on the fast group to want to change their group membership.

These novel-group studies indicate the importance of even limited explicit messages about group characteristics. Although it would be extremely unusual for a teacher to make broad statements about members of a particular social group, teachers should be aware of the impact of even relatively minor stereotypical statements. For example, it is unlikely that a teacher would tell her students "women are materialistic." A teacher might, however, make a comment such as "women love diamonds" in teaching her students how to spell "diamonds." Explicit statements about members of social groups can both make group membership salient and teach stereotype content.

Implicit Curricular Messages About Groups

Most stereotype content is likely to be acquired via the detection of correlations between social groups and attributes within educational curricula. So, for example, children learning about presidents of the United States of America are exposed exclusively to European American males. Do children notice this correlation, and if so, does it lead to the belief that men are more suited or qualified for this position than women?

Bigler and Liben (2006) hypothesize that children attend to the links between psychologically salient social groups and attributes and in the process create stereotypic beliefs. This knowledge is also hypothesized to affect their group attitudes, self-conceptions, and vocational goals. Research by Bigler and colleagues suggests that children are sensitive to indirect messages about group status, and that these subtle messages can also influence children's perceptions of groups.

For example, Bigler, Brown, and Mark Markell (2001) gave children implicit messages about the status of classroom groups in the form of classroom posters depicting winners of academic and athletic contests. Colored T-shirts were again used to mark novel-group membership. The study contained three conditions: labeling and use of groups with status messages (that is, posters), labeling and use without status messages, and status messages (posters) without labeling and use. Results indicated that status manipulations affected children's intergroup attitudes only when teachers made use of the novel groups. When teachers labeled and used groups, members of high-status groups developed in-group–biased attitudes, whereas members of low-status groups developed nonbiased attitudes. When teachers did not make use of groups, members of both high- and low-status groups developed nonbiased attitudes.

A recent study by Bigler, Meagan M. Patterson, and William B. Swann (2004) suggests a complex relationship between messages about group status, intergroup attitudes, and self-conceptions. The authors again used a novel-group paradigm in which children wore colored T-shirts to indicate their group membership and teachers labeled and used the color groups in the classroom. Before being assigned to novel groups, children reported their perceived self-competence in academic and athletic domains. Immediately after being assigned to groups, children reported on the perceived competences of their in-group and out-group, allowing for a test of whether children project their self-conceptions onto their in-group. Next, messages about group status were manipulated via posters hung in the classrooms that depicted one color group as the winners of all the school's academic contests and the other color group as the winners of all the school's athletic contests. After six weeks, children were again asked to report their academic and athletic self-competence, as well as academic and athletic competence and trait ratings of the color groups.

Overall, children showed a tendency to project their self-views onto their in-group (but not out-group), indicating a belief that they were more similar to their in-group than their out-group. Furthermore, children whose self-views were confirmed by the posters (for example, children who perceived themselves to be good at academics and saw that their in-group won all of the academic contests) were significantly more content with their group membership than children whose self-views were not confirmed. Children's levels of intergroup bias did not, however, vary as a function of self-confirmation; all children showed evidence of in-group bias. Consistent with the results of earlier studies, the frequency with which teachers labeled and made use of the color groups in the classrooms was positively correlated with children's in-group bias on a trait-rating scale. Overall, however, children in this study showed lower levels of intergroup bias than children in earlier studies whose teachers made use of the novel classroom groups. This finding suggests that receiving both positive and negative messages about one's own group *and* the out-group may discourage the formation of intergroup bias.

This study replicates other work in showing that subtle messages about the status of their own and other groups can have significant effects on children's attitudes and preferences, particularly when labeling or minority status makes group membership salient (Brown and Bigler 2002). Posters depicting contest winners, historical figures, and well-known community members are common in children's educational settings, so it is important to consider the messages inherent in these media and their potential effects on children's perceptions of themselves and their groups.

With respect to educational policy and procedures, research on the effects of implicit and explicit messages about social groups suggests that educational curricula are likely to make children aware of links between social categories such as race and gender and specific traits and roles. In other words, educational materials (books, films) might potentially teach children the content of gender and racial stereotypes, such as "only men can be astronauts" or "whites are smarter than blacks." The formation of such stereotypes, in turn, appears to affect children's feelings about their group membership. As a consequence, we argue that teachers should be thoughtful about the types of curricular messages that they select for use in their classrooms. Specifically, teachers should strive to associate roles and attributes with individuals from diverse social groups.

We recognize, however, that it is impossible to de-couple social groups from all traits and roles. For example, there have been no African American or female presidents of the United States, and thus no such models are available to children. For this reason, we also recommend that teachers discuss the historical, economic, and societal factors that have contributed to existing associations between social groups and particular roles or attributes. In the case of the presidency, for example, teachers should address the presence of gender and racial discrimination in past and current political systems. Information about discrimination gives children an alternative to assuming that the associations between certain roles and social groups are natural or inevitable.

Evidence that such a strategy can have positive effects comes from a recent study of children's responses to learning about racism. Julie Milligan Hughes, Rebecca S. Bigler, and Sheri R. Levy (forthcoming) presented European American and African American elementary-school-age children with history lessons that included information about racism experienced by African Americans (racism condition), or otherwise identical lessons that omitted this information (control condition). Among European American children, participants in the racism condition showed less bias toward African Americans than participants in the control condition. Among African American children, attitudes did not vary by condition.

Conclusions and Directions for Future Research

The effects of children's social identities on their school-related choices and outcomes and the reciprocal effects of school environments on children's social identities and related attitudes are remarkably complex. Experimental manipulations of specific aspects of school environments and social identities can, we have argued, be used to identify causal mechanisms that link social-group membership, schooling, and academic outcomes. In this chapter we have described some of the theoretical and empirical work produced by intergroup researchers and have outlined some of the important implications of this research for educational and social policies.

In addition, we argued that developmental intergroup theory (Bigler and Liben 2006) is a useful framework for understanding the influence of school characteristics on children's intergroup attitudes. The theory, and supporting empirical work, suggests that social groups that are routinely labeled, segregated, and of disproportionate sizes are likely to become psychologically salient to children, and thus likely to become the basis of stereotyping and prejudice (as in Goldstein et al. 1979). The theory also posits that children construct stereotypes and prejudices on the basis of implicit and explicit environmental messages about groups.

A strength of DIT is that it allows for predictions about the consequences of particular social policies and procedures. As an example, we apply the theory to the school integration process adopted in Shaker Heights, Ohio, and described in detail by Galletta and Cross in this volume (chapter 1). As Galletta and Cross note, teachers did not explicitly use race to label students or organize the classroom environment. Nonetheless, race became a psychologically salient social category for Shaker Heights students, a result (according to DIT) of racial segregation. Galletta and Cross report that prior achievement (grades, standardized test scores, teacher recommendations) and student preferences were used to place students into academic "levels" within schools. This practice created de facto racial segregation within the district's schools.

DIT predicts that once a particular social category (such as race) has become salient via a process such as segregation, children notice the traits and roles associated with category membership. Thus, children in Shaker Heights schools were very likely to notice the association between race and academic achievement (and other traits) within their schools, even if authority figures ignored such correlations. Indeed, Galletta and Cross note that students published a report about race differences in the student newspaper. Of course, for students reading the paper, the link between race and achievement was explicitly stated. In both explicit and implicit ways, the environment provided content for racial stereotypes among students and teachers. So, for example, a student named Mark stated: "I think the general judgment is, if you're in, if you're a white kid in CP [lower-level] classes, you're lazy, and if you're a black kid in CP classes—[tap] it's expected" (Galletta and Cross, chapter 1).

Galletta and Cross present additional evidence of implicit messages about racial groups presented by teachers. Nika, a former student, reports the following experience: "[The educator] called all the black students' names and told us—in front of the whole class–that we were in the wrong class, that we were supposed to be in the other teacher's and [the educator] said [the other teacher's] name, and the other kids in the class knew that wasn't the enriched class." According to DIT, it was not necessary for the teacher to explicitly label the "errant" students as African American for their race to be noted by onlookers. The psychological salience of race guaranteed that students would process the connection between race and (assumed) membership in advanced-level classes. Furthermore, according to DIT, children who are minorities in their classrooms are highly likely to note that status and are likely to find it unpleasant. Consistent with this prediction, Galletta and Cross cite several examples of African American students in advanced courses feeling alienated or excluded by their peers.

Finally, the Shaker Heights system appeared to lack, or even to suppress, open discussions of race and discrimination. Many teachers asserted that "color-blind" teaching is sufficient to remedy racial inequality, as exemplified by the teacher who stated, "I'm treating everyone equally. . . . I don't see what their problem is (Galletta and Cross, chapter 1, this volume)." The lack of discussion of race meant students were probably left to construct their own reasons for the racial segregation—and lower levels of achievement among African American students—in their schools. In sum, the ways in which race was treated by the Shaker Heights district were, according to DIT, unlikely to result in the development of positive racial attitudes or true integration.

There is, however, a great deal left to learn about the relations between schooling and social identity. Perhaps most pressing is the need for intergroup research to address issues of academic choice and performance. In what ways—and how—does membership in a social group affect children's academic self-conceptions and performance? Studies of issues such as stereotype threat and academic disidentification can conceivably be tested in especially clear and rigorous ways via the use of novel social groups. In addition, intergroup methodologies might be used to explore novel questions about the ways in which teachers' and peers' social-group membership affects children's academic interests and goals. Novel groups might also be used to examine many unexplored questions about identity and schooling. For example, how does their prototypicality as group members affect children's attitudes, peer relations, and school outcomes?

Further research using controlled experimental manipulations of both novel and existing social groups is likely to be useful for solving many of the pressing educational problems facing our country. We believe, for example, that such research is likely to help educators design educational programs and curricula that both minimize social stereotyping and prejudice and maximize the potential of children regardless of their social-group membership.

References

Aberson, Christopher L., Carl Shoemaker, and Christina Tomolillo. 2004. "Implicit Bias and Contact: The Role of Interethnic Friendships." *Journal of Social Psychology* 144(3): 335–47.

Aboud, Frances E., Morton J. Mendelson, and Kelly T. Purdy. 2003. "Cross-Race Peer Relations and Friendship Quality." *International Journal of Behavioral Development* 27(2): 165–73.

American Association of University Women. 1998. *Gender Gaps: Where Schools Still Fail Our Children.* Washington, D.C.: American Association of University Women.

Aronson, Elliot, and Shelly Patnoe. 1997. *The Jigsaw Classroom: Building Cooperation in the Classroom.* New York: Longman.

Bae, Yupin, Susan Choy, Claire Geddes, Jennifer Sable, and Thomas Snyder. 2000. *Trends in Educational Equity of Girls and Women.* Washington, D.C.: National Center for Education Statistics.

Bem, Sandra L. 1981. "Gender Schema Theory: A Cognitive Account of Sex Typing." *Psychological Review* 88(4): 354–64.

Bigler, Rebecca S. 1995. "The Role of Classification Skill in Moderating Environmental Influences on Children's Gender Stereotyping: A Study of the Functional Use of Gender in the Classroom." *Child Development* 66(4): 1072–87.

Bigler, Rebecca S., Cara J. Averhart, and Lynn S. Liben. 2003. "Race and the Workforce: Occupational Status, Aspirations, and Stereotyping Among African American Children." *Developmental Psychology* 39(3): 572–80.

Bigler, Rebecca S., Christia Spears Brown, and Mark Markell. 2001. "When Groups Are Not Created Equal: Effects of Group Status on the Formation of Intergroup Attitudes in Children." *Child Development* 72(4): 1151–62.

Bigler, Rebecca S., Lecianna C. Jones, and Debra Beth Lobliner. 1997. "Social Categorization and the Formation of Intergroup Attitudes in Children." *Child Development* 68(3): 530–43.

Bigler, Rebecca S., and Lynn S. Liben. 2006. "A Developmental Intergroup Theory of Social Stereotypes and Prejudice." In *Advances in Child Development and Behavior*, edited by Robert V. Kail. San Diego: Elsevier.

Bigler, Rebecca S., Meagan M. Patterson, and Christia Spears Brown. Forthcoming. "Can Separate Be Equal? Effects of Segregation on Children's Intergroup Attitudes." Unpublished manuscript. University of Texas at Austin.

Bigler, Rebecca S., Meagan M. Patterson, and William B. Swann, Jr. 2004. "Reciprocal Relations Between Social Stereotypes and Children's Self Views." Poster presented at the annual conference of the American Psychological Association. Honolulu (July).

Billig, Michael, and Henri Tajfel. 1973. "Social Categorization and Similarity in Intergroup Behavior." *European Journal of Social Psychology* 3(1): 37–52.

Borman, Geoffrey D., Samuel Stringfield, and Laura Rachuba. 2000. *Advancing Minority High Achievement: National Trends and Promising Programs and Practices*. New York: College Board.

Brewer, Marilynn B., and Rupert J. Brown. 1998. "Intergroup Relations." In *The Handbook of Social Psychology*, edited by Daniel T. Gilbert, Susan T. Fiske, and Gardner Lindsey. 4th edition. Volume 2. New York: McGraw-Hill.

Brown, Christia Spears, and Rebecca S. Bigler. 2002. "Effects of Minority Status in the Classroom on Children's Intergroup Attitudes." *Journal of Experimental Child Psychology* 83(2): 77–110.

Crocker, Jennifer, and Brenda Major. 1989. "Social Stigma and Self-Esteem: The Self-Protective Properties of Stigma." *Psychological Review* 96(4): 608–30.

Dion, Kenneth L. 1979. "Intergroup Conflict and Intragroup Cohesiveness." In *The Social Psychology of Intergroup Relations*, edited by William G. Austin and Steven Worchel. Monterey, Calif.: Brooks/Cole.

Doise, Willem, Gyorgy Csepeli, Hans D. Dann, Celia Gouge, Knud S. Larsen, and Alistair Ostell. 1972. "An Experimental Investigation into the Formation of Intergroup Representations." *European Journal of Social Psychology* 2(2): 202–4.

Dustin, David S., and Henry P. Davis. 1970. "Evaluative Bias in Group and Individual Competition." *Journal of Social Psychology* 80(1): 103–8.

Goldstein, Carole G., Elizabeth J. Koopman, and Harold H. Goldstein. 1979.

"Racial Attitudes in Young Children as a Function of Interracial Contact in the Public Schools." *American Journal of Orthopsychiatry* 49(1): 89–99.

Hanushek, Eric A., John F. Kain, and Steven G. Rivkin. 2002. *New Evidence About Brown v. Board of Education: The Complex Effects of School Racial Composition on Achievement.* Cambridge, Mass.: National Bureau of Economic Research.

Hughes, Julie Milligan, Rebecca S. Bigler, and Sheri R. Levy. Forthcoming. "Consequences of Learning About Racism Among European American and African American Children." *Child Development.*

Johnson, Robert C., and Debra Viadero. 2000. "Unmet Promise: Raising Minority Achievement." *Education Week*, March 15, 2000.

Kao, Grace, and Jennifer S. Thompson. 2003. "Racial and Ethnic Stratification in Educational Achievement and Attainment." *Annual Review of Sociology* 29: 417–42.

Khmelkov, Vladimir T., and Maureen T. Hallinan. 1999. "Organizational Effects on Race Relations in Schools." *Journal of Social Issues* 55(4): 627–45.

Kober, Nancy. 2001. *It Takes More Than Testing: Closing the Achievement Gap.* Washington, D.C.: Center on Education Policy.

Leaper, Campbell, and Rebecca S. Bigler. 2004. "Gendered Language and Sexist Thought." *Monographs of the Society for Research in Child Development* 69(1, serial no. 275): 128–42.

Liben, Lynn S., Rebecca S. Bigler, and Holleen R. Krogh. 2001. "Pink and Blue Collar Jobs: Children's Judgments of Job Status and Job Aspirations in Relation to Sex of Worker." *Journal of Experimental Child Psychology* 79(4): 346–63.

Lott, Albert J., and Bernice E. Lott. 1965. "Group Cohesiveness as Interpersonal Attraction: A Review of Relationships with Antecedent and Consequent Variables." *Psychological Bulletin* 64(4): 259–309.

Maccoby, Eleanor E., and Carol N. Jacklin. 1987. "Gender Segregation in Childhood." In *Advances in Child Development and Behavior*, edited by Hayne W. Reese. Volume 20. New York: Academic Press.

Major, Brenda, Steven Spencer, Toni Schmader, Connie Wolfe, and Jennifer Crocker. 1998. "Coping with Negative Stereotypes About Intellectual Performance." *Personality and Social Psychology Bulletin* 24(1): 34–50.

Martin, Carol Lynn, Lisa Eisenbud, and Hilary Rose. 1995. "Children's Gender-Based Reasoning About Toys." *Child Development* 66(5): 1453–71.

Mayer, Susan E. 2002. "How Economic Segregation Affects Children's Educational Attainment." *Social Forces* 81(1): 153–76.

Messick, David M., and Diane M. Mackie. 1989. "Intergroup Relations." *Annual Review of Psychology* 40: 45–81.

Nesdale, Drew, and Debbie Flesser. 2001. "Social Identity and the Development of Children's Group Attitudes." *Child Development* 72(2): 506–17.

Orfield, Gary. 2001. *Schools More Separate: Consequences of a Decade of Resegregation.* Cambridge, Mass.: Civil Rights Project.

Osborne, Jason W. 1997. "Race and Academic Disidentification." *Journal of Educational Psychology* 89(4): 728–35.

Oyserman, Daphna, Deborah Bybee, and Kathy Terry. 2003. "Gendered Racial Identity and Involvement with School." *Self and Identity* 2(4): 307–24.

Patterson, Meagan M., and Rebecca S. Bigler. 2006. "Preschool Children's Attention to Environmental Messages About Groups: Social Categorization and the Origins of Intergroup Bias." *Child Development* 77(4): 847–60.

Peters, William. 1971. *A Class Divided*. Garden City, N.Y.: Doubleday.

Sherif, Muzafer, O. J. Harvey, B. Jack White, William R. Hood, and Carolyn W. Sherif. 1961. *Intergroup Conflict and Cooperation: The Robbers Cave Experiment*. Norman, Okla.: University Book Exchange.

Shrum, Wesley, Neil H. Cheek, and Saundra M. Hunter. 1988. "Friendship in School: Gender and Racial Homophily." *Sociology of Education* 61(4): 227–39.

Simon, Bernd, and Rupert Brown. 1987. "Perceived Intragroup Homogeneity in Minority/Majority Contexts." *Journal of Personality and Social Psychology* 53(4): 703–11.

Swanson, Christopher B. 2004. *Who Graduates? Who Doesn't?* Washington, D.C.: Urban Institute.

Tajfel, Henri, Michael G. Billig, R. P. Bundy, and Claude Flament. 1971. "Social Categorization and Intergroup Behaviour." *European Journal of Social Psychology* 1(2): 149–78.

Wigfield, Allan, Ann Battle, Lisa B. Keller, and Jacquelynne S. Eccles. 2002. "Sex Differences in Motivation, Self-Concept, Career Aspiration, and Career Choice: Implications for Cognitive Development." In *Biology, Society, and Behavior: The Development of Sex Differences in Cognition*, edited by Ann McGillicuddy–De Lisi and Richard De Lisi. Westport, Conn.: Ablex Publishing.

Yee, Mia D., and Rupert Brown. 1992. "Self-Evaluation and Intergroup Attitudes in Children Aged Three to Nine." *Child Development* 63(3): 619–29.

PART II

How Social Identities Facilitate or Challenge Achievement and Engagement in School

Chapter 4

Racial-Ethnic Identity: Content and Consequences for African American, Latino, and Latina Youths

Daphna Oyserman, Daniel Brickman,
and Marjorie Rhodes

A large number of sociologists and psychologists have argued that racial-ethnic identity is a central part of self-concept for racial-ethnic minority adolescents. While these scholars have proposed that positive racial-ethnic identity should be related to general positive self-regard as well as specific positive outcomes, such as academic attainment (for example, Akbar 1991; Asante 1987; Asante 1988, Cross 1991; Gibson and Ogbu 1991; McAdoo 1988; Parham 1989; Phinney 1996; Porter and Washington 1989). Research to date more consistently provides empirical evidence of a link between racial-ethnic identity and self-esteem than evidence of a link between racial-ethnic identity and academic outcomes. In the current chapter, we conceptualize racial-ethnic identity within a self-schema formulation. We then address when and how racial-ethnic identity is associated with and predictive of positive academic outcomes.

We define self-concept as a set of knowledge structures that provide working answers to basic identity questions about meaning ("Who am I?" and "Where do I belong?") and process ("What am I trying to achieve?") and self-schemas as cognitive structures that organize experience as well as structure motivation and behavior by identifying goals as either relevant or irrelevant to how the self is defined. Using this framework, we focus on how racial-ethnic identity may bolster academic attainment and promote well-being for racial-ethnic minority youths. We propose that social identities, including racial-ethnic identity, influence behavior both by providing information about the norms, expectations, and behaviors relevant to group membership and by influencing the sense made of social and contextual feedback (Oyserman 2007). Thus, racial-ethnic identity serves to parse experience and create sense and meaning from the flow of everyday life by (1) making sense of the self as a group member; (2) lending meaning to current and historical racism and the limited opportunities and successes of racial-ethnic in-group members; and (3) organizing self-relevant knowledge about personal effort and its meaning to oneself and members of one's racial-ethnic in-group.

Thus, racial-ethnic identity is likely to matter because it serves to protect youths from negative social contextual influences and motivates persistent pursuit of important goals. Because academic attainment is both a central focus of adolescence and a key pathway to attaining future adult success, we are particularly interested in what distinguishes the content of the racial-ethnic identities of adolescent youths who are more and less successful at school. In subsequent sections, we outline our model of racial-ethnic identity and the nature of empirical support for the proposition that racial-ethnic identity has a positive effect on school outcomes, concluding with a more general theoretical model of adolescent racial-ethnic identity as a self-schema.

The Social Context of Racial-Ethnic Identity

Even young children are aware of race and ethnicity as social groups (see Patterson and Bigler, chapter 3, this volume; Hirschfeld 1996; Brown and Bigler 2005) and may include membership in social groups within their self-concepts (Harter 1997). During adolescence, when individuals wrestle with critical identity questions that impact subsequent life choices (Erikson 1950), racial-ethnic identity is likely to take on new meaning. Adolescence is a time when teens' attention turns outside the home to peer and other social groups (for example, racial-ethnic groups) and the larger world (Brown 2004). These social contexts provide feedback about how others see one's racial-ethnic group and role models for engagement in the world ("What others like me can do, I can do too"). Indeed, youth actively seek to make sense of their lives and share their created meaning with their peers (Corsaro and Eder 1990). In the following sections we consider two features of the broader social context that are likely to influence adolescent identity development for racial-ethnic minority youths: demographic racial concentration and school contexts that communicate negative academic stereotypes. We propose that as youths face these contexts, content of racial-ethnic identity is likely to importantly influence their responses and behavior.

Racial-Ethnic Concentration

In spite of gains in integration and increased representation of African Americans and Hispanic Americans in the middle and upper classes, social contexts are not randomly distributed across racial-ethnic groups. About 87 percent of African Americans lived in metropolitan areas in 2000 (U.S. Census Bureau 2000), such that African Americans are most concentrated within urban, as opposed to rural or suburban, areas and when African Americans live in rural areas, they are likely to be southern. Hispanic Americans are also concentrated in particular social contexts; although the population of Hispanics in other parts of the country is increasing rapidly, over half of all Hispanics live in California and Texas (Population Resource Center 2001). This racial-ethnic concentration means that racial-ethnic minority youth rarely experience being a lone member of their racial or ethnic group. The consequences of racial-ethnic concentration for the racial composition of neigh-borhoods, schools, and peer groups is that racial-ethnic in-group members are likely to form the local majority within the schools and neighborhoods of low- and moderate-income African American and Hispanic American youths (see discussion regarding the importance of "home fronts" in Moje and Martinez, chapter 9, this volume). As youths seek out connections beyond the family, the peer groups with which they are likely to engage will, for the most part, contain racial-ethnic in-group members. Therefore, developing a sense of connection to racial-ethnic in-groups and wrestling with how in-groups relate to broader society are important identity-development tasks for racial-ethnic minority adolescents.

School as Social Context

School is an important social context for many youths throughout adolescence. Teens are required by law to attend school until age sixteen and are commonly expected to remain in school until at least age eighteen. Given the nature of these requirements and expectations, issues related to school will likely be central to teens' identities, whether they are in school or not, and whether they are high or low achieving. In support of the proposal that school remains important to adolescent identity even for youths who disengage from academic contexts, in our own work with low-income African American and Hispanic youth we find that students not attending school are unlikely to claim an identity of "dropout." Rather, even if youths are currently not attending school, they often imagine themselves to be potentially going to school, and will self-identify as high school students. By the time their peers are completing high school, most nonattending students still see school as a potential identity.

Academic Engagement and Racial-Ethnic Stereotypes   The social context of school is a place to create a self separate from family (Chavous et al. 2004). School is an important context for identity development during adolescence, yet creating a positive school identity may be more challenging for African American and Hispanic youths, who must cope with negative academic stereotypes about their racial-ethnic groups (see examples in Galletta and Cross, chapter 1, this volume). Research in moderate-to-low-income middle and high school contexts demonstrates that academic stereotypes about African Americans (for a review see Oyserman, Gant, and Ager 1995) and Mexican Americans (Conchas 2001; Gonzales et al. 2004; Hudley and Graham 2001; Kao 2000; Secada 1999) are common. For both groups, these negative academic stereotypes focus on inability, laziness, and lack of interest and curiosity.

There is consistent evidence that negative academic stereotypes can undermine academic attainment. Simply bringing these stereotypes to mind leads to decreased attainment for African American (Spencer, Steele et al. 1999; Steele 1997) and Hispanic American (Gonzales, Blanton, and Williams 2002; McKown and Weinstein 2003; Schmader and Johns 2003) students. These negative effects of salient stereotypes have been termed "stereotype threat," with the implied threat being the possibility that one might behave in a stereotype confirming way, and the assessed consequence being lower academic performance. The impact of stereotype-threat effects is not dependent on one's personally accepting the stereotype as self-defining, though the negative effects may be stronger when the relevant stereotype is incorporated into self-definition. Unfortunately, middle and high school students are at risk of doing just that—incorporating stereotypes about their group as self-defining and thus relevant to their future possibilities. Thus, the psychologists Cynthia Hudley and Sandra Graham (2001) report that youths from diverse racial-ethnic groups rated Latino and African American males as least likely to succeed. Students also rated Latino and African American males (in that order) as least likely to work hard, follow school rules, and attain good grades (Graham 2001).

Other research also supports the proposal that middle school and high school students internalize negative stereotypes about academic attainment as in-group defining. Hudley and Graham's (2001) results suggest that Latino and African American boys' assessment of their own chances for future success matched their low assessment of their racial-ethnic group as a whole. They also report that Latino and African American middle school boys' role models are boys of their own racial-ethnic group that don't try hard, don't follow school rules, and receive poor grades (Graham 2001). Effects for girls appear to be less severe; African American and Latina girls choose role models who are girls of their race-ethnicity who are moderately high (though not very high) performing. Moreover, compared with African American boys, African American girls are more likely to view academic attainment as a status marker, whereas African American boys are more likely to view some degree of aggressive or delinquent behavior as a means to achieve popularity (LaFontana and Cillessen 2002).

Taken together, these data suggest that African American and Latino adolescents, especially boys, are at risk of incorporating negative academic stereotypes into their racial-ethnic identity. Youths face the challenge of coping with these negative contexts as they seek answers to critical identity development questions ("Who am I?" and "Who can I become?"). Despite these challenges, many racial-ethnic minority youths succeed in developing positive school-focused identities and achieving academically (see Galletta and Cross, chapter 1, this volume; Moje and Martinez, chapter 9, this volume). Feeling a strong sense of connection to racial-ethnic in-groups appears to be an important element of school engagement. For example, African American and Latino boys living in high-poverty neighborhoods are less at risk of disengagement from school (as evidenced by low grades and behavior problems) when they feel they look like members of their own racial group (Oyserman et al. 2006). We propose that the content and structure of racial-ethnic identity are key determinants of how youths respond to or cope with the contextual challenges described, with important consequences for their academic attainment. In the following sections, we outline relevant content of racial-ethnic identity and suggest how this content is likely to influence youths' responses to their contexts.

Content of Racial-Ethnic Identity in Adolescence

Racial-ethnic identity serves to help youths organize experiences related to race, guides their behavior within important domains, and may be critical to predicting how they will respond to the challenges they face in schools. Much of the previous research on racial-ethnic identity has focused on two broad components of identity: the importance of race-ethnicity to an individual's self-concept and an awareness of societal racism. While these two components are important to consider when describing the role of race-ethnicity within the self-concept, neither specifies how racial-ethnic identity may facilitate, or impede, academic engagement. Therefore, social scientists Daphna Oyserman, Larry Gant, and Joel Ager (1995) suggested that a third component be added to models of racial-ethnic identity, "Embedded Achievement." Embedded Achievement describes the inclusion of positive beliefs about academic engagement within the conceptualization of racial-ethnic identity.

Believing that academic achievement is an in-group goal and that members of one's racial-ethnic group have an expectation for group members to succeed makes engaging in school-related behaviors part of being an in-group member. Embedded Achievement is thought to be helpful for youths in conjunction with awareness of racism and strong feelings of connection to racial-ethnic in-group. Indeed, Daphna Oyserman and her colleagues hypothesized an interaction model such that individuals who are high in in-group connection and aware of racism but also see academic achievement as in-group defining would do better in school than would individuals whose racial-ethnic identity does not include all three components (Oyserman et al. 1995). Before summarizing the empirical work testing this interaction model against simpler main-effects models, we define each component of racial-ethnic identity and briefly provide a rationale for including the component as part of racial-ethnic identity and for hypothesizing a "value-added" interaction model, such that positive impact on school outcomes occurs when youths include all three components within their racial-ethnic identity.

Connectedness

Connectedness describes the extent to which individuals feel a positive sense of connection to their racial-ethnic in-group. In our own field work, we find that youths frequently describe their racial-ethnic identity as involving a strong sense of connection. For example, when asked what it means to be African American, youths commonly say things like "To be black is wonderful. I am a member of my community" (Oyserman, Bybee, and Terry 2003).

If membership in a social group is to move beyond a social fact and become a social identity, one must feel connected with the social group; groups that one feels positively connected with are posited to contribute to positive feelings of self-worth (Tajfel and Turner 1986). Indeed, in their review, Dena Swanson, Margaret Spencer, and Vinay Harpalani (2003) find that measures of racial-ethnic identity that assess feelings of connection consistently yield positive correlations between racial-ethnic identity and self-esteem. Feeling of positive connection to the in-group has been described using multiple terms; these include feeling that one is part of a group's history (Quintana and Segura-Herrera 2003), "centrality" and "private regard" (Crocker, Luhtanen, Blaine, and Broadnaz 1994; Sellers et al. 1997), and feelings of belonging (Phinney 1996). With respect specifically to African American racial identity, Connectedness to the in-group has been described as including a sense of self as a member of an African American community, heir to a tradition of communalism, familialism, and kin support (Akbar 1991; Asante 1987, 1988), and as endorsing a worldview focused on spiritualism and connection with the social environment (Akbar 1991; Parham 1989).

Broadly defined, the Connectedness component of racial-ethnic identity focuses on positive valence, feeling good about being an in-group member. Connectedness may provide motivation to engage in behaviors that are associated with belonging to the in-group; however, the Connectedness component of racial-ethnic identity does not provide specific direction for appropriate in-group behavior or motivation. While racial-ethnic Connectedness and related racial-ethnic identity constructs have been consistently associated with self-esteem, this component of racial-ethnic identity has not been consistently associated with academic outcomes. Feeling a strong sense of connection alone does not guide youths toward engaging in school.

Awareness of Racism

Awareness of racism is a second important element of racial-ethnic identity that is common across diverse models. This aspect of racial-ethnic identity involves the need to grapple with how out-group members view the in-group (Oyserman, Gant, and Ager 1995). Awareness of racism provides a framework for understanding others' negative responses, suggesting that others do not see the self in an individualized fashion, but rather through a lens of low or negative expectations. A number of authors have described awareness of racism as central to racial-ethnic identity (for example, Stevenson 1995), using terms such as awareness of others' prejudice (Quintana and Segura-Herrera 2003), or public regard (for example, Chavous, Bernat, and Schmeelk-Cone 2003; Crocker et al. 1994; Sellers et al. 1997). Similarly, African American identity has been described as involving a sense of self as subject to prejudice, racism, and exclusion from opportunities by white society (Gibson and Ogbu 1991; Tripp 1991). Youths commonly describe their racial-ethnic identity as containing elements of awareness of racism. In our own field work, we find that when asked what it means to be African American, youth generate statements such as "Being African American means that there are no easy way outs, one should be ready for each obstacle."

Broadly defined, the awareness-of-racism component of racial-ethnic identity focuses on deflecting negative assumptions that otherwise may be cued by negative experiences. That is, when racial-ethnic identity contains an awareness of racism, youths are posited to be less likely to simply incorporate negative feedback as self-relevant and more likely to be able to defend their self-esteem from failure feedback because such feedback may be viewed with skepticism, depending on the source and nature of the feedback. Awareness of racism is important, but it does not identify the specific goals, behaviors, or strategies relevant to the in-group; with regard to academic engagement specifically, awareness of racism does not in itself imply that focus on school is in-group relevant. Thus, although we hypothesize that the awareness-of-racism component of racial-ethnic identity is necessary for maintaining engagement with school, it is not sufficient. Just as with the Connectedness component of racial-ethnic identity, the Awareness of Racism component does not by itself guide individuals toward engagement in academic behaviors.

Embedded Achievement

The Connectedness and Awareness of Racism components of racial-ethnic identity may motivate youths to act in ways that allow them to express their positive sense of identity as group members, but neither of these components specifies what behaviors are appropriate means to enact this positive sense of in-group identity. Therefore, predicting particular types of behaviors from these two components is difficult because neither Connectedness nor Awareness of Racism identifies particular goals as targets for the motivation derived from group membership. To address this problem, Oyserman and her colleagues (Oyserman, Gant, and Ager 1995; Oyserman and Harrison 1998), described a third component of racial-ethnic identity, which they termed "embedded achievement," which comprises beliefs that achievement is a goal that is valued by the in-group and therefore provides a specific goal (such as doing well in school) for motivation derived from the desire to enact group identity. For individuals who believe that doing well in school is part of being a good group member, engaging in pro-school behaviors becomes an avenue for enacting racial-ethnic identity. In our own field work, we find that youths do describe their racial-ethnic identity in terms of the in-group relevance of achievement. For example, when asked what it means to be African American, youths say things like "To be an African American means to me being strong, intelligent and very proud of where I came from. Many African Americans have been successful and I plan to be the same way."

Although an embedded-achievement component of racial-ethnic

identity has not been directly articulated within other racial-ethnic identity formulations, the idea that achievement may be in-group defining is itself not new. Such an element of racial-ethnic identity is referred to by Anne Galletta and William E. Cross Jr. (chapter 1, this volume) in their description of an African American legacy of valuing education, and has been alluded to by research describing some groups as "model minorities" for whom academic achievement is assumed to be an in-group marker (for a review, see Oyserman and Sakamoto 1997). Moreover, research on stereotypes and stereotype threat is predicated on the idea that it is easy to create conditions in which a group is tagged with a nonachieving identity (for example, Steele 1997).

Structure of Racial-Ethnic Identity: An Interaction Model   Oyserman, Gant, and Ager (1995) proposed a tripartite model of racial-ethnic identity, whereby three components of racial-ethnic identity—Connectedness, Awareness of Racism, and Embedded Achievement—interact to promote well-being and academic achievement. Specifically, they hypothesized that youths who strongly endorse all three racial-ethnic identity components would be better equipped to succeed in school over time than those who didn't. They proposed that defining one's racial-ethnic identity in terms of any one of these components alone was insufficient to maintain the focused effort that school success requires and that defining one's racial-ethnic identity as composed of all three components was necessary for school success over time.

Sense of Connectedness to the racial-ethnic in-group was assumed to be critical if youths are to be motivated to engage in group-relevant behaviors. However, connectedness alone does not provide information about what in-group members do. This behavioral-guide function is served by the Embedded Achievement component of racial-ethnic identity, which focuses attention on school engagement as a way to enact one's in-group identity. Especially to the extent that race-based unfair treatment may be part of youths' social context, but even if only as a way to make sense of their group's history, the third component of racial-ethnic identity, an awareness of racism, is necessary to help youths maintain persistence in the face of failures, obstacles, and implicit or explicit negative expectations. Thus, the positive impact of the Embedded Achievement component of racial-ethnic identity should occur only in the presence of the Connectedness and Awareness of Racism components of racial-ethnic identity. Evidence for this model is summarized in the next section. The appendix provides information on how these components are measured, on scale reliability, and on construct validity.

The Relationship Between Racial-Ethnic Identity and Academic Outcomes in Adolescence

As described in the previous section, the tripartite interactive model of racial-ethnic identity posits that adolescents whose racial-ethnic identity simultaneously contains feelings of in-group connectedness, an awareness of racism, and a belief that achievement is embedded in in-group membership will attain better academic outcomes. An initial test of this hypothesis was conducted by experimentally priming racial-ethnic identity among eighth-grade African American students. They were asked to respond, either before or after working on a math task, to (open-ended) questions about what it means to be black or African American. Racial-ethnic identity was expected to have a positive influence on effort on the subsequent math task only when racial-ethnic identity was brought to mind before doing the math task and when the racial-ethnic identity brought to mind included all three components of racial-ethnic identity (Connectedness, Awareness of Racism, and Embedded Achievement). Indeed, youths who wrote about their racial-ethnic identity before the math task and described their racial-ethnic identity in terms of all three identity components performed better on the math task than youths in all other conditions (Oyserman, Gant, and Ager 1995). None of the identity components alone had a significant effect.

This initial test focused on an immediate effect of salient racial-ethnic identity on a school task. Subsequent tests focused on more ecologically valid questions about the effects of racial-ethnic identity in classroom contexts over time, using the brief close-ended rating scales included in table 4A.1. In a series of one-year longitudinal studies that included controls for prior school grades, Oyserman and colleagues found that over the course of the school year, African American eighth grade youth high in all three elements of racial-ethnic identity became more concerned about school (Oyserman, Bybee, and Terry 2003) and did not experience decline in school efficacy (Oyserman, Harrison, and Bybee 2001). Not all effects supported the full three-way interaction model. The authors also found gendered effects of racial-ethnic identity. The Connectedness component had positive effects for boys (predicting improved grades, increased study time, better attendance, and more numerous strategies to attain academic possible selves), and the Embedded Achievement component had positive effects for girls (predicting improved grades) (Oyserman, Bybee, and Terry 2003). A two-year longitudinal study focused on stability of the relationship between the three components of racial-ethnic identity and grades (from school report card) (Altschul, Oyserman, and Bybee 2006). This study included both African American and Latino youths and showed that youths high in Connectedness and Embedded Achievement had better grades at each point in time and that this relationship was stable across gender, race-ethnicity, and time (from the beginning of eighth grade to the end of ninth grade).

Racial-Ethnic Identity as a Socially Contextualized Self-Schema

The program of research described above underscores the utility of conceptualizing racial-ethnic identity in terms of Connectedness, Embedded Achievement, and Awareness of Racism when the goal is to predict the role of racial-ethnic identity in promoting academic attainment and persistence. Oyserman and her colleagues have recently attempted to broaden their conceptualization of the content of racial-ethnic identity (Oyserman et al. 2003). How might responses to the "Who am I, where do I belong, and what am I trying to achieve?" questions be understood more broadly, outside the specific context of school?

Following a social-identity approach (for instance, Tajfel and Turner 1986) a first assumption is that though race-ethnicity is usually a part of self-concept or identity, it is not necessarily a part of self-concept or identity. Thus a basic issue minority youths must resolve is whether race-ethnicity is part of identity—something that frames who they are, where they belong, and what they are trying to achieve. In their reconceptualization, Oyserman and colleagues first asked the basic question of whether race-ethnicity is part of self-definition for all youths. Then, as outlined below, they asked how in-group connection, difficulties integrating into larger society, and valuation of the same goals as the larger society might be differentially combined in various types of racial-ethnic self-schemas.

A first question is whether all youths do in fact incorporate race-ethnicity into identity. Although race-ethnicity, like gender and weight, is commonly used by others to define the self, not everyone self-defines in terms of their race, gender, or weight (Oyserman et al. 2003). When information about the self is incorporated into the self-concept, it may become part of an organized cognitive structure, or self-schema (Markus 1977). Self-schemas are likely to develop in domains that are contextually valued or made salient (Oyserman and Markus 1993). Therefore, though racial-ethnic self-schemas are likely to be common, literature following a self-schema approach suggests that not all youths will incorporate race-ethnicity into identity and that some youths will be aschematic for race-ethnicity while other youth will have a race-ethnicity self-schema (RES).

Being Aschematic for Race-Ethnicity

When asked what it means to be African American or Latino, youth sometimes say things like "Doesn't matter. I was born in America so it doesn't really matter to me," or "It doesn't mean anything to me" (Latino youth). African American male teenagers said: "Really, my race does not matter to me"; "Nothing"; "It means nothing to me. I think it does not matter how you feel about your ethnic group" (see Oyserman et al. 2003). Oyserman operationalized these responses as being aschematic for race-ethnicity, meaning that these individuals are aware of their racial-ethnic group membership and their membership in larger society but see these as simply social "facts" rather than as self-defining and meaningful information. They are likely to consider themselves simply as individuals or as members of other kinds of groups and have not formed a coherent cognitive structure integrating thoughts, feelings, and beliefs about these memberships as part of self-concept.

In segregated contexts in which one's racial-ethnic group is the local majority, being aschematic may mean not feeling connected to one's racial-ethnic in-group, which can be socially isolating, increasing risk of various adjustment problems (see also Cross 1991). In heterogeneous contexts, others are likely to use race-ethnicity to make predictions about the kind of person one is now and is likely to become. Because those who are aschematic for race-ethnicity have not developed a cognitive structure organized around racial-ethnic group membership, they cannot automatically fend off negative implications of racially tinged feedback or social information, which makes them more vulnerable to incorporating negative feedback as self-defining. Given the nature of racial-ethnic stereotypes and race-based unfair treatment, individuals who are aschematic for race-ethnicity are hypothesized to be at risk of simply incorporating negative feedback as self-defining. This is likely to lead to self-blame, increased stress, worse mental health, and reduced effort and engagement with school. Therefore, being aschematic for race-ethnicity is hypothesized to increase risk of academic disengagement and vulnerability to stress and depression among minority youths.

Being Schematic for Race-Ethnicity but Focused Only on One's Racial-Ethnic In-Group

Incorporating the in-group in a racial-ethnic self-schema (RES) without wrestling with the connection between one's racial-ethnic in-group and broader society does not itself resolve the problem of vulnerability to responding to stereotypes by disengaging from school. Youth whose RES focuses solely on in-group membership have a positive focus on their in-group but do not recognize that an aspect of their racial-ethnic identity is their connection to broader society. This racial-ethnic self-schema was termed "in group RES" and is relatively common (almost 60 percent of responses in a middle school sample) (Oyserman et al. 2003). When asked what it means to be African American (or Latino), such youths say things like "It means the world to me. I'm glad of my ethnicity. I wouldn't want to be anything else." A number of separate models draw identical conclusions about the risky nature of simply incorporating the in-group into identity (see Oyserman et al. 2003 for a review).

Being in-group RES can increase risk of vulnerability to stereotypes and disengagement from school. From a social-identity perspective (Tajfel and Turner 1986), out-group stereotypes motivate minorities to devalue and disengage from stereotyped domains and find alternative domains in which to positively self-define (for example, Lemaine 1974; Mummendey et al. 1999; for reviews see Blanton, Christie, and Dye 2002 and Branscombe and Ellemers 1998). Because the stereotyped domain is school, this tendency to disengage from sterotyped domains has the unfortunate consequence of leading youths who feel strongly connected to their in-group but disconnected from broader society to disengage from school and tacitly accept the notion that certain positive attributes such as academic success "belong" to majority- not minority-group members. Thus, we hypothesize that having an In-group RES makes individuals vulnerable to disengagement from school and other mainstream institutions they view as not self-defining. This disengagement is hypothesized to lead to academic difficulties.

Moreover, we suspect that as youths disengage from important social institutions and future goals, they are more likely to sense that the future holds limited opportunities, leading to increased risk for mental health problems. Our formulation is consistent with proposals made by Cross (1991) and research reported by Carlton Pyant and Barbara Yanico (1991)—all of them social scientists—indicating that when individuals are fully immersed in their own culture and are isolated from broader society, they have increased risk for mental health problems. Thus, having an in-group-only racial-ethnic self-schema is hypothesized to be associated with increased risk for both academic and mental health difficulties.

Being Schematic for Race-Ethnicity and Making Connections Between the In-Group and the Larger Society

Given that being either aschematic for race-ethnicity or in-group-only schematic is hypothesized to increase risk of disengagement from school and vulnerability to negative stereotypes about in-group academic ability, what alternatives remain? Oyserman and her colleagues posited that including both the connection to the in-group and the relation between the in-group and broader society within one's racial-ethnic self-schema, termed "Bridging RES," will reduce vulnerability to negative academic stereotypes and reduce the risk of disengagement from school (Oyserman et al. 2003; see LaFramboise, Colman, and Gerton 1993 for another description of the benefits of feeling connected to both the in-group and broader society). Individuals who are Bridging RES focus on both positive connection to the in-group and the connection with the larger society—so that they have a feeling that they are either members of both the in-group and of larger society (Dual RES) or members of an in-group that must struggle to overcome obstacles and barriers to success in larger society (Minority RES).

Dual RES   A person who has a Dual RES focuses attention on his or her status as both an in-group member and a member of the larger society and focuses on the positive consequences of this Dual status (this conceptualization resonates with prior work of Gaertner et al. 1999 and Moran et al. 1999). When asked what it means to be a member of their racial-ethnic group, youths sometimes make statements describing a Dual RES such as "To me, being Latino means that I'm not only part of American culture but that I also belong to another group."

   We hypothesize that the Dual RES provides a buffer against the negative effects of stereotypes about the in-group by connecting individuals to positive larger societal roles and values as well as in-group roles and values. Because those with Dual RES define them selves as members of larger society, they can dismiss stereotypes about the in-group as not self-relevant because the self is a member of larger society for which these stereotypes do not apply (see Hornsey and Hogg 2000). Moreover, eager focus on the attainment of goals and a belief in membership in the larger society should be energizing for individuals with Dual RES, reducing the risk of depression.

Minority RES   Individuals with Minority RES focus attention on their status as members of both the in-group and a group that is discriminated against or obstructed by larger society and they focus on ways to prevent or avoid the negative consequences of minority status within the larger society. When asked what it means to be a member of their racial-ethnic group, youths who are Minority RES sometimes make statements such as "To me being an African American is great because I'm part of a generation that overcame so many obstacles."

   We hypothesize that the Minority RES provides a buffer against the negative effects of stereotypes about the in-group by means of automated strategies for noticing and handling stereotypic and prejudicial responses while remaining engaged in the larger society. Both the Dual and Minority RESs promote a focus on school, but they were posited to have different emotional effects. In individuals with Minority RES, vigilance regarding possible prejudicial responses and heightened awareness of discrimination is likely to be emotionally draining, together increasing risk of depression for these youths.

Evidence for the RES Approach

To examine the effect of RES on academic outcomes, initial studies operationalized each of the four RES types (In-group, Minority, Dual, and Aschematic) from content-coded responses to open-ended questions (Oyserman et al. 2003), allowing participants to say what they mean rather than simply to respond to the categories provided by the researcher. The first test of the RES model included Arab Israeli high school students, who were asked either before or after working on a math task to describe what it meant to them to be Arab Israeli (Oyserman et al. 2003). As expected, students performed better on a math task when racial-ethnic identity was brought to mind before they worked on the task and when it was organized as a Bridging RES. Bringing to mind racial-ethnic identity undermined performance when racial-ethnic identity was organized as an In-group RES or when youths were RES aschematic and race-ethnicity was not organized as a schema at all (Oyserman et al. 2003, study 1). The second and third tests of the RES model involved a more ecologically valid assessment of effects of RES on academic attainment over the course of the school year (Oyserman et al. 2003, studies 2 and 3). The studies demonstrate that American Indian, African American, and Latino youths with racial-ethnic schemas that include both connection to one's racial-ethnic in-group and connection to larger society (Bridging RES) have significantly better academic outcomes by the end of the school year than youths with an in-group-only RES or youths who are aschematic for race-ethnicity. One-year longitudinal follow-up studies using a close-ended rating scale version of the RES scales replicates these school performance findings using school report card grades and teacher reported class participation for Latino and African American youths in the eighth grade (Oyserman, Rhodes, and Brickman 2007). Moreover, among twelfth grade students, only Dual RES also has a positive effect on well-being by reducing risk of depression, whereas minority and In-group-only RES are both associated with increased risk of depression over the high school years (Oyserman, Rhodes, and Brickman 2007). With regard to Latino youths, having a Bridging RES predicts better grades and also mediates the positive effect of length of stay in the United

States and English proficiency on grades. That is, the main effects of being longer in the United States and being proficient in English on grades are mediated by the positive relationship between length of stay in U.S. and English proficiency on likelihood of having a Bridging RES. Youths longer in the United States and youths who are more proficient in English are more likely to have a Bridging RES, a racial-ethnic self-schema that articulates both in-group membership and connection to larger society, and once likelihood of having a Bridging RES is entered as a mediator, effects of length of stay in the United States and English proficiency on grades is significantly reduced (Altschul, Oyserman, and Bybee 2006a).

A General Model of Racial-Ethnic Identity

We have presented here two working operationalizations of racial-ethnic identity. In our first operationalization, we focused on feeling connected to an in-group, being aware of racism, and believing that the in-group values academic achievement. We summarized research showing that youths high in all three of these components of racial-ethnic identity (termed Connectedness, Awareness of Racism, and Embedded Achievement) were in fact more likely to do better in school, whereas when racial-ethnic identity was conceptualized in terms of the main effects of Connectedness or Awareness of Racism without Embedded Achievement, racial-ethnic identity is not predictive of improved academic outcomes.

We then turned to a second operationalization of racial-ethnic identity, the goal of which was threefold: first, to link racial-ethnic identity with broader theorizing about self-concept (self-schemas); second, to include an explicit test of whether youths do define themselves in terms of racial-ethnic identity; third, to articulate racial-ethnic identity in terms of the extent to which minority youths view themselves as connected to larger society more generally rather than focusing only on one aspect of this connection: the relationship between the in-group and the social institution of school. We summarized research showing that youths who define themselves in terms of racial-ethnic identity and see the in-group as connected with larger society do better in school. Moreover, we summarized research suggesting that how youths see the connection between their in-group and larger society matters for their well-being. Youths who see this connection positively are at reduced risk of depression; youths who see it as something that they must struggle to achieve by overcoming barriers and prejudice are at increased risk of depression.

Thus, both conceptualizations provide predictions as to when racial-ethnic identity should be related to academic attainment. The second operationalization provides evidence that racial-ethnic identity also predicts well-being. Moreover, the second operationalization holds promise for predicting positive attainments in life tasks beyond schooling, such as in higher education or in career, as well as a broader sense of well-being, beyond measures of depressive symptoms. By moving beyond explicit focus on academic attainment, the racial-ethnic schema conceptualization of racial-ethnic identity provides a more general model that holds promise for both future research and for articulating effective intervention focuses.

Our general model of racial-ethnic identity postulates that not all youths will incorporate race-ethnicity into self-concept, and that even if they do incorporate race-ethnicity into identity, they are likely to differ in terms of what racial-ethnic content is incorporated into self-concept and how this content is structured. Youths who focus only on the in-group, whether operationalized as being high in connectedness only or as having an In-group RES, are vulnerable to incorporating negative stereotypes about the in-group into their self-concept. Youths who focus on the in-group as well as other important aspects of being a minority-group member are better able to buffer these negative representations. We have articulated what these other aspects are in two ways. We have argued that if the goal is to promote motivation for academic success, then racial-ethnic identity must contain not only a sense of connection to the in-group but also the belief that the in-group values educational attainment. More generally, we have argued that if the goal is to promote successful attainment of developmentally appropriate life tasks, then racial-ethnic identity must contain not only sense of connection to in-group but also a positive belief in one's membership in larger society.

Appendix: Measurement and Construct Validity of the Racial-Ethnic Identity Scales

We present here details of how to measure racial-ethnic identity and the construct validity of the racial-ethnic identity scales.

Measurement

No matter how interesting, a model is only as useful as its operationalization and measurement allows it to be. With regard to the racial-ethnic identity scales, to avoid social desirability and experimenter demand characteristics, initial research utilized open-ended probes such as "What does it mean to you to be a _____?" Responses were content-coded (Oyserman, Gant, and Ager 1995; Oyserman, Bybee, and Terry 2003). To improve ease of use, close-ended scales were operationalized as extent of agreement to common responses generated from these open-ended probes. Each of the three components of racial-ethnic identity (Connectedness, Awareness of Racism, and Embedded Achievement) can be assessed with a four-item scale. Each scale uses a five-point Likert response-scale. (1 = strongly disagree, 2 = disagree, 3 = neither agree nor disagree, 4 = agree, 5 = strongly agree). Scale items are provided in the first column of table 4A.1. Scales are intentionally brief so they can be used in school-based research, which often requires that research take no more than a single classroom period.

Though brief, the racial-ethnic identity Connectedness, Awareness of Racism, and Embedded Achievement scales are adequately reliable. Reliability refers to the consistency, or "repeatability," of a measure. One way to measure reliability is to compute Cronbach's alpha, a measure of the level of association among items within a subscale and another way to measure reliability is to compute the test-retest reliability, or level of association between scales, over time. Perfect association would result in a reliabilty of 1.00. The Cronbach's alpha for Racial-Ethnic Identity scales ranges from 0.58 to 0.79 across samples (Altschul, Oyserman, and Bybee 2006b; Lesane 2003; Oyserman, Harrison, and Bybee 2001; Oyserman, Bybee, and Terry 2003; Oyserman, Bybee, and Dai 2006). Over eight months, test-retest reliability: 0.78 for Connectedness, 0.81 for Awareness of Racism, and 0.65 for Embedded Achievement (Altschul, Oyserman, and Bybee 2006).

Structural Validity

Structural validity is typically examined by conducting a confirmatory factor analysis (CFA). CFA allows for examining whether the scale structure is similar across groups and the degree of correlation between scales. For the Racial-Ethnic Identity scales, we asked whether scale items loaded as expected on the scales and whether the items loaded on the factors the same way for younger and older youths, for boys and girls, and for African Americans and Latinos. Testing for stability is important because if the scales are stable across these groups, then findings from one group (for instance, older teens) could be used to make predictions about another group (younger teens), but if the scales are not stable, it is not possible to make such predictions or to use the same scale over time as teens age.

Similarly, if the scales are not stable across racial-ethnic groups then what is learned from one group cannot be generalized to another. Since ascertaining that the structure of the factors is as assumed is important for continued use of the scale and interpretation of results, we conducted a CFA for this chapter, utilizing data from Oyserman, Rhodes, and Brickman 2007. This relatively large data set (N = 348) was adequate for the overall CFA and for each of the targeted compar-

Table 4A.1   Three-Factor Racial-Ethnic Identity Confirmatory Factor Analysis: Items, Unstandardized and Standardized Coefficients

		Unstandarized Coefficient[a]	Standardized Coefficient[a]
Connectedness	It is important to think of myself as ——.	1[b]	0.61
	I feel a part of the —— community.	1.13	0.76
	I have a lot of pride in what —— have done and achieved.	0.97	0.70
	I feel close to ——.	1.12	0.71
Embedded achievement	If I am successful it will help other ——.	1[b]	0.71
	It is important for my family and the —— community that I succeed in school.	0.78	0.65
	It helps me when other —— do well.	0.96	0.70
	If I work hard and get good grades, other —— will respect me.	0.74	0.49
Awareness of racism	Some people will treat me differently because I am ——.	1[b]	0.71
	The way I look and speak influences what others expect of me.	0.64	0.52
	Things in the —— community are not as good as they could be because of lack of opportunity.	0.56	0.47
	People might have negative ideas about my abilities because I am a(n) ——.	1.14	0.85

Source: Oyserman, Harrison, and Bybee (2001) for racial-ethic identity scales. Original analysis for CFA.
[a]All coefficients are significantly different from zero.
[b]Coefficients constrained to 1.
p < .001.

isons, but did not allow for simultaneous comparison of all subgroups. Consequently each comparison is presented as a separate analysis.

Specifically, we performed a three-factor CFA of our twelve-item Racial-Ethnic Identity scale with maximum likelihood estimation using the Amos 4.0 statistical package. Our goal was to determine whether the three-factor structure of Racial-Ethnic Identity (Connectedness,

Embedded Achievement, and Awareness of Racism) that we posited is a good fit to the patterning of responses. This "goodness of fit" is assessed using multiple indices. Following the standard procedure recommended by Li-Tzi Hu and Peter M. Bentler (1998), we used three indices, the standardized root mean square residual (SRMR), the comparative fit index (CFI) and the root mean square error of approximation (RMSEA). For the SRMR, values below .08, for the RMSEA, values below .06, and for the CFI values at or above .95 indicate "good fit," respectively (Hu and Bentler 1998). On the basis of this set of goodness-of-fit indicators, the three-factor racial-ethnic identity model is a good fit overall and for younger and older adolescents (eighth and twelfth grade), boys and girls, and Latino and African American youths.

Overall Fit   Overall we found good fit for the three component racial-ethnic identity model (SRMR = .059; CFI = .947; RMSEA = .061). Table 4A.1 presents nonstandardized and standardized loadings in columns two and three respectively. All coefficients are significant, p < .001, and all are greater than .45, which means that each item is adequately associated with its subscale. Awareness of Racism is moderately correlated with both Connectedness (r = .45, p < .001); Embedded Achievement (r = .41, p < .001); Connectedness and Embedded Achievement are highly correlated (r = .78, p < .001).

Measurement Structure Fit by Subgroup   To test whether the racial-ethnic identity model has the same measurement structure across age, gender, and race-ethnicity groups, we performed three separate multigroup CFAs. In each case the test was relatively stringent as we required that factor loadings, factor variances, and covariances not differ. For each set, we compared a model where these values were free to vary (that is, were different for younger versus older teens, were different for boys versus girls, or were different for African Americans versus Latinos) with a model where these values were constrained to equality (that is, were the same for both age groups, were the same for both genders, were the same for both African Americans and Latinos). If the models do not differ significantly, it is reasonable to assume that the structure of the racial-ethnic identity components is similar. Indeed, the models did not differ significantly. The results of the models comparing the two ages ($\Delta\chi^2(15) = 17.91$, p > .25), the models comparing boys and girls ($\Delta\chi^2(15) = 15.34$, p > .4), and the models comparing African American and Latino race-ethnicity ($\Delta\chi^2(15) = 8.43$, p = .91) were not significant, suggesting that the racial-ethnic identity components were similarly structured within each subgroup. This means that it is possible to use the measures across these different groups and assume that they have similar meanings across these groups. It should be noted that the race-ethnicity analyses focus only on eighth-grade youths because this sample had a roughly even split between Latinos (n = 95) and African Americans (n = 84), whereas the twelfth-grade sample was mostly African American (Oyserman, Rhodes, and Brickman 2007).

References

Akbar, Na'im. 1991. *Visions for Black Men*. Nashville, TN: Winston–Derek.

Altschul, Inna, Daphna Oyserman, and Deborah Bybee. 2006a. "Racial-Ethnic Identity and the Academic Achievement of Low-Income Latino Youths: Comparing Segmented Assimilation and Racial-Ethnic Self-Schema Predictions." Manuscript under editorial review. Ann Arbor: University of Michigan.

Altschul, Inna, Daphna Oyserman, and Deborah Bybee. 2006b. "Racial-ethnic Identity in Mid-Adolescence: Content and Change as Predictors of Academic Achievement." *Child Development* 77: 1155–69.

Asante, Molefi Kete. 1987. *The Afrocentric Idea*. Philadelphia: Temple University Press.

———. 1988. *Afrocentricity*. Trenton, N.J.: African World Press.

Blanton, Hart, Charlene Christie, and Maureen Dye. 2002. "Social Identity Versus Reference Frame Comparisons: The Moderating Role of Stereotype Endorsement." *Journal of Experimental Social Psychology* 38(3): 253–67.

Branscombe, Nyla R., and Naomi Ellemers. 1998. "Coping with Group-Based Discrimination: Individualistic Versus Group-Level Strategies." In *Prejudice: The Target's Perspective*, edited by Janet K. Swim and Charles Stangor. San Diego: Academic Press.

Brown, B. Bradford. 2004. "Adolescents' Relationships with Peers." In *Handbook of Adolescent Psychology*, edited by Richard M. Lerner and Lawrence Steinberg. Hoboken, N.J.: Wiley.

Brown, Christia S., and Rebecca S. Bigler. 2005. "Children's Perceptions of Discrimination: A Developmental Model." *Child Development* 76(3): 533–53.

Chavous, Tabbye M., Deborah H. Bernat, Karen Schmeelk-Cone, Cleopatra H. Caldwell, Laura Kohn-Wood, and Marc A. Zimmerman. 2003. "Racial Identity and Academic Attainment Among African American Adolescents." *Child Development* 74(4): 1076–90.

Chavous, Tabbye M., Angel Harris, Deborah Rivas, Lumas Helaire, and Laurette Green. 2004. "Racial Stereotypes and Gender in Context: African-Americans at Predominantly Black and Predominantly White Colleges." *Sex Roles* 51(1–2): 1–16.

Conchas, Gilberto Q. 2001. "Structuring Failure and Success: Understanding the Variability in Latino School Engagement." *Harvard Educational Review* 71(3): 475–504.

Corsaro, William A., and Donna Eder. 1990. "Children's Peer Cultures." *Annual Review of Sociology* 16: 197–220.

Crocker, Jennifer, Riia Luhtanen, Bruce Blaine, and Stephanie Broadnax. 1994. "Collective Self-Esteem and Psychological Well-Being Among White, Black, and Asian College Students." *Personality and Social Psychology Bulletin* 20(5): 503–13.

Cross, William E. 1991. *Shades of Black: Diversity in African-American Identity*. Philadelphia: Temple University Press.

Erikson, Erik H. 1950. *Childhood and Society.* New York: W. W. Norton.

Gaertner, Samuel L., John F. Dovidio, Jason A. Nier, Christine M. Ward, and Brenda S. Banker. 1999. "Across Cultural Divides: The Value of a Superordinate Identity." In *Cultural Divides: Understanding and Overcoming Group Conflict,* edited by Deborah A. Prentice and Dale T. Miller. New York: Russell Sage Foundation.

Gibson, Margaret, and John Ogbu. 1991. *Minority Status and Schooling.* New York: Garland.

Gonzales, Nancy A., Larry E. Dumka, Julianna Deardorff, Sara J. Carter, and Adam McCray. 2004. "Preventing Poor Mental Health and School Dropout of Mexican American Adolescents Following the Transition to Junior High School." *Journal of Adolescent Research* 19(1): 113–31.

Gonzales, Patricia M., Hart Blanton, and Kevin J. Williams. 2002. "The Effects of Stereotype Threat and Double-Minority Status on the Test Performance of Latino Women." *Personality and Social Psychology Bulletin* 28(5): 659–70.

Graham, Sandra. 2001. "Inferences About Responsibility and Values: Implication for Academic Motivation." In *Student Motivation: The Culture and Context of Learning,* edited by Faridi Salili and Chi-yue Chiu. Dordrecht, Netherlands: Kluwer Academic Publishers.

Harter, Susan. 1997. "The Development of Self-Representations." In *Handbook of Child Psychology,* edited by William Damon. 5th ed. Volume 3, *Social, Emotional, and Personality Development,* edited by Nancy Eisenberg. New York: Wiley.

Hirschfeld, Lawrence A. 1996. "Race in the Making: Cognition, Culture, and the Child's Construction of Human Kinds." Cambridge, Mass.: MIT Press.

Hornsey, Matthew J., and Michael A. Hogg. 2000. "Assimilation and Diversity: An Integrative Model of Subgroup Relations." *Personality and Social Psychology Review* 4(2): 143–56.

Hu, Li-Tze, and Peter M. Bentler. 1998. "Fit Indices in Covariance Structure Modeling: Sensitivity to Underparameterized Model Misspecification." *Psychological Methods* 3(4): 424–53.

Hudley, Cynthia, and Sandra Graham. 2001. "Stereotypes of Achievement Striving Among Early Adolescents." *Social Psychology of Education* 5(2): 201–24.

Kao, Grace. 2000. "Group Images and Possible Selves Among Adolescents: Linking Stereotypes to Expectations by Race and Ethnicity." *Sociological Forum* 15(3): 407–30.

LaFontana, Kathryn M., and Antonius H. N. Cillessen. 2002. "Children's Perceptions of Popular and Unpopular Peers: A Multimethod Assessment." *Developmental Psychology* 38(5): 635–47.

LaFramboise, Teresa, Hardin L. K. Coleman, and Jennifer Gerton. 1993. "Psychological Impact of Biculturalism: Evidence and Theory." *Psychological Bulletin* 114(3): 395–412.

Lemaine, Gerard. 1974. "Social Differentiation and Social Originality." *European Journal of Social Psychology* 4(1): 17–52.

Lesane, Cheryl. 2003. "Ethnic Identity-Oyserman." Fast Track technical report. Available online at http://www.fasttrackproject.org/techrept/e/eio/eio9tech.pdf.

Lovaglia, Michael J., Jeffrey W. Lucas, Jeffrey A. Houser, Shane R. Thye, and

Barry Markovsky. 1998. "Status Processes and Mental Ability Test Scores." *American Journal of Sociology* 104(1): 195–228.

Markus, Hazel R. 1977. "Self-Schemata and Processing Information About the Self." *Journal of Personality and Social Psychology* 35(2): 63–78.

McAdoo, Harriette P. 1988. Black families. 2nd ed. Newbury Park, Calif.: Sage.

McKown, Clark, and Rhona S. Weinstein. 2003. "The Development and Consequences of Stereotype Consciousness in Middle Childhood." *Child Development* 74(2): 498–515.

Moran, James R., Candace M. Fleming, Philip Somervell, and Spero M. Manson. 1999. "Measuring Bicultural Ethnic Identity Among American Indian Adolescents: A Factor Analysis Study." *Journal of Adolescent Research* 14(4): 405–26.

Mummendey, Amélie, Thomas Kessler, Andreas Klink, and Rosemarie Mielke. 1999. "Strategies to Cope with Negative Social Identity: Predictions by Social Identity Theory and Relative Deprivation Theory." *Journal of Personality and Social Psychology* 76(2): 229–45.

Ogbu, John U. 1992. "Understanding Cultural Diversity and Learning." *Educational Researcher* 21(8): 5–14.

Oyserman, Daphna. 2007. "Social Identity and Self-Regulation." In *Handbook of Social Psychology, Second Edition*, edited by Arie W. Kruglanski and E. Tory Higgins. New York: Guilford Press.

Oyserman, Daphna, Daniel Brickman, Deborah Bybee, and Aaron Celious. 2006. "Fitting in Matters: Markers of In-group Belonging and Academic Outcomes." *Psychological Science* 17: 854–61.

Oyserman, Daphna, Deborah Bybee, and Haijing Dai. 2006. "Neighborhood Effects on Content of Racial-ethnic Identity in Adolescence." Under editorial review. Ann Arbor: University of Michigan.

Oyserman, Daphna, Deborah Bybee, and Kathy Terry. 2003. "Gendered Racial Identity and Involvement with School." *Self and Identity* 2(4): 307–24.

Oyserman, Daphna, Larry Gant, and Joel Ager. 1995. "A Socially Contextualized Model of African American Identity: Possible Selves and School Persistence." *Journal of Personality and Social Psychology* 69(6): 1216–32.

Oyserman, Daphna, and Kathy Harrison. 1998. "Implications of Cultural Context: African American Identity and Possible Selves." In *Prejudice: The Target's Perspective*, edited by Janet K. Swim and Charles Stangor. San Diego: Academic Press.

Oyserman, Daphna, Kathy Harrison, and Deborah Bybee. 2001. "Can Racial Identity Be Promotive of Academic Efficacy?" *International Journal of Behavioral Development* 25(4): 379–85.

Oyserman, Daphna, Markus Kemmelmeier, Stephanie Fryberg, Hazi Brosh, and Tamera Hart-Johnson. 2003. "Racial-Ethnic Self-Schemas." *Social Psychology Quarterly* 66(4): 333–47.

Oyserman, Daphna, and Hazel R. Markus. 1993. "The Sociocultural Self." In *The Self in Social Perspective*, edited by Jerry Suls. Volume 4. Hillsdale, N.J.: Lawrence Erlbaum.

Oyserman, Daphna, Marjorie Rhodes, and Daniel Brickman. 2007. "Racial-Ethnic Self-Schemas: Engagement Well-Being, and School." Under editorial review. Ann Arbor: University of Michigan.

Oyserman, Daphna, and Izumi Sakamoto. 1997. "Being Asian American: Identity, Cultural Constructs, and Stereotype Perception." *Journal of Applied Behavioral Science* 33(4): 435–53.

Parham, Thomas A. 1989. "Cycles of Psychological Nigrescence." *The Counseling Psychologist* 17(2): 187–226.

Phinney, Jean S. 1996. "Understanding Ethnic Diversity: The Role of Ethnic Identity." *American Behavioral Scientist* 40(2): 143–52.

Population Resource Center. 2001. "Executive Summary: A Demographic Profile of Hispanics in the U.S." Available at: http://www.prcdc.org/summaries/hispanics/hispanics.html (accessed December 9, 2006).

Porter, Judith R., and Robert E. Washington. 1989. "Developments in Research on Black Identity and Self-Esteem: 1979–1988." *Revue Internationale de Psychologie Sociale* 2(3): 339–53.

Pyant, Carlton T., and Barbara J. Yanico. 1991. "Relationship of Racial Identity and Gender-Role Attitudes to Black Women's Psychological Well-Being." *Journal of Counseling Psychology* 38(3): 315–22.

Quintana, Stephen M., and Theresa A. Segura-Herrera. 2003. "Developmental Transformations of Self and Identity in the Context of Oppression." *Self and Identity* 2(4): 269–85.

Schmader, Toni, and Michael Johns. 2003. "Converging Evidence That Stereotype Threat Reduces Working Memory Capabilities." *Journal of Personality and Social Psychology* 85(3): 440–52.

Secada, Walter G. 1999. "Lessons Learned by the Hispanic Dropout Project. *Clearing House* 73(2): 93–95.

Sellers, Robert M., Stephane A. J. Rowley, Tabbye M. Chavous, J. Nicole Shelton, and Mia A. Smith. 1997. "Multidimensional Inventory of Black Identity: A Preliminary Investigation of Reliability and Construct Validity." *Journal of Personality and Social Psychology* 73(4): 805–15.

Spencer, Steven J., Claude M. Steele, Diane M. Steele, and Steve Quinn. 1999. "Stereotype Threat and Women's Math Performance." *Journal of Experimental Social Psychology* 35(1): 4–28.

Steele, Claude M. 1997. "A Threat in the Air: How Stereotypes Shape Intellectual Identity and Performance." *American Psychologist* 52(6): 613–29.

Stevenson, Howard C. 1995. "Relationship of Adolescent Perceptions of Racial Socializations to Racial Identity." *Journal of Black Psychology* 21(1): 49–70.

Swanson, Dena P., Margaret B. Spencer and Vinay Harpalani. 2003. "Psychosocial Development in Racially and Ethnically Diverse Youth: Conceptual and Methodological Challenges in the 21st Century." *Development and Psychopathology* 15(3): 743–71.

Tajfel, Henri, and John C. Turner. 1986. "The Social Identity Theory of Intergroup Behavior." In *The Social Psychology of Intergroup Relations*, edited by William G. Austin and Stephen Worchel. Chicago: Nelson-Hall.

Tripp, Luke. 1991. "Race Consciousness Among African-American Students, 1980s." *The Western Journal of Black Studies* 15(3): 159–68.

U.S. Census Bureau. 2000. "Housing Patterns. Percent of Persons Who Are Black or African American Alone, Map by Metropolitan Area." Available at http://factfinder.census.gov.

Chapter 5

Social Identity, Stereotype Threat, and Self-Theories

Catherine Good, Carol S. Dweck, and Joshua Aronson

Each of us possesses multiple social identities. For example, our sex, age, race, social class, religion, political beliefs, and professions are all potential social identities. In certain contexts in which we find ourselves, that social identity may be devalued. For example, Democrats at the Republican National Convention, gays and lesbians at a custody hearing, a lone woman at a corporate board of directors meeting, black people in an all-white, southern neighborhood, or an Arab flight attendant with an American or European airline—all are at risk of having a component of their social identities devalued in the respective contexts. In response to this devaluation, they may find that their behavior or sense of self changes. Perhaps the female corporate board member speaks less persuasively than she is capable of speaking, or perhaps the Arab flight attendant chooses a different occupation, thus changing his professional identity.

One need not be in an extreme situation to feel the weight of a devalued social identity. More subtle situations may also place a burden upon individuals who are in some way stigmatized. For example, when a woman takes a math test in the presence of men, she may be reminded about the stereotype of male superiority in mathematics that is alive in our culture (Spencer, Steele, and Quinn 1999; Steele and Aronson 1995). Being a woman, and thus, having a social identity that is devalued vis-à-vis mathematics ability, she may have a sense that she could be judged or treated in terms of the stereotype or that she might inadvertently confirm the stereotype. This sense can disrupt her ability to perform up to her potential, a predicament known as "stereotype threat" (Steele and Aronson 1995).

In this chapter we will review the literature on stereotype threat as it relates to social identity. Specifically, we will discuss not only how people's social identity can either protect them from or create vulnerability to stereotype threat, but also how the experience of stereotype threat can influence their social identity. Thus, we will show that social identity and stereotype threat have a reciprocal relationship. Finally, we will discuss methods of protecting both social identity and achievement from the negative effects of stereotypes.[1]

Social Identity Affects Vulnerability to Stereotype Threat

Over a decade of research has shown that when an individual's social identity includes a group that is negatively stereotyped in a domain, or area of study, the person is vulnerable to underperformance in that domain (see Steele, Spencer, and Aronson 2002 for a review). This research has also shown, however, that not all members of a stigmatized group have the same degree of vulnerability to stereotype threat. Rather, differences in the degree to which people base their identities on their group membership or on achievement in the stereotyped domain can influence the degree to which they are vulnerable to stereotype-based underperformance.

Identification with the Stereotyped Group

Some studies suggest that stigmatized individuals whose social identity is strongly aligned with the stereotyped group may be most vulnerable. For example, Toni Schmader (2002) has shown that females who are highly identified with their gender group are most vulnerable to threat. In her study, women and men took a diagnostic math test and in one condition, were told that their scores would be used to compare women to men. Thus, in one condition their performance was linked to their social identity, and in the other condition it was not. For women whose gender was a strong part of their social identity, connecting their math outcomes to their gender suppressed their performance on the math test—they performed worse than the men in this condition. But women who did not consider their gender to be central to their social identity performed just as well as men, regardless of whether or not their math performance was linked to their gender.

The opposite happened for men—men who had a strong gender identity benefited from the thought of comparing men's and women's math scores. Clearly, the stereotype of men's greater ability in math was a boon to their performance.

Thus the results of this study provide evidence that not all negatively stereotyped individuals are equally vulnerable to stereotype threat. Rather, in this case, those who were the most invested in the component of their social identity that was devalued were also the most vulnerable to stereotype threat.

Yet research with other stereotyped groups, such as African Americans, suggests that the opposite can sometimes occur: that identifying with the stereotyped group can buffer a person from stereotype-threat effects (Davis and Aronson 2005; Oyserman, Harrison, and Bybee 2001). For example, Claytie Davis and Joshua Aronson (2005) found that a strong racial identity protected African American students against stereotype threat, although this occurred only when the threat was relatively weak. When the threat was increased, the benefit of having a strong racial identity was reduced.

Daphna Oyserman, Kathy Harrison, and Deborah Bybee (2001) also found evidence for the benefits of having a strong racial identity. These researchers found that even when African American adolescent girls believed that their racial group was devalued by out-group members, they showed the greatest sense of academic achievement efficacy when they felt connected with their racial group. A strong racial identity, however, was protective only when the females also believed that being African American is associated with achievement. When stereotyped individuals make this identity-achievement link, then the stereotype may be disarmed, even though they may find themselves in situations in which the prevailing negative cultural stereotype is alive.

What might account for the fact that females who are highly identified with their group appear to be more vulnerable to negative stereotypes (as in Schmader 2002), whereas African Americans who are highly identified with their group appear to be less vulnerable (as in Davis and Aronson 2005 and Oyserman, Harrison, and Bybee 2001)? Consider for a moment what it means for these two groups to be highly identified. For females, a high identification with being female may often mean that they buy into societal prescriptions for what it means to be female and therefore will be more sensitive to messages that say females may not have a particular competency. However, for African Americans, a high identification with being black may mean that they reject the definitions that the larger white society may try to impose on them—and therefore might be more rejecting of messages about their competencies.

Furthermore, as Oyserman, Daniel Brickman, and Marjorie Rhodes discuss in chapter 4 of this volume, both identifying with and not identifying with one's stereotyped in-group can increase vulnerability to negative stereotypes. They argue, however, that when in-group identification also includes either the larger society or an awareness of the need to overcome negative societal expectations, having a strong in-group identity can be protective. In the context of racial identity,

Oyserman, Brickman, and Rhodes define these two types of social identity as Dual Racial Ethnic Schematic and Minority Racial Ethnic Schematic, respectively. Studies that fail to measure these forms of racial (or gender) identity may draw spurious conclusions about the relationship between in-group identity and vulnerability to negative stereotypes.

Furthermore, as Julie A. Garcia and Jennifer Crocker (chapter 7, this volume) discuss, another source of potential discrepancy in the relationship between social identity and vulnerability to negative stereotypes may be the degree to which stigmatized individuals base their self-worth on academic achievement. Stigmatized individuals are particularly susceptible to state variations in academic contingencies, especially when they are highly identified with their stereotyped group. Although having self-worth that is contingent on academic success can be motivating in some situations, it also comes at a price. For example, high contingencies of self-worth can lead to the goal of maintaining self-esteem, often at the expense of learning. Consequently, stigmatized individuals who are high in contingent self-worth and also highly identified with their stereotyped group may be more susceptible to academic setbacks.

In sum, the extent to which one identifies with the stereotyped group is a factor in vulnerability to stereotype threat. In some situations, however, identification can be protective. In other situations, it can create vulnerabilities. A fruitful avenue for future research would be to probe more deeply into the circumstances under which strong identification with a group leads to increased versus decreased vulnerability to stereotypes.

Is a Historically Valued Social Identity Protective?

Clearly, having a devalued social identity creates vulnerability to stereotype threat, and perhaps even more so when that component of your social identity is a fundamental part of who you are. However, having a social identity that is the chronic target of stigmatization and stereotypes is not necessary to create vulnerability. For example, even white males—who do not face a history of stigmatization or chronic negative stereotypes about their intellectual abilities—can experience threat. In a study by Aronson et al. (1999), white males took a math test and in the stereotype-threat condition were told that the purpose was to better understand Asian superiority in math achievement. Thus, stereotype threat was created for these participants by casting their social identity in the shadow of a more valued social identity in the domain of math—Asians. The results showed that the white men whose social identities were called into question performed less well on the math test than those whose social identities were not devalued by comparison to a more competent group. This study is important because it illustrates that vulnerability to stereotype threat is not an internalized trait nor is it predicated upon a chronically devalued social identity. Rather, it is a situational predicament that could beset any- one when faced with a situation in which his or her social identity is devalued.

Multiple Social Identities and Conflicting Stereotypes

As noted earlier, however, people's social identities have many components, some of which may be more or less valued in any given situation. What happens, then, when multiple social identities are associated with conflicting stereotypes? For example, females are considered to be poor mathematicians, but Asians are considered talented in math. Are Asian females vulnerable to stereotype threat in math, or do the positive stereotypes about their race protect them from it? To answer this question, consider the following study (Shih, Pittinsky, and Ambady 1999): Asian American women took a math test after having one component of their social identity primed. In one condition, the women answered survey questions designed to prime their Asian identity—a social identity that is positively associated with math achievement in American culture. In the other condition, the women answered survey questions designed to prime their gender identity—a social identity that is negatively associated with math achievement. Results showed that the women's performance on the math test depended on which component of their social identity was made salient. Specifically, compared to a third condition in which no identity was made salient, women's math performance in the race-salient condition improved, whereas women's math performance in the gender-salient condition was impaired.

These results underscore the interesting role that multiple social identities can play in vulnerability to stereotype threat. Although all the participants were women and thus were potentially vulnerable to stereotype threat, their Asian identity not only protected them from the threat, it lifted their performance above baseline. Clearly, simply possessing a social identity that is devalued in a context does not necessarily lead to underperformance in a threatening situation, such as when one's abilities are being measured. This study illustrates that when a valued social identity is made salient, the stereotype associated with the devalued social identity may lose its bite.

Situations That Increase the Link Between
Social Identity and Stereotype Threat

That identity salience plays such a pivotal role in determining whether or not a person is vulnerable to stereotype-based underperformance raises the question: How are devalued social identities made salient? Research has shown that situational cues, such as the proportion of people in a setting who share (or do not share) the same social identity, can affect not only the activation of stereotypes associated with one's social identity but also the likelihood of underperformance caused by stereotype threat. In one study that elegantly illustrates this possibility (Inzlicht and Ben-Zeev 2000), men and women took a math test in three-person groups, either three women, two women and one man, or one woman and two men. The authors argued that for women taking the test with two men, the mere distinctiveness of being in the minority should focus their attention on their gender, and along with it, the negative stereotypes about women and math. Conversely, women who take the test in the presence of other women should be less likely to spontaneously notice their gender and related negative stereotypes. In other words, being outnumbered by men should be sufficient to bring to mind not only their social identity, but also the negative stereotypes associated with that identity. This is precisely what happened, even when the women were in the presence of just one man (Inzlicht and Ben-Zeev 2000, study 2).

If increases in the relative number of out-group members in the environment can increase the salience of social identity and stereotypes (Inzlicht and Ben-Zeev 2003; McGuire et al. 1978), then it would not be surprising if women's math performance in this study dropped as a function of the number of men in the room. And indeed, women who took the math test in the presence of one man performed worse than women test takers in the presence of only women, but better than women test takers in the presence of two men. Thus, a seemingly innocuous contextual cue—such as the number of men in a room—can create a "threatening intellectual environment" (Inzlicht and Good 2006) in which a devalued social identity and negative stereotypes combine to undermine women's math test performance. Similar results have been found with other stigmatized groups: when black participants were the only minority person trying to remember a verbal presentation, they remembered less of the presentation than when the majority of participants were black (Sekaquaptewa and Thompson 2002).

Other situational factors have also been found that link identity salience and vulnerability to stereotype threat. For example, in both real-world and laboratory settings, the simple act of having participants indicate their gender or race prior to taking a test—and thus, making their social identity about that group salient—led to lower performance. In a controlled laboratory experiment (Steele and Aronson 1995), for example, black and white participants either indicated their race on the test booklet prior to taking a difficult verbal test or did not indicate their race. In the race-salient condition, the black participants scored significantly worse than both black and white participants in all conditions. But when black participants did not indicate their race, their performance equaled that of their white peers. The results of this carefully controlled laboratory experiment were replicated in a real-world test-taking situation. Researchers at the Educational Testing Service had students indicate their gender either before or after taking the advanced placement (AP) calculus examination (Stricker 1998). The female test takers who were asked about their gender before the test scored significantly lower than those asked about their gender after the test. Similar (albeit weaker) results were found when minority students were asked to indicate their race either before or after the test. Thus, the simple act of specifying a stigmatized component of social identity can create vulnerability to stereotype threat.

The salience of one's stigmatized social identity need not always undermine test performance, however. Recent research (Marx, Stapel, and Muller 2005) showed, in line with past research, that stereotype threat can heighten the accessibility of the collective self, especially as it centers on membership in a stereotyped group. Female participants in the stereotype-threat condition listed more group-based pronouns, such as "we" and "us," and indicated more overlap between the self and their gender group. However, the authors went on to demonstrate that this heightened sense of "we-ness" could be used to benefit math test performance when they provided females with examples of other females who had been successful in mathematics. Thus, when females' collective self is heightened and the stereotype is refuted, females may actually perform better under stereotype-threat conditions than under non-threat conditions.

Identification with the Stereotyped Domain

As we have seen, in many cases the salience and strength of a stigmatized social identity can create vulnerability to stereotype threat. In addition, seemingly innocuous situational factors, such as the number of non-stigmatized individuals who are in the room or indicating group membership prior to taking a test, can make that social identity salient and consequently injurious to academic achievement. Perhaps, however, a social identity that is aligned with the task can protect against stereotype threat. Is it the case that individuals who are strongly identified with achievement in a stereotyped domain—that is, those who are invested in their competence and belonging in a domain—are shielded from the negative effects of their stigmatized status? Ironically, the answer is no. Their identification with the domain does not protect them from stereotype threat. Moreover, it is often precisely the people who are most identified with the domain who are the most vulnerable to depressed performance.

For example, Catherine Good, Joshua Aronson, and Jayne Ann Harder (forthcoming) tested whether or not stereotype threat could undermine the performance of women who aspired to become mathematicians, engineers, or scientists. They found that even among this highly selective sample of women who were enrolled in the most difficult college mathematics courses, stereotype threat suppressed their calculus performance. However, alleviating the threat by ensuring women that the same diagnostic test was free of gender-bias unleashed their mathematics potential. Not only did the women in the non-threat condition outperform women in the stereotype-threat condition, but they also outperformed the men in either testing condition. Thus, when the threat of being evaluated on a diagnostic math task is removed by ensuring women that the test is gender-fair, women can outperform men even on the most difficult of math tests. However, when faced with a stereotype-threat situation, these women underperform—they lose their competitive edge over men, despite their talent, their love of math, and their desire to pursue mathematics-oriented professions.

This study suggests that having a social identity aligned with the stereotyped domain (such as mathematician or scientist) does not protect against stereotype threat. Moreover, it is precisely those whose social identities are most invested in high achievement in the domain who are sometimes the most vulnerable (Aronson et al. 1999). For example, in the study showing that white males can experience stereotype threat when faced with the stereotype of Asian superiority in math (Aronson et al. 1999), this pattern only occurred for the males who were highly identified with math achievement—those who indicated that math ability is an important component of their self-concept.

In sum, those whose social identities are based on achievement in and belonging to the stereotyped domain are sometimes also most vulnerable to stereotype-based underachievement (Aronson et al. 1999; Good, Dweck, and Rattan 2006a).

Stereotype Threat Affects Social Identity

Social identity does not only determine vulnerability to stereotype threat. It is also a consequence of it. As we will see, stereotype threat can lead people to alter their sense of self. For example, research has shown that stereotype-threatened individuals often feel less like valued members of the domain in which they are stereotyped (Good, Dweck, and Rattan 2006a), avoid the stereotyped domain (Good, Dweck, and Rattan 2006a), stop caring about achievement in the domain (Steele, Spencer, and Aronson 2002), or distance themselves from the stereotyped group (Pronin, Steele, and Ross 2004; Steele and Aronson 1995). Although some of these results may involve short-term effects, others have more long-term consequences that can influence the career opportunities and directions of people's lives.

Stereotype Threat and Professional Identity

An extremely serious consequence of stereotypes for social identity is that they can make an academic community an uncomfortable place to be, consequently altering stereotyped students' professional identities by redirecting the career paths that they pursue. For example, women who perceived that their college calculus classes conveyed negative stereotypes about women's math abilities reported a lower sense of belonging to the math community—that is, they felt less like accepted members of the math community whose presence was valued—than those who did not perceive a stereotypical climate (Good, Dweck, and Rattan 2006a). Moreover, this threat to their identity as a future mathematician (or scientist) had real consequences for their achievement and career aspirations: when women's sense of belonging was reduced by their perceptions of a stereotypical environment, they earned lower grades in the course and were less likely to intend to take any more math classes in the future.

Thus, stereotypes can cause individuals enough discomfort to lead them to drop out of the domain and redefine their professional identities. When the domain is something as fundamental as mathematics, domain avoidance essentially shuts the door to potentially lucrative careers in science, engineering, and technology. Moreover, the effects of stereotypes on professional identity has roots early in schooling, for it has been found that stereotypes can undermine sense of belonging for girls in math as early as middle school (Good, Dweck, and Rattan 2006b). This has important consequences for girls' identities as future mathematicians and scientists, because it is precisely the middle school years when girls' confidence in and liking of mathematics begins to wane.

Removing the Stereotyped Domain
from Self-Definition

Another consequence for social identity is what Crocker and Brenda Major and their colleagues (Crocker, Major, and Steele 1998; Major et al.

1998) have called "disengagement." Disengagement occurs when, in order to protect themselves, people's self-views become disconnected from how they perform in the domain. Disengagement is related to domain avoidance in that they both involve a distancing of the self from the task in which a threat is felt. However, domain avoidance is typically more of a long-term reaction to the threatening situation—simply avoiding the domain (Steele, Spencer, and Aronson 2002). Disengagement, on the other hand, is typically a more short-term psychological adjustment to stereotype threat that involves weakening the dependence of one's self-views on one's performance.

At first blush, disengagement may seem like a healthy and protective strategy in the face of stereotype threat. And sometimes this is true. For example, Major et al. (1998) found that black participants were unaffected by the negative feedback they received on an intelligence test after the possibility of racial bias was primed—possibly an adaptive response. Thus some forms of disengagement—such as removing the dependence of self-worth on performance in the domain—can be protective and possibly even beneficial. In fact, Jason Lawrence, Jennifer Crocker, and Carol Dweck (2005) make the point that disengagement can sometimes be good and can sometimes simply mean that one's worth is not on the line—not that one doesn't care about achievement in the domain. This form of disengagement has been called noncontingent self-esteem (see Crocker and Wolfe 2001).

We worry about disengagement when detaching oneself from a domain means that the domain is no longer important to students' identities. For example, when a female math student ceases to think of herself as "a math person"—perhaps in response to a less-than-desirable performance on a math task—she has disengaged her social identity from mathematics. This kind of disengagement is called "disidentification (Steele, Spencer, and Aronson 2002) and is another example of a long-term reaction to the threatening situation. An illustration of someone who is firmly "disidentified" from mathematics would be a person who not only discounts low math achievement by saying, "Oh, that's okay. I'm just not a 'math person'" but also has no desire to change this self-appraisal. Disidentified individuals not only maintain self-esteem in the face of an immediate failure, but they also no longer care about their achievement in the domain and no longer incorporate the domain into their identities.

Distancing the Self from the Stereotyped Group

As we have seen, stereotypes and stereotype threat can alter people's social identities by causing them to feel as though they do not fit in in an academic community, to avoid the stereotyped domain and perhaps professions that are related to the domain, and to remove the stereotyped domain from their self-definition. But an individual's sense of self often includes more than professional and academic components. It can also include the activities that people enjoy, activities that are associated with their social group and make them more a part of it. Does stereotype threat affect components of social identity in this sense? Steele and Aronson (1995) found that the answer is yes.

In their classic study (Steele and Aronson 1995), African American and white students took a difficult verbal test under one of two conditions. In the stereotype-threat condition, they were told that their performance on the test would be a good indicator of their underlying intellectual abilities. In the non-threat condition, they were told that the test was simply a problem-solving exercise and was not diagnostic of ability. After the test, they completed a measure of activity preferences. The well-known performance results—that African American participants performed less well than their white counterparts in the stereotype-threat condition, but as well as the white students in the non-stereotype-threat condition—were coupled with similar results on the activities-preference measure. That is, under stereotype threat, African Americans avoided expressing preferences for stereotypically African American activities, such as jazz, hip-hop, and basketball. As Steele and Aronson reasoned, this avoidance illustrated a distinct desire not to be seen through the lens of a racial stereotype.

In a similar study, women under stereotype threat disavowed feminine characteristics that were strongly associated with the stereotype of women's math potential but not feminine characteristics that were weakly associated with the stereotype (Pronin et al. 2004). This process is known as "identity bifurcation" because of the split along stereotypical lines of the personality traits that can contribute to one's identity. What's more, the previous discussion concerning the fact that strength of domain identification predicts vulnerability to stereotype threat also applies to identity bifurcation: only the women who were strongly identified with mathematics achievement bifurcated their identity in response to stereotype threat. These studies (Steele and Aronson 1995; Pronin et al. 2004) illustrate that in order to preserve their identity as competent persons in a domain, stereotyped people sometimes distance themselves from another aspect of their social identity, one that bears the burden of the negative stereotype.

In short, we have seen that stereotype threat can lead people to alter their social identities in ways that distance them not only from the stereotype but also from the domain in which the stereotype applies. Although these strategies may confer short-term protective benefits to self-esteem, the potential long-term consequences could include low representation and success in the stereotyped domain. This may partly explain why men outnumber women in the upper echelons of science and mathematics professions. For black and Hispanic students, for whom the stereotype is more broadly applicable to achievement in general, the consequences could be even more widespread.

Remedies from the Achievement Motivation Literature

That a stigmatized social identity can so easily lead to stereotype threat—for example, simply by means of the makeup of a group—and that stereotype threat seems to affect more than just achievement but also people's fundamental sense of self could paint a bleak picture. There is hope, however, both for student achievement and protection of social identity. One beneficial strategy has come from the achievement-motivation literature, which for many years has been dealing with the same issue as the stereotype-threat literature: the consequences for students' performance when they are oriented toward proving their ability and their ability is called into question.

Self-Theories

The achievement-motivation literature has spelled out the mind-sets that are created and has illuminated the processes that accompany impaired performance when students focus on proving their abilities rather than improving them (Diener and Dweck 1978, 1980; Elliott and Dweck 1988; Elliot, McGregor, and Gable 1999; Pintrich and Garcia 1991; Utman 1997). Thus, research on achievement motivation can help us understand the processes through which messages of fixed, limited ability, including those conveyed by negative stereotypes, affect academic achievement and, as we will see, social identity. In particular, Dweck and her colleagues have shown that people's theories about the nature of intelligence or ability influence a host of academic variables, including sustained motivation and achievement in the face of challenge or difficulty (see, for example, Dweck and Sorich 1999; see Dweck 1999 for a review).

As Dweck has shown, people may believe their intelligence is a fixed trait (an "entity theory" of intelligence) or a more malleable quality that can be developed (an "incremental theory" of intelligence). Because of their belief that intelligence is a fixed trait, entity theorists are highly concerned with messages and outcomes that convey what their "true" abilities are (Dweck and Leggett 1988; Dweck and Sorich 1999). Although this view can certainly be motivating in certain circumstances, research has shown that in the face of academic setbacks, students with this view see their setbacks as a reflection of their abilities (Dweck and Sorich 1999; Henderson and Dweck 1990; compare Mueller and Dweck 1998). Furthermore, in the wake of negative conclusions about their capabilities, entity theorists often exhibit a "helpless response" to challenge, characterized by a decrease in meta-cognitive processes (such as planning and strategy generation), and by an increase in distracting thoughts (such as off-task thoughts and ability-related worries), accompanied by a decline in performance (Diener and Dweck 1978, 1980). In other words, entity theorists' concern with their abilities interferes with their capabilities to perform well.

Incremental theorists, in contrast, believe that intellectual skills are largely expandable. Because this belief system implies that one can influence one's level of intellectual skill, incremental theorists focus on improving rather than proving their intellectual ability (Dweck and Leggett 1988; Dweck and Sorich 1999). In the face of challenge, they show a "mastery"- oriented pattern characterized by increasing meta-cognitive activity, enhanced task focus, and an absence of off-task thoughts, accompanied by maintained or improved performance (Diener and Dweck 1978). Compared to entity theorists, who are focused more on their ability, incremental theorists are focused more on effort, as a way to further learning and as a way to overcome obstacles (Dweck and Sorich 1999; see Mueller and Dweck 1998).

These differences have been consistently found in laboratory studies, in which students' theories of intelligence have been measured as more chronic individual-differences variables (for example, Dweck and Leggett 1988) and have been manipulated experimentally (for example, Hong et al. 1999), and in real-world academic settings (for example, Dweck and Sorich 1999). In summary, much research shows that students' implicit theories of intelligence can have important effects on academic achievement, and that incremental theorists generally fare better than entity theorists in the face of ability-threatening academic challenges.

Incremental Theories Can Protect Against Stereotype-Based Underperformance

Encouraging evidence has begun to emerge suggesting that incremental theories of intelligence can protect against the negative effects of stereotype threat. Specifically, a series of studies in which the idea of expandable ability was explicitly invoked has shown sharply reduced vulnerability to stereotype threat (Aronson 2006; Aronson, Fried, and Good 2001; Good, Aronson, and Inzlicht 2003).

In one laboratory study (Aronson 2006), African American students' conceptions of ability as fixed versus expandable were manipulated and participants then took a challenging verbal test under stereotype-threat conditions. One-third of the participants were told that the abilities being tested were highly expandable, one-third were told that the abilities were fixed, and one-third simply were told that the test measured verbal ability. In the fixed-ability condition, participants solved fewer items than participants in the control condition, whereas those in the malleable-ability condition solved more items. Moreover, in the control group, performance correlated with the test takers' own views of intellectual ability as measured prior to the test: the more malleable they thought it was, the better was their performance on the test. Thus, believing that the test is one on which people can improve their abilities appreciably reduced vulnerability to stereotype threat.

In a recent field study, Aronson, Carrie Fried, and Good (2002) sought to determine whether teaching an incremental theory of intelligence would affect college students' academic engagement and achievement outside the laboratory. Three groups of African American and Caucasian undergraduates participated in the study. One group participated in an intervention that used various attitude-change techniques designed to teach them, help them internalize, and make cognitively available the notion that intelligence is expandable (malleable condition). The achievement outcomes for this group were compared to those of two control groups, one that participated in a comparable intervention with a different intelligence orientation (the idea that there are many kinds of intelligence), and a third group that did not participate in any intervention. The results showed that African American students who were taught that intelligence is malleable received significantly higher grades that semester than those in the other conditions. Interestingly, African Americans in the malleable condition did not report fewer stereotypes in their environment. That is, the intervention did not change their perception of their stereotyped environment; rather it appeared to reduce their vulnerability to the stereotype when they later encountered it.

In a similar study, Good, Aronson, and Inzlicht (2003) designed an intervention that they hypothesized would reduce children's vulnerability to stereotype threat by encouraging them to view intelligence as something that could increase and expand with effort rather than something that was a fixed trait. In this program, college students mentored Latino and Caucasian junior high students over the course of a year and endorsed one of the following educational messages: the expandability of intelligence or the perils of drug use. The mentors also helped the students design and create a web page in which the students advocated, in their own words and pictures, the experimental message conveyed by the mentor.

At the year's end, results showed that girls mentored in the malleability of intelligence performed better on the statewide standardized math achievement test and Latinos in this condition performed better on the statewide standardized reading test than students in the antidrug condition. Not only did girls' math performance increase in the malleability condition, but they narrowed the gap between boys' and girls' math performance in this condition. Taken together, these studies provide encouraging evidence of the potential benefits of holding an incremental theory of intelligence—especially when faced with a stereotype suggesting limited ability. As shown in the Aronson et al. (2002) study, it is not that the group taught the incremental theory subsequently reported encountering less stereotype threat—it did not make them see the world through rose-colored glasses. Rather, learning the incremental theory appeared to reduce their vulnerability to the debilitating aspects of the stereotype on achievement.

Incremental Theories Can Facilitate the Maintenance of Social Identity in the Presence of Stereotypes

Incremental theories also can protect against the unsettling effects of stereotypes on social identity (Aronson et al. 2002). For example, in the intervention involving college students, the researchers included a measure of identification with academics. After the intervention period, students were asked, "Considering all the things that make you who you are, how important is academic achievement?" Results showed that in the control condition, black students were less identified with academics than were white students—an indication that the process of disidentification had begun. However, after participating in the malleability training, black students' academic identification significantly increased. The results of these studies provide strong evidence that directly teaching an incremental theory of intelligence protects against the effects of stereotypes not only on performance but also on one's social identity.

The Effects of Perceiving an Incremental-Oriented Environment and Stereotyping on Social Identity and Achievement

In these studies (Aronson et al. 2002; Good, Aronson, and Inzlicht 2003) the researchers went to great lengths to explicitly teach students that intellectual skills are attainable. Yet this is unlikely to be the way that fixed and malleable views are typically communicated in the real world. Indeed, many educators who espouse the view that skills are expandable and that all students can learn may contradict these views with their day-to-day actions.

For example, teachers may unwittingly convey fixed-ability messages to their students through their classroom discourse and pedagogical practices, especially in math. This often may occur inadvertently through statements or practices that are actually meant to motivate students, perhaps specifically girls. For example, teachers may attempt to make a math lesson more engaging and human by discussing the life of prominent mathematicians such as Pythagoras in a way that stresses their mathematical genius, or that implies that great discoveries came to these mathematicians naturally and without great effort. However, extolling the genius or talent of great mathematicians may operate in a similar fashion as praising individual students' ability (see Mueller and Dweck 1998; Kamins and Dweck 1999). That is, it may convey an entity theory to students, which in turn can make them vulnerable to impaired motivation and performance when they later encounter difficulty. Indeed, the day-to-day messages embedded in the environment may be just as powerful as explicit messages in conveying the idea that intellectual skills are relatively fixed—or the opposite, that they are relatively acquirable.

Furthermore, although the effect of such (direct) messages on achievement is well known, how messages embedded in the environment affect aspects of social identity is less well understood. As mentioned earlier, stereotypes can undermine students' sense of belonging—their feelings that they are respected members of the academic community—and their intent to remain in the field (Good, Dweck, and Rattan 2006a). Do environments focused on fixed ability exacerbate this effect? Alternatively, can academic contexts focused on malleable ability protect against the threat of negative stereotypes?

To answer these questions, Good, Dweck, and Aneeta Rattan (2006a) conducted a longitudinal study of calculus students in which participants completed the Sense of Belonging to Math Scale during their calculus classes at three times during the semester: at the beginning of the semester, after midterms, and just before finals. The questionnaires also included a measure of the extent to which students perceived their math classes as sending messages of a fixed view of math intelligence and of gender stereotyping about math ability.

Results showed that at the beginning of the semester, the most important determinant of whether females felt a sense of belonging to math was their prior math ability. Specifically, females with higher SAT scores reported a greater sense of belonging to math than did females with lower SAT scores. Over time, however, the educational environment in which the students were immersed began to influence the degree to which they felt that they belonged to the math domain. By the end of the semester, females' perceptions of both the amount of stereotyping in their environment and the extent to which the environment was focused on fixed ability undermined their sense of belonging to math. Furthermore, an interaction effect emerged that suggested that high perceptions of gender stereotyping combined with high perceptions of a fixed-ability learning environment constituted a particular threat to females' sense of belonging to math: females who perceived both fixed-ability messages and gender stereotyping in their learning environment were the most vulnerable to lowered sense of belonging to math, regardless of their prior ability. Moreover, when women's sense of belonging was undermined by their perceptions of their learning environment, they were also less likely to indicate an intention to pursue math in the future.

Alternatively, evaluative contexts that portrayed skills as acquirable created resiliency to the negative stereotypes' debilitating message of fixed ability: females with these perceptions maintained a sense of belonging to math even when they perceived their environment to be highly gender-stereotypical. When their sense of belonging was high, they were also more likely to indicate a desire to pursue math in the future.

In summary, messages about the expandable nature of intelligence can mitigate stereotype-threat effects, on both achievement and social identity. Moreover, subtle messages about the nature of intelligence that are conveyed in the learning environment may operate in the same way as explicit messages in exacerbating or mitigating stereotype-threat effects. When women perceived both stereotyping and fixed-ability messages in their math classes, their social identity was threatened—they felt less like valued members of the math community and were more likely to abandon the field. When women perceived malleable-ability messages, they were able to maintain their identity as valued members of the math community and were more likely to continue their math studies in the future.

Conclusions

As we have seen, having a social identity that is devalued in a particular context can lead to underperformance in that context. What is more, factors such as the strength of identification with the devalued identity or with the stereotyped domain, as well as contextual factors that increase the salience of one's devalued social identity, can influence one's vulnerability to stereotype threat. At the same time, stereotype threat can affect one's social identity. In threatening situations—those for which the stereotype is relevant—people often disavow the very likes, dislikes, personality traits, and professional goals that make them who they are.

Remedies to these effects can be found in lessons from the achievement-motivation literature. By encouraging students to adopt a malleable view of intelligence—either through directly teaching students about this perspective or by creating learning environments that embrace the incremental view rather than entity view of intelligence—we can help students overcome stereotype threat. The value of this approach is that it can redress the achievement gap in immediate achievement situations. For example, a malleable orientation may help protect stigmatized students when they are faced with a potentially threatening testing situation, and it may transform learning environments from exclusionary settings, in which only certain students are expected to succeed, to safe havens in which all students are valued and everyone's learning is supported. The benefits include increased achievement in the domain, increased valuing and enjoyment of the domain, and a stronger sense of being a valued member of that domain.

Note

1. Before we begin, however, we would like to point out one way in which our chapter may differ from the other chapters in this book. Much of our discussion of the relationship between stereotypes, social identities, and achievement involves the immediate achievement situation, such as the act of taking an important test or the environment in which learning and assessment occur. Other chapters of this book also address how social identity can affect achievement, but their focus is more on factors not directly related to an achievement setting, such as family influences. As we will show, however, these immediate achievement contexts often provide the impetus not only for the identity-stereotype threat relationship that we detail here, but also for the subsequent effects on achievement.

References

Aronson, Joshua. 2006. "The Effects of Conceiving Ability as Fixed or Malleable on Responses to Stereotype Threat." Unpublished paper. New York University.

Aronson, Joshua, Carrie Fried, and Catherine Good. 2002. "Reducing the Effects of Stereotype Threat on African American College Students by Shaping Theories of Intelligence." *Journal of Experimental Social Psychology* 38(2): 113–25.

Aronson, Joshua, Michael Lustin, Catherine Good, Kelly Keough, Claude Steele, and Joseph Brown. 1999. "When White Men Can't Do Math: Necessary and Sufficient Factors in Stereotype Threat." *Journal of Experimental Social Psychology* 35(1): 29–46.

Crocker, Jennifer, Brenda Major, and Claude Steele. 1998. "Social Stigma." In *The Handbook of Social Psychology*, edited by Daniel Gilbert, Susan Fiske, and Gardner Lindzey. 4th ed. Volume 2. Boston: McGraw-Hill.

Crocker, Jennifer, and Connie Wolfe. 2001. "Contingencies of Self-Worth." *Psychological Review* 108(3): 593–623.

Davis, Claytie, and Joshua Aronson. 2005. "Black Racial Identity as a Moderator of Stereotype Threat: Identity in Context." Unpublished paper.

Diener, Carol, and Carol S. Dweck. 1978. "An Analysis of Learned Helplessness:

Continuous Changes in Performance, Strategy and Achievement Cognitions Following Failure." *Journal of Personality and Social Psychology* 36(5): 451–62.

———. 1980. "An Analysis of Learned Helplessness II. The Processing of Success." *Journal of Personality and Social Psychology* 39(5): 940–52.

Dweck, Carol S. 1999. *Self-Theories: Their Role in Motivation, Personality and Development*. Philadelphia: Taylor & Francis/Psychology Press.

Dweck, Carol S., and Ellen Leggett. 1988. "A Social-Cognitive Approach to Motivation and Personality." *Psychological Review* 95(2): 256–73.

Dweck, Carol, and Lisa Sorich. 1999. "Mastery-Oriented Thinking." In *Coping*, edited by C. Richard Snyder. New York: Oxford University Press.

Elliot, Andrew, Holly McGregor, and Shelly Gable. 1999. "Achievement Goals, Study Strategies, and Exam Performance: A Mediational Analysis." *Journal of Educational Psychology* 91(3): 549–63.

Elliott, Elaine, and Carol S. Dweck. 1988. "Goals: An Approach to Motivation and Achievement." *Journal of Personality and Social Psychology* 54(1): 5–12.

Good, Catherine, Joshua Aronson, and Jayne Ann Harder. Forthcoming. "Problems in the Pipeline: Women's Achievement in High-Level Math Courses." Manuscript submitted to the *Journal of Applied Developmental Psychology*.

Good, Catherine, Joshua Aronson, and Michael Inzlicht. 2003. "Improving Adolescents' Standardized Test Performance: An Intervention to Reduce the Effects of Stereotype Threat." *Journal of Applied Developmental Psychology* 24(6): 645–62.

Good, Catherine, Carol S. Dweck, and Aneeta Rattan. 2006a. "The Effects of Perceiving Fixed-Ability Environments and Stereotyping on Women's Sense of Belonging to Math. Unpublished paper. Barnard College, Columbia University.

———. 2006b. "Do I Belong Here? Middle School Girls' Sense of Belonging to Math." Unpublished paper. Barnard College, Columbia University.

Henderson, Valanne L., and Carol S. Dweck. 1990. "Achievement and Motivation in Adolescence: A New Model and Data." In *At the Threshold: The Developing Adolescent*, edited by S. Shirley Feldman and Glenn R. Elliott. Cambridge, Mass: Harvard University Press.

Hong, Ying-yi, Chi-yue Chiu, Carol S. Dweck, D. Linn, and W. Wan, 1991. "Implicit Theories, Attributions, and Coping: A Meaning System Approach." *Journal of Personality and Social Psychology* 77(3): 588–99.

Inzlicht, Michael, and Talia Ben-Zeev. 2000. "A Threatening Intellectual Environment: Why Females Are Susceptible to Experiencing Problem-Solving Deficits in the Presence of Males." *Psychological Science* 11(5): 365–71.

———. 2003. "Do High-Achieving Female Students Underperform in Private? The Implications of Threatening Environments on Intellectual Processing." *Journal of Educational Psychology* 95(4): 796–805.

Inzlicht, Michael, and Catherine Good. 2006. "How Environments Threaten Academic Performance, Self-Knowledge, and Sense of Belonging." In

Stigma and Group Inequality: Social Psychological Approaches, edited by Colette van Laar and Shana S. Levin. Mahwah, N.J.: Lawrence Erlbaum.

Kamins, Melissa, and Carol S. Dweck. 1999. "Person Versus Process Praise and Criticism: Implications for Contingent Self-Worth and Coping." *Developmental Psychology* 35(3): 835–47.

Lawrence, Jason, Jennifer Crocker, and Carol S. Dweck. 2005. "Stereotypes Negatively Influence the Meaning Students Give to Academic Settings." In *Navigating the Future: Social Identity, Coping, and Life Tasks*, edited by Geraldine Downey, Jaquelynne Eccles and Celina M. Chatman. New York: Russell Sage Foundation.

Major, Brenda, Stephen J. Spencer, Toni Schmader, Connie T. Wolfe, and Jennifer Crocker. 1998. "Coping with Negative Stereotypes About Intellectual Performance: The Role of Psychological Disengagement." *Personality and Social Psychology Bulletin* 24(1): 34–50.

Marx, David, Diederik Stapel, and Dominique Muller. 2005. "We Can Do It: The Interplay of Construal Orientation and Social Comparison Under Threat." *Journal of Personality and Social Psychology* 88(3): 432–46.

McGuire, William J., Claire V. McGuire, Pamela Child, and Terry Fujoko. 1978. "Salience of Ethnicity in the Spontaneous Self-Concept as a Function of One's Ethnic Distinctiveness in the Social Environment." *Journal of Personality and Social Psychology* 36(5): 511–20.

Mueller, Claudia M., and Carol S. Dweck. 1998. "Intelligence Praise Can Undermine Motivation and Performance." *Journal of Personality and Social Psychology* 75(1): 33–52.

Oyserman, Daphna, Kathy Harrison, and Deborah Bybee. 2001. "Can Racial Identity Be Promotive of Academic Efficacy?" *International Journal of Behavioral Development* 25(4): 379–85.

Pintrich, Paul, and Teresa Garcia. 1991. "Student Goal Orientation and Self-Regulation in the College Classroom." In *Advances in Motivation and Achievement*, edited by Martin L. Maehr and Paul Pintrich. Volume 7. Greenwich, Conn.: JAI Press.

Pronin, Emily, Claude Steele, and Lee Ross. 2004. "Identity Bifurcation in Response to Stereotype Threat: Women and Mathematics." *Journal of Experimental Social Psychology* 40(2): 152–68.

Schmader, Toni. 2002. "Gender Identification Moderates Stereotype Threat Effects on Women's Math Performance." *Journal of Experimental Social Psychology* 38(2): 194–201.

Sekaquaptewa, Diane, and Mischa Thompson. 2002. "The Differential Effects of Solo Status on Members of High- and Low-Status Groups." *Personality and Social Psychology Bulletin* 28(5): 694–707.

Shih, Margaret, Todd Pittinsky, and Nalini Ambady. 1999. "Stereotype Susceptibility: Identity Salience and Shifts in Quantitative Performance." *Psychological Science* 10(1): 80–83.

Spencer, Stephen, Claude Steele, and Diane Quinn. 1999. "Stereotype Threat and Women's Math Performance." *Journal of Experimental Social Psychology* 35(1): 4–28.

Steele, Claude, and Joshua Aronson. 1995. "Stereotype Threat and the Intellectual Test Performance of African-Americans." *Journal of Personality and Social Psychology* 69(5): 797–811.

Steele, Claude M., Stephen Spencer, and Joshua Aronson. 2002. "Contending with Images of One's Group: The Psychology of Stereotype and Social Identity Threat." In *Advances in Experimental Social Psychology*, edited by Mark Zanna. San Diego: Academic Press.

Stricker, Lawrence J. 1998. "Inquiring About Examinees' Ethnicity and Sex: Effects on AP Calculus AB Examination Performance." ETS Research Report no. 98-5. New York: College Entrance Examination Board.

Utman, Christopher. 1997. "Performance Effects of Motivational State: A Meta-Analysis." *Personality and Social Psychology Review* 1(2): 170–82.

Chapter 6

Ethnicity, Ethnic Identity, and School Valuing Among Children from Immigrant and Non-Immigrant Families

Jason S. Lawrence, Meredith Bachman,

and Diane N. Ruble

Ethnic-group differences in school achievement in the United States are distressing. At all school levels, African American and Latino students have lower grades, lower graduation rates, higher dropout rates, and lower standardized achievement test scores than do white and Asian students (see Burton and Jones 1982; Jencks and Phillips 1998; Kao and Thompson 2003; Sue and Okazaki 1990; Steele 1997). This achievement gap is particularly worrisome because it portends a sustained economic gap between low-achieving and high-achieving ethnic groups. That is, compared to whites and Asians, blacks and Latinos will be less likely to have stable well-paying jobs and own homes or achieve other signs of economic success (see Jacobson et al. 2001; Gyourko 1998; Jencks and Phillips 1998; Thernstrom and Thernstrom 2003).

Reasons for ethnic-group differences in school achievement are numerous and complex (see Kao and Thompson 2003), but, like many of the chapters in this book, the present chapter examines how such group differences may be explained by ethnic-group differences in school values and also by individuals' ethnic identities. A popular hypothesis is that blacks and Latinos do not value school achievement as much as whites and Asians do (see Cook and Ludwig 1997; Sue and Okazaki 1990; Tyson 2002), and this hypothesis stems from various beliefs: Asian families socialize their children to value school and hard work

(Mordkowitz and Ginsburg 1987); Latino families encourage their children to find jobs instead of going to college (Perez 2002); blacks and some Latino groups devalue school achievement because they believe that it conflicts with their ethnic identity, that those who strive for school achievement are not being true members of their ethnic group (see Fordham and Ogbu 1986; Fordham 1988; Gibson and Ogbu 1991).

It is critical to note that empirical evidence for this hypothesis is inconclusive. Some studies support it, whereas other studies show that black and Latino students do value school and that their ethnic identity can facilitate valuing of school. Moreover, as Carla O'Connor, Sonia DeLuca Fernández, and Brian Girard note in chapter 8 of this volume, studies are unable to address all the aspects of this hypothesis. In particular, these studies often have limited samples. Although comparisons of different ethnic groups and of immigrant and non-immigrant groups are both essential to testing this hypothesis (see Ogbu 1978), many studies examine only one ethnic group (particularly blacks), and few studies include immigrants. Most studies also focus on adolescents and college-aged students; it is unclear whether children from different ethnic groups differ in school valuing, and whether ethnic identity influences their school valuing. Testing these ideas with children is important because we know little about how children's emerging constructions about ethnicity and ethnic identification during middle childhood influence their own achievement-related choices and behaviors (Ruble et al. 2004). Moreover, conclusions drawn from the specific information available during relatively circumscribed periods of acquiring the information may exert continued and profound influence and thus be difficult to change (Ruble 1994).

In this chapter we discuss research on the hypotheses that cultural values lead students from certain ethnic groups to either value or devalue school, and that blacks' and Latinos' ethnic identities lead them to devalue school. We also offer explanations for some inconsistent findings. Then we present the results of a study of these hypotheses we undertook with an ethnically diverse group of elementary school–aged children from immigrant and non-immigrant families.

Ethnicity, Ethnic Identity, and School Valuing

How do theorists explain the proposed differences in school valuing among different ethnic groups? There is little explanation as to why whites presumably value school. This assumption seems to involve circular reasoning: white students value school because on average their achievement is higher than that of black and Latino students. But implicit in John Ogbu and colleagues' theory (Fordham and Ogbu 1986) is that white students value school because their parents socialize them to believe that working hard in school will lead to desirable jobs and economic success.

Explanations for why minorities value or devalue school are more explicit. Some theorists propose that family socialization leads Asians to value school (Mordkowitz and Ginsburg 1987). Interview studies show that Asian parents engage in the following practices: "demands and expectations for achievement and upward mobility, induction of guilt about parental sacrifices and the need to fulfill obligations, respect for education, social comparisons with other Asian-American families in terms of educational success, and obedience to elders such as teachers" (Sue and Okazaki 1990, 915–16). Family obligation is particularly important in Asian children's beliefs about the importance and utility of education and putting forth academic effort even in difficult situations (see Fuligni et al. 2005; Fuligni and Pedersen 2002).

Such family socialization theories implicitly suggest that if certain practices lead Asians to value school, then these practices must be at least somewhat absent in families from ethnic groups where students often do not persist nor excel in school. Ogbu and colleagues' "oppositional culture" theory (Fordham and Ogbu 1986; Gibson and Ogbu 1991) is more explicit: it argues that black and Latino parents are likely to socialize their children to view academic efforts as futile. This occurs because involuntary minorities (that is, groups historically enslaved, colonized, or conquered) experience and observe discrimination in American society and see that for their group members, in contrast to white Americans, school achievement does not result in desirable jobs and economic success. Involuntary minorities then teach this perspective to their children.

Although experiencing discrimination alone might be enough to lead individuals to devalue school, Ogbu and colleagues further argue that discrimination has led blacks and some Latino groups to develop an ethnic identity that is in opposition to whites and, consequently, to school valuing (Gibson and Ogbu 1991). According to this perspective, to keep their identity distinct, blacks and Latinos try to ensure that in-group members adhere to group norms and reject "white" characteristics. In school this means that when a minority student tries to achieve, other group members will view this as a repudiation of the ethnic identity and an acceptance of "white" characteristics and will pressure the student to conform by way of ridicule, alienation, or physical attack. Ogbu (2003) also proposes that for black Americans this oppositional identity stems in part from their experience with slavery and segregation—a proposition that Anne Galletta and William E. Cross critique in chapter 1 of this volume. Our chapter focuses more on blacks' and Latinos' current experiences and perceptions of discrimination.

As O'Connor, DeLuca Fernández, and Girard note (chapter 8 of this volume), the idea that ethnic identity is incompatible with school valuing among minorities, especially black students, has popular support and is propagated in the media (see Cook and Ludwig 1997; Tyson 2002). In his keynote address at the 2004 Democratic Convention, Barack Obama, soon to be an Illinois senator, argued that to improve black student achievement, society must "eradicate the slander that says a black youth with a book is acting white." Because of the ubiquity and popularity of this notion, it is imperative that research address its accuracy. If inaccurate and unchecked this notion can mislead those making public policy and planning interventions intended to deal with ethnic-group differences in achievement. Moreover, because it is popular this notion risks taking on mythical dimensions and consequently becoming even more difficult to discredit (see Wise 2004).

Evidence Concerning Group Differences in School Valuing

As noted before, some studies show that blacks and Latinos do not value school as much as do whites and Asians, whereas other studies show no ethnic-group differences in school valuing or show that whites value school less than do other ethnic groups (see Ainsworth-Darnell and Downey 1998; Fuligni et al. 2005). This may be due to the different ways that researchers measure school valuing. When researchers ask whether a good education is important, leads to good jobs, and is a means to overcome poverty, blacks, Latinos, Asians, and whites equally believe these to be true (see Fuligni, Witkow, and Garcia 2005; Steinberg, Dornbusch, and Brown 1992; Mickelson 1990; Ogbu 1978; also see Ford and Harris 1996).

What do students from different ethnic groups believe are their chances of success if they get a poor education? Laurence Steinberg, Sanford Dornbusch, and B. Bradford Brown (1992) found that relative to black and Latino adolescents, Asian American adolescents were more likely to believe that a good job was unlikely to follow a poor education. This suggests that black and Latino students are "too" optimistic. In other words, they do believe a good education is important, but not so much that they worry about the implications of a poor education. This is distressing because Steinberg, Dornbusch, and Brown also found that believing a poor education would not lead to a good job was more strongly related to academic success than was believing a good education would lead to a good job.

Awareness of Discrimination and School Valuing

Although there is evidence that involuntary minorities often value school, oppositional-culture theory posits that black and Latino students will devalue school when they perceive discrimination against their group (Fordham and Ogbu 1986). But evidence for this hypothesis is also mixed. Research suggests that the more involuntary minorities think about themselves experiencing discrimination the lower their school valuing. For example, black adolescents show less school valuing the more they report experiencing discrimination at school (Wong, Eccles, and Sameroff 2003) and the more they believe they will experience future job discrimination (Taylor et al. 1994).

However, involuntary minorities may be more likely to value school when they think about discrimination against their group. In an interview study, for example, Carla O'Connor (1997) found that black adolescents who were aware of black Americans' struggle against racism were more motivated to achieve in school than black adolescents who were less aware of racism. Similarly, Daphna Oyserman, Larry Gant, and Joel Ager (1995) found that black adolescents showed more academic persistence if their ethnic identity included knowledge of racism against their group. Clearly, more research is needed to test this hypothesis, especially given the scarce research on how knowledge of discrimination affects Latinos' and Asians' school valuing.

Sanctioning High-Achieving In-Group Peers

Research is not only mixed as to whether involuntary minorities devalue school and whether knowledge of discrimination leads involuntary minorities to devalue school, but also as to whether black and Latino students sanction high-achieving in-group peers. There is evidence for peer sanctioning among involuntary minorities when researchers determine each student's popularity by asking students to list their best friends or peers whom they admire. Using this method, Sandra Graham, April Taylor, and Cynthia Hudley (1998) found that black and Latino adolescent males showed less admiration for high-achieving peers than did females (black, Latino, or white) and white males. Similarly, Roland Fryer and Paul Torelli (2005) found that, at interracially mixed schools, black and Latino adolescents were less popular after they reached a certain GPA (3.5 for blacks and 2.5 for Latinos). But as O'Connor, DeLuca Fernández, and Girard show, context is important: contrary to oppositional-culture theory, Fryer and Torelli also found no relationship between school performance and popularity for black students attending predominantly black schools and private schools, and that high-achieving white students were less popular at private schools.

There is little evidence for peer sanctioning when involuntary minority students indicate whether they have experienced peer sanctioning (see Ford and Harris 1996). For example, research finds that high-achieving black adolescents were the most popular with their peers (Ainsworth-Darnell and Downey 1998; Cook and Ludwig 1997) and were no more likely to be disparaged by their peers than were low-achieving peers and high-achieving white adolescents (Cook and Ludwig 1997; Downey and Ainsworth-Darnell 2002; for a contrary view, see Farkas, Lleras, and Maczuga 2002).

High-achieving involuntary minorities may not experience peer sanctioning because they use strategies to deflect attention from their high achievement, such as keeping their achievement unknown to their peers or engaging in extracurricular activities (see Fordham 1988; Farkas, Lleras, and Maczuga 2002). Carmen Arroyo and Edward Zigler (1995) tested this idea and found that, contrary to oppositional-culture theory, both high-achieving black and white adolescents reported using strategies to deflect attention from their high achievement in order to avoid peer sanction (see also Gross 1989; Phelan, Davidson, and Cao 1991; Steinberg, Brown, and Dornbusch 1996).

Does Ethnic Identity Relate to School Valuing?

Examining peer sanctioning is one way to test whether involuntary minorities' culture opposes school valuing. Another way to test this idea is to examine the relationship between involuntary minorities' ethnic identity and their school valuing. Research using this method tends to show that, in contrast to the oppositional-culture theory, the stronger involuntary minorities' ethnic identity is, the more they value school. Importantly, researchers show this relationship with several different conceptions of ethnic identity. Carol Wong, Jacquelynne Eccles, and Arnold Sameroff (2003), for example, found that the stronger black adolescents' ethnic-group belonging was, the higher their ratings of the importance of school, utility value of school, and beliefs about academic competence. Ronald Taylor and colleagues (1994) found that the more black adolescents felt committed to their ethnic identity, the higher their school engagement. And two studies show that the more importance involuntary minorities place on their ethnic identity (centrality) and the more positive they feel about their ethnic group (regard), the more likely they are to value school (Chavous et al. 2003; Fuligni et al. 2005).

Why would ethnic identity be positively related to school valuing? Some theorists believe that a strong ethnic identity buffers against discrimination's impact on school valuing (Cross 1991; Phinney 1996). Similarly, Catherine Good, Joshua Aronson, and Carol Dweck (chapter 5, this volume) argue that the more blacks identify with their group, the more they reject white Americans' presumed negative views of blacks. In support of this notion, Wong, Eccles, and Sameroff (2003) found that the negative relationship between discrimination and school valuing was diminished among black adolescents who felt a strong sense of belonging to their ethnic group.

The Current Study

In summary, research shows that involuntary minorities' ethnic identity is often positively related to school valuing, but the evidence is mixed concerning the notions that different ethnic groups differ in school valuing, that knowledge of discrimination lowers school valuing, and that involuntary minorities sanction high-achieving in-group peers. One possible reason for the mixed findings is that different studies assess the variables in different ways. Thus, further research is needed to clarify issues of ethnicity, ethnic identity, and school valuing.

The current study addressed these issues with samples that are largely missing in the literature: children and multiple ethnic groups including immigrants. Studying elementary-school-age children can help clarify parental socialization's impact on students' school valuing (see also Fuligni, Rivera, and Leininger, chapter 10, this volume). With adolescents—who have likely had many experiences with academic feedback and who are increasingly concerned with peer acceptance—it is difficult to explain ethnic-group differences in school valuing. But with younger children, ethnic-group differences in school valuing suggest parental and family socialization (see Bachman, Ruble, and Fuligni 2005) because parents have less competition from socializing forces such as media, teachers, and peers (see Spencer et al. 1990).

Studying elementary-school-age children is also useful when looking for links between ethnic identity and school valuing. Individuals' self-representations become increasingly complex between the ages of seven and ten (for example, Damon and Hart 1988; Harter 1998), and during this time a "true" sense of ethnic identification is likely to be emerging (see Ruble et al. 2004). Moreover, O'Connor, DeLuca Fernández, and Girard (chapter 8, this volume) note that it is important to examine, at different time points, the relationship between ethnic identity and achievement attitudes. As such, it is difficult to predict the significance of children's ethnic identity for school valuing. On the one hand, during middle childhood ethnic identities may be too nascent to have consequences for personal values and motivation. On the other hand, Diane Ruble (1994) suggests that individuals who are actively acquiring new identities often go through a period of rigidity, when adherence to perceived group norms becomes particularly important. In this case, if children perceive that their ethnic group either values or devalues school while their ethnic identity is emerging as an important social identity, then the children may strongly endorse group norms.

It is also important to study both immigrant and non-immigrant children. Such a diverse sample allows for testing the hypothesis that voluntary minorities (that is, immigrants) are less likely than are involuntary minorities to devalue school (Fordham and Ogbu 1986). Moreover, for a variety of reasons second-generation immigrant children are especially aligned with their families' cultural values (see Fuligni et al. 2005). Finally, when looking at ethnic identity and school valuing, it is important to study students from immigrant and non-immigrant families and minority and non-minority families because these students are all likely to experience ethnic identity differently (Fuligni, Witgow, and Garcia 2005). Therefore, ethnic identity may play a key role in some groups' school valuing and be unrelated for other groups.

This study included children from five different groups, some of which clearly fit into Ogbu's categories. For instance, the white children represent the majority group, the black children represent an involuntary minority, and the Chinese children represent a voluntary minority (or voluntary immigrants). But the study also includes groups that are not as easily classified, such as Dominicans and Russians. Dominicans are a voluntary minority, but because they have academic difficulties, are often racially black, and may perceive themselves to be discriminated against, their experiences may be more like that of involuntary minorities (Ellen et al. 2001; Lopez 2002). Russians are voluntary immigrants but racially white, which are both categories that should be linked to school valuing, according to oppositional culture theory.

Method

In this study, a diverse sample of second- and fourth-grade children responded to questions relevant to the key hypotheses such as their school valuing, academic motivation, ethnic identity, peers' school valuing, peer sanctioning, and discrimination experiences.

Participants

Study participants were 89 white American (55 percent female), 44 black American (77 percent female), 120 Chinese[1] (49 percent female), 106 Dominican (63 percent female), and 77 Russian (52 percent female) children who were in the second and fourth grades. The white and black children were third-generation American or later, and the Chinese, Dominican, and Russian children were first- or second-generation immigrants. The black, Dominican, and Chinese children attended schools in which their ethnic group was in the majority, whereas the white American and Russian children attended schools that were more ethnically heterogeneous.

Procedure

The study consisted of three separate sessions that lasted approximately forty minutes each. Each child was interviewed by an adult female whose racial background matched the child's. The interviewer read the questions and recorded each child's responses. This study was part of a larger study on social development and academic engagement, and so the children responded to several measures not reported here.

School Valuing

Because ethnic-group differences in school valuing may depend on the type of school valuing, this study included two school-valuing measures. To assess the importance of school achievement, the children reported their belief in the importance of five achievement-related behaviors—getting good grades; doing homework; going to school every day; graduating from high school; trying hard in school—using a scale from 1 to 5, with 1 = "not at all important" and 5 = "very important." On the second school-valuing measure, the children were asked whether they could get a job even if they did poorly in school, to which they answered yes or no.

Other School-Related Variables

It is also informative to ask the children about other school-related attitudes and beliefs. To assess the extent that they did their schoolwork for extrinsic reasons the children were asked, "Why do you believe it is important to do your schoolwork?" They were given three answers: (1) Your parents told you that you have to; (2) The teacher says you have to; (3) You will get into trouble if it's not done. To assess the extent they did their schoolwork for intrinsic reasons they were asked the same question and responded to the following: (1) You want to learn new things; (2) It's fun and interesting. The children responded to these items on a scale ranging from 1 ("not at all true") to 5 ("very true').

If children are concerned with school achievement, they may feel anxious about performing poorly. Four questions were asked to assess the children's level of school anxiety: How much do you worry about doing badly in school? When taking a test, how nervous do you get? How much do you worry about what your parents will say if you don't do well at school? How nervous do your parents make you feel about doing well in school? The children responded to these questions on a scale ranging from 1 ("not at all") to 5 ("very much").

In-Group School Valuing and Sanctioning

According to oppositional-culture theory, black and Latino students believe that in-group peers devalue school achievement and that their peers sanction high achievers. Two questions measured the children's assessment of their in-group peers' attitudes toward school achievement. Specifically, the children reported whether their in-group peers believed it was important to achieve in school, and how many in-group peers worked hard to achieve in school. The children used a five-point scale to respond to all the above items.

To assess peer sanctioning, one question measured the degree to which the children believed in-group peers like high-achieving members. Another question asked whether or not kids are teased for school performance. Children who responded yes then described the teased kids' school performance, which we coded into three categories: teased for doing well, teased for doing poorly, teased for some other reason (for example, acting strangely in class).

Ethnic Centrality and Private Regard Measure

Oppositional-culture theory also suggests that black and Latino students' ethnic identity conflicts with school valuing (see Fordham and Ogbu 1986). But, as several theorists propose, ethnic identity consists of a few related yet unique dimensions, each of which may differentially predict different outcomes (see Ashmore, Deaux, and McLaughlin-Volpe 2004; Sellers et al. 1997). Thus, this study focused on two ethnic-identity dimensions: centrality (the degree to which individuals' ethnicity is important to their sense of self) and regard (individuals' level of positive feelings about their ethnicity).

The ethnic identity measure (centrality and regard) resembled Susan Harter's (1985) Self-Perception Profile for Children (SPPC). In this measure the children learned about two groups of kids: the first group of kids felt their ethnic identity was important (or felt good about their ethnic identity) and the second group of kids felt their ethnic identity was not important (or did not feel good about their ethnic identity). Then the children indicated which kids they were most like, and the extent to which they were like the kids ("really" versus "sort of"); thus, the response scale was four points. More specifically, for the ethnic centrality items the children reported the degree to which they believed being their ethnicity is an important part of self and believed being their ethnicity is a big part of who they were. For the regard items the children reported the degree to which they are happy to belong to their ethnic group, proud to be what they are, and like being whatever ethnicity they are.

Discrimination: Messages and Experiences

Oppositional-culture theory suggests that the black and Dominican children will be more likely to devalue school when they are aware of discrimination against their group. Often this awareness comes from parents' telling their children about discrimination against their ethnicity. To test this idea, we asked the children to indicate how often their parents say the following: [child's ethnicity] people are more likely to be treated poorly or unfairly than other people; some people may treat you badly or unfairly because you are [child's ethnicity]; it is harder to succeed in America if you are [child's ethnicity]. The children responded to these items on a scale of 1 to 3: 1 ("never"), 2 ("a few times"), 3 ("a lot of times").

Children may also experience discrimination directly. To test whether black and Dominican children experienced discrimination and whether these experiences lowered school valuing, the children responded to two questions: Do grown-ups ever treat you unfairly or badly? Do kids ever treat you badly or unfairly? Children who said yes also reported whether or not the unfair treatment was due to their ethnicity. We combined the children's responses to these questions in order to examine whether or not children experienced discrimination either by grown-ups or kids.

Results

The goals of the analyses are to examine whether there are group differences in school values and motivation and to examine Ogbu's hypotheses that involuntary minorities experience peer sanctioning of school valuing, that discrimination is related to school devaluing, and that ethnic identity is negatively related to school valuing and motivation.

There were few differences between second- and fourth-graders. Therefore we will not describe the results separately for grades.

School Valuing

Did the data support the hypothesis that black and Dominican students value school achievement less than white, Chinese, and Russian students? On the contrary, in line with results of past research, not only did the ethnic groups not differ in these ratings but all the groups rated the importance of school achievement highly (see table 6.1)—that is, all the groups had an average rating of over 4.5 on a 5-point scale, with little variation (also see Fuligni et al. 2005; Mickelson 1990; Steinberg, Dornbusch, and Brown 1992). As several theorists argue, most people in the United States are socialized to value education (Major and Schmader 1998; Mickelson 1990).

Although the ethnic groups equally agreed that school achievement is important, past research suggests that the black and Dominican children would be more likely than the other groups to believe that they can get a job even if they do poorly in school (Steinberg, Dornbusch, and Brown 1992). But the present study did not support previous research: only 34 percent of the black children and 51 percent of the Dominican children said that they could get a job even if they do poorly in school. In contrast, the white, Chinese, and Russian children were equally optimistic about getting a job even if they do poorly in school, with 82 percent, 73 percent, and 71 percent, respectively, answering yes to this question.

These results may differ from Laurence Steinberg, Sanford M. Dornbusch, and B. Bradford Brown's (1992) results because of methodological differences between the two studies. One difference is that we examined children, whereas Steinberg, Dornbusch, and Brown examined adolescents. Perhaps when blacks and Latinos become adolescents and are closer to joining the workforce and are performing more poorly than other groups, the idea that they will not get a job with a poor education is distressing. In order to relieve this threat they become more optimistic about their prospects of getting a job even with a poor education. Longitudinal research, however, is needed to determine whether black and Latino students become more optimistic over time. Another difference is that Steinberg, Dornbusch, and Brown asked students whether they would be able to get a good job with a poor education, whereas we did not specify that the job be good. A reasonable response to our question is that one can get a job with a poor education, though it may not be a good job. This may be why the majority of white, Chinese, and Russian children responded yes to the question.

If this is the most likely response it is telling that so many black and Dominican children reported that they would be unable to get a job with a poor education. Perhaps they receive the message that they will not get a job if they do poorly in school, and this message may seem realistic to them, given the unemployed adults they are likely to see in their communities.

Motivation and Anxiety

Although members of both ethnic groups were in equal agreement that school achievement is important, there may be ethnic-group differences as to why they think it is important. Theorists suggest that white children and voluntary minorities are pushed to achieve more than black and Latino children (for a review see Graham 1994). Yet, contrary to this notion, analysis of the extrinsic-motivation measure shows that black and Dominican children more often reported that it is important to achieve because others (teachers and parents) think they should achieve than white children did (see table 6.1). The only other difference was that black children reported more extrinsic motivation than the Russian children. This finding suggests that parents and teachers do push black and Dominican children to achieve in school, and that black and Dominican children care what their parents and teachers think.

It is one thing for students to want to achieve because they think this is what their parents and teachers want and another thing for students to want to achieve for intrinsic reasons such as liking to learn (see Deci and Ryan 1995). Do the ethnic groups also differ in the degree to which they want to achieve for intrinsic reasons? Results show that black and Dominican children were more likely to report that they wanted to achieve for intrinsic reasons than were Chinese, Russian, and white children; the latter three groups reported equal amounts of intrinsic motivation (see table 6.1).

These results suggest that black and Dominican children are motivated to achieve in school, but do they worry about performing poorly? The current study suggests that they do (see table 6.1). In a test of ethnic-group differences in school anxiety, the Dominican and Chinese children reported the most school anxiety. The black and Russian children reported marginally lower school anxiety than did the Dominican children, but they did not report significantly less school anxiety than the Chinese children. The white children reported the least amount of school anxiety.

In-Group School Valuing and Sanctioning

Oppositional-culture theory proposes that black and Latino children's in-group peers devalue school achievement. We first tested this idea by asking the children whether in-group peers thought school achieve-

Table 6.1 Group Differences in School-Related Attitudes and Beliefs, and Discrimination Messages

	Black	Dominican	Chinese	Russian	White
School importance	4.77 (.41)	4.8 (.35)	4.69 (.48)	4.7 (.48)	4.78 (.40)
Extrinsic motivation	3.99[a] (1.2)	3.87[ab] (1.2)	3.63[ab] (1.1)	3.49[bc] (1.3)	3.25[c] (1.3)
Intrinsic motivation	4.5[a] (.74)	4.6[a] (.8)	4.05[b] (.94)	4.11[b] (.89)	3.9[b] (1.04)
School anxiety	3.56[a] (.98)	3.85[a] (.84)	3.69[a] (.88)	3.61[a] (.93)	2.99[b] (.92)
In-group school values	4.45 (.71)	4.5 (.75)	4.28 (.67)	4.48 (.65)	4.38 (.66)
Peer liking for achievers	3.64 (1.3)	4.1 (1.03)	3.81 (.94)	3.86 (1.02)	3.9 (.90)
Discrimination messages	1.77[ab] (.56)	1.8[a] (.51)	1.65[bc] (.51)	1.56[c] (.43)	1.21[d] (.32)

Source: Authors' compilation.
Note: Mean scores with different superscripts are significantly different from each other at a probability level of $p < .05$. The Dominican children were marginally higher in school anxiety ratings than Russian and black children ($p < .10$).

ment was important. In contrast to the hypothesis, not only did the ethnic groups not differ in these ratings but all reported that they thought their in-group peers strongly believed school achievement was important (see table 6.1).

Another way to test whether black and Latino children's in-group peers devalue school achievement is to examine whether in-group peers dislike and sanction high achievers. In contrast to the hypothesis, the different ethnic groups believed equally that in-group peers liked high-achieving group members (see table 6.1). In terms of active sanctioning of high achieving peers, at first glance the teasing results seem to support Ogbu's hypothesis (see table 6.2): compared to the other ethnic groups, a higher percentage of black children reported that their schoolmates tease other children for good school performances. However, it is very important to note that a higher percentage of black children than of the other ethnic groups also reported that their schoolmates tease other children for poor school performances. These results are important for two reasons. First, they highlight how the specific questions that researchers do and do not ask greatly impact outcomes as to whether hypotheses are supported or rejected. Second, these findings suggest that black children may simply tease each other more for

Table 6.2   Group Differences in Number of Reports of Performance-Related Teasing (Percentage of Students Within Groups Reporting Teasing)

	No Teasing	Teasing For Doing Well	Teasing For Doing Poorly	Teasing For Other
Black	13 (29.5)	11 (25)	17 (38.6)	3 (6.8)
Dominican	40 (42.6)	11 (10.6)	31 (25.7)	22 (21.2)
White	44 (50)	12 (13.6)	19 (21.6)	13 (14.8)
Chinese	43 (42.6)	12 (11.9)	26 (25.7)	20 (19.8)
Russian	38 (49.4)	12 (15.6)	20 (26)	7 (9.1)

Source: Authors' compilation.

any behavior that makes an individual stand out than do children from other ethnic groups.

Ethnic Identity and School Attitudes and Beliefs

Thus far the results do not strongly support the notion that black and Latino children's culture prevents school valuing. Another way to test this idea is to examine the degree to which the children's ethnic identity relates to school valuing. According to the oppositional-culture theory, black and Dominican children's ethnic identity should be negatively related to school valuing and other school-related beliefs and attitudes. We examined this relationship, for each ethnic group, with two different ethnic-identity dimensions, centrality and regard, and school-related attitudes and beliefs such as the amount of importance placed on school achievement, beliefs about getting a job with a poor education, extrinsic motivation, intrinsic motivation, and school anxiety. These relationships are presented in tables 6.3 and 6.4.

Table 6.3   Pearson Correlations Between Centrality and the School-Valuing Measures, by Ethnicity

	Black	Chinese	Dominican	Russian	White
School importance	.42*	.14	.22*	.29*	−.08
Extrinsic motivation	.08	.05	−.18	−.04	−.22*
Intrinsic motivation	.29†	.23*	.07	−.01	.02
School anxiety	−.04	.21*	−.20*	−.03	−.12

Source: Authors' compilation.
*p < .05; †p < .10

Table 6.4   **Pearson Correlations Between Regard and the School-Valuing Measures, by Ethnicity**

	Black	Chinese	Dominican	Russian	White
School importance	.45*	.09	.18†	.13	.00
Extrinsic motivation	.07	−.11	−.11	.06	−.06
Intrinsic motivation	.36*	.10	.25*	−.03	.04
School anxiety	−.10	.23*	−.06	−.15	−.02

Source: Authors' compilation.
*p < .05; †p < .10

Generally, these relationships are the reverse of what oppositional-culture theory predicts. For both black and Dominican children, the more central their ethnic identity is, the higher they rated school importance. Similarly, the more positively the black children regarded their ethnicity, the higher they rated school importance. The Dominican children showed a similar pattern, although this relationship was marginally significant statistically. Moreover, both black and Dominican children showed that the more positively they regarded their ethnicity, the higher their intrinsic motivation.

Interestingly, the Chinese children's ethnic identity (both centrality and regard) was positively related to school anxiety. This result fits with the notion that Asian culture pressures children to achieve academically (see Mordkowitz and Ginsburg 1987). More specifically, the more Chinese children identify with their ethnicity, the more susceptible they may be to cultural pressures to achieve.

Discrimination: Messages and Experiences

Although there was little support for the notion that black and Dominican children's ethnic identity prevented school valuing, perhaps black and Dominican children who are aware of discrimination against their group are more likely to devalue school (Fordham and Ogbu 1986). First we examined whether black and Dominican children were more likely to report that their parents talk about discrimination against their group. As can be seen in table 6.1, the Dominican children reported more discrimination messages than any other group except for the black children; the black children reported more discrimination messages than the Russian and the white children; the Chinese and the Russian children did not differ from each other, and both reported more discrimination messages than did the white children.

But do discrimination messages influence children's school valuing and other school-related beliefs and attitudes? The results suggest that discrimination messages do not decrease students' school valuing and motivation (see table 6.5). For all ethnic groups, discrimination messages were unrelated to importance of school achievement. The only significant relationships to emerge were positive: the more their parents discussed discrimination, the higher was Chinese children's extrinsic and intrinsic motivation and Russian children's extrinsic motivation and school anxiety.

Perhaps black and Dominican children's perceived discrimination experiences will predict their school valuing and other school-related beliefs and attitudes. Before we test this hypothesis it is important to note that the data do not show that black and Dominican children are more likely than the other children to report experiences of ethnic discrimination. Russian children reported the most experiences with discrimination (20 percent), followed by black and Chinese children (13 percent each), and Dominican and white children reported the least (5 percent and 3 percent, respectively). Although we did not initially expect the Russian children to report discrimination, it is possible that they experienced discrimination as immigrants and because of their religion, given many were Jewish. Moreover, the Russian children had more opportunity to experience discrimination because they attended more diverse schools than the black, Dominican, and Chinese children.

We then examined whether the children's discrimination experiences related to their school valuing for the different ethnicities. Among all the ethnic groups, there was no relationship between discrimination experiences and school valuing, intrinsic motivation, and school anxiety. The only significant relationship to emerge was that the black children's reports of discrimination were linked with lowered extrinsic motivation. However, this result does not mean that they did not value school achievement but only that they were less likely to want to achieve because they believed that is what their parents and teachers

Table 6.5   Pearson Correlations Between Discrimination Messages and the School-Valuing Measures, by Ethnicity

	Black	Chinese	Dominican	Russian	White
School importance	.19	−.02	−.03	−.16	−.01
Extrinsic motivation	.27†	.24*	.01	.34*	.04
Intrinsic motivation	.25	.27*	.09	−.03	−.01
School anxiety	.18	−.09	−.001	.34	−.14

Source: Authors' compilation.
*p < .05; †p < .10

want. Overall, these results provide little support for the oppositional-culture theory's predictions.

Discussion

This study did not find support for many of oppositional-culture theory's central tenets. Not only did the black and Dominican children believe school achievement was as important as the white, Chinese, and Russian children did, but also the black and Dominican children were more likely than these latter groups to want to achieve for intrinsic reasons, and were less likely to report that they could get a job if they did poorly in school. Moreover, black and Dominican children were higher in extrinsic motivation than the white children.

The present findings also did not generally support the hypothesis that in-group peers make it difficult for black and Dominican children to value school achievement. The children from the different ethnic groups reported equally that their peers believed school achievement was important and liked high-achieving in-group members. The Dominican children also did not differ from white, Chinese, and Russian children in reporting that other children tease high achievers.

Black children, however, more often reported that other children tease high achievers than did the other ethnic groups. But, as discussed earlier, when this finding is put into context, it becomes clear that it may not support oppositional-culture theory, because black children also reported more than any other ethnic group that other children tease low achievers (also see Tyson 2002). This finding suggests that it is important to consider cultural differences in teasing more generally and even cultural differences in sanctioning of other behaviors.

There was also little evidence that the black and Dominican children's ethnic identity was incompatible with school valuing and other school-related attitudes and beliefs. For both groups, centrality of ethnic identity was linked to more school valuing, and for blacks, positive regard for their ethnic group was linked to more school valuing. Perhaps the more positive black and Dominican children feel toward their groups, the more they want to do well in order to make their group proud.

However, several dimensions of ethnic identity were missing from the current study. For example, we did not measure the degree to which the children's ethnic identity was salient to them, their sense of group belonging, nor the meaning they give to their ethnic identity (Sellers et al. 1997). The meaning individuals give to their ethnic identity may be especially influential to school valuing. Oyserman, Kathy Harrison, and Deborah Bybee (2001) found that black adolescents high in ethnic identity that included a sense of achievement were more likely to persist on an academic task than were those who excluded this meaning.

Some caution is necessary in generalizing the present findings. This study is limited in that the sample of black children was small and predominantly female. In addition, the black and Dominican children attended schools in which they were in the majority. Black and Dominican children who attend more racially diverse schools or schools in which they are in the minority may have different school-related attitudes, particularly those school-related attitudes that link with ethnic identity. O'Connor, DeLuca Fernández, and Girard (chapter 8, this volume) found evidence that black students who attended predominantly white schools were more likely to perceive a disconnect between their ethnic identity and school valuing than their counterparts who attended predominantly black schools.

School Valuing and Achievement

Although the current study did not measure school achievement, the results suggest that ethnic-group differences in school achievement are not due to ethnic-group differences in school valuing. This may be because we measured students' abstract school valuing. According to Roslyn Mickelson (1990), most people endorse abstract notions about the value of education, and so belief in these values should neither differ by ethnic group nor predict school achievement. A better predictor of ethnic differences in school achievement, she further argues, is students' beliefs about whether school achievement will pay off for them in the future, beliefs that develop in response to in-group members' discrimination experiences. The more that black and Latino children believe in-group members experience discrimination, the less likely it is that these children will be motivated to work hard in school. But the present study provided little support for this notion. Even though black and Dominican children were more likely to report hearing parental messages of discrimination than the other ethnic-group children, this did not affect their school valuing. In addition, the children's reports of discrimination experiences were unrelated to school valuing.

If there are no ethnic-group differences in school valuing then other factors account for black and Latino student underachievement. One possible factor is structural. Black and Latino students are likely to attend poorer schools with fewer resources and less educated teachers (Ellen et al. 2001). Even when black and Latino students attend diverse schools, they are often in lower tracks and thus experience a lower quality education than their white and Asian counterparts (Oakes and Guiton 1995; Kao and Thompson 2003).

Teachers' expectations may also play a part in black and Latino underperformance. If teachers have low expectations, they may treat black and Latino children in ways that lead the children to confirm these expectations (Rosenthal and Jacobson 1968). Black and Latino children may also perform poorly if they worry about confirming their teachers' low expectations (Steele 1997; see also Good, Dweck, and Aronson, chapter 5, this volume).

Conclusion

The aim of this chapter is to add to the literature on ethnicity and school valuing. We emphasized the importance of how researchers measure ethnic identity and school valuing, and that measurement variety may explain conflicting results. Also, by examining multiple ethnic groups, immigrant and non-immigrant, we found different relationships among different groups. Often these relationships contradicted oppositional-culture theory predictions. Finally, the present study adds to the literature by focusing on ethnic identity and school valuing during middle childhood. The findings suggest that such an oppositional process might not be present during middle childhood, even though there is evidence of emerging ethnic understanding and identification in such children. Thus, it is possible that the observed relationships might change if we followed the sample over time. Taken together, our study suggests that much research is needed on this issue; given our results it is distressing that the media and public seem to accept as truth the notion that blacks and Latinos devalue school achievement.

Note

1. For simplicity's sake we use the labels "Chinese" and "Russian," but it is important to note that children from Taiwan and Hong Kong were included in the "Chinese" sample and children from countries that were part of the former Soviet Union, such as Ukraine, were included in the "Russian" sample.

References

Ainsworth-Darnell, W. James, and Douglas B. Downey. 1998. "Assessing the Oppositional Culture Explanation for Racial/Ethnic Differences in School Performance." *American Sociological Review* 63(4): 536–53.

Arroyo, G. Carmen, and Edward Zigler. 1995. "Racial Identity, Academic Achievement, and the Psychological Well-Being of Economically Disadvantaged Adolescents." *Journal of Personality and Social Psychology* 69(5): 903–14.

Ashmore, Richard, Kay Deaux, and Tracy McLaughlin-Volpe. 2004. "An Organizing Framework for Collective Identity: Articulation and Significance of Multidimensionality." *Psychological Bulletin* 130(1): 80–114.

Bachman, Meredith, Diane N. Ruble, and Andrew J. Fuligni. 2005. "Academic Identity in Middle Childhood: Exploring Developmental Trajectories in Diverse Contexts." Unpublished manuscript. New York: New York University.

Burton, Nancy W., and Lyle V. Jones. 1982. "Recent Trends in Achievement Levels of Black and White Youth." *Educational Researcher* 11(4): 10–17.

Chavous, M. Tabbye, Debra H. Bernat, Karen Schmeelk-Cone, Cleopatra H. Caldwell, Laura Kohn-Wood, and Marc A. Zimmerman. 2003. "Racial Identity and Academic Attainment Among African American Adolescents." *Child Development* 74(4): 1076–90.

Cook, J. Phillip, and Jens Ludwig. 1997. "Weighing the 'Burden of "Acting White'": Are There Race Differences in Attitudes Toward Education." *Journal of Policy Analysis and Management* 16(2): 256–78.

Cross, E. William, Jr. 1991. *Shades of Black: Diversity in African-American Identity.* Philadelphia: Temple University Press

Damon, William, and Daniel Hart 1988. "Self-Understanding in Childhood and Adolescence." New York: Cambridge University Press

Deci, Edward L., and Richard M. Ryan. 1995. "Human Autonomy: The Basis for True Self-Esteem." In *Efficacy, Agency, and Self-Esteem*, edited by Michael H. Kernis. New York: Plenum.

Downey, Douglas B., and James W. Ainsworth-Darnell. 2002. "The Search for Oppositional Culture Among Black Students." *American Sociological Review* 67(1): 156–64.

Ellen, Ingrid G., Katherine O'Regan, Amy E. Schwartz, and Leanna Stiefel. 2001. *Immigrant Children and Urban Schools: Evidence from New York City on Segregation and Its Consequences for School.* working paper 2001-20. New York: Taub Urban Research Center.

Farkas, George, Christy Lleras, and Steve Maczuga. 2002. "Does Oppositional Culture Exist in Minority and Poverty Peer Groups?" *American Sociological Review* 67(1): 148–55.

Ford, Donna Y., and John J. Harris. 1996. "Perceptions and Attitudes of Black Students Toward School Achievement, and Other Educational Variables." *Child Development* 67(3): 1141–52.

Fordham, Signithia. 1988. "Racelessness as a Factor in Black Students' School Success: Pragmatic Strategy or Pyrrhic Victory?" *Harvard Educational Review* 58(1): 54–84.

Fordham, Signithia, and John U. Ogbu. 1986. "Black Students' School Success: Coping with the 'Burden of "Acting White.'"" *The Urban Review* 18(3): 176–206.

Fryer, G. Roland, Jr., and Paul Torelli. 2005. "An Empirical Analysis of 'Acting White.'" Unpublished manuscript. Cambridge, Mass.: Harvard University.

Fuligni, J. Andrew, Jeannette Alvarez, Meredith Bachman, and Diane N. Ruble. 2005. "Family Obligation and the Academic Motivation of Young Children from Immigrant Families." In *Hills of Gold: Rethinking Diversity and Context as Resources for Children's Developmental Pathways*, edited by Catherine R.

Cooper, Cynthia Garcia Coll, Todd Bartko, H. Davis, and Celina Chatman. Mahwah, N.J.: Lawrence Erlbaum.

Fuligni, J. Andrew, and Sara Pedersen. 2002. "Family Obligation and Transition to Young Adulthood." *Developmental Psychology* 38(5): 856–68.

Fuligni, Andrew, Melissa Witkow, and Carla Garcia. 2005. "Ethnic Identity and the Academic Adjustment of Adolescents from Mexican, Chinese, and European backgrounds." *Developmental Psychology* 41(5): 799–811.

Gibson, Margaret A., and John U. Ogbu. 1991. *Minority Status and Schooling: A Comparative Study of Immigrant Involuntary Minorities.* New York: Garland.

Graham, Sandra 1994. "Motivation in African Americans." *Reviews of Educational Research* 64(1): 55–118.

Graham, Sandra, and April Z. Taylor. 2001. "Ethnicity, Gender, and the Development of Achievement Values." In *Development of Achievement Motivation*, edited by Allan Wigfield and Jacquelynne S. Eccles. New York: Academic Press.

Graham, Sandra, April Z. Taylor, and Cynthia Hudley. 1998. "Exploring Achievement Values Among Ethnic Minority Early Adolescents." *Journal of Educational Psychology* 90(4): 606–20.

Gross, Miraca U. 1989. "The Pursuit of Excellence or the Search for Intimacy? The Forced-Choice Dilemma of Gifted Youth." *Roeper Review* 11(4): 189–94.

Gyourko, Joseph. 1998. "The Changing Strength of Socioeconomic Factors Affecting Home Ownership in the United States: 1960–1990." *Scottish Journal of Political Economy* 45(4): 466–90.

Harter, Susan. 1985. *Manual for the Self-Perception Profile for Children.* Denver: University of Denver.

———. 1998. "Developmental Processes in the Construction of the Self." In *Integrative Processes and Socialization: Early to Middle Childhood*, edited by Thomas D. Yawkey and James E. Johnson. Hillsdale, N.J.: Lawrence Erlbaum.

Hauser, Robert M., and Douglas K. Anderson. 1991. "Post–High School Plans and Aspirations of Black and White High School Seniors." *Sociology of Education* 64(00): 263–77.

Jacobson, Jonathan, Cara Olsen, Jennifer King Rice, Stephen Sweetland, and John Ralph. 2001. *Educational Achievement and Black-White Inequality.* Statistical Analysis Report, NCES2001-061. Washington: U.S. Department of Education, National Center for Education Statistics, Office of Educational Research and Improvement, available at http://nces.ed.gov/pubsearch/pubinfo.asp?pubid=2001061.

Jencks, Christopher, and Meredith Phillips. 1998. *The Black-White Test Score Gap.* Washington, D.C.: Brookings Institution Press.

Kao, Grace, and Jennifer S. Thompson. 2003. "Racial and Ethnic Stratification in Educational Achievement and Attainment." *Annual Review of Sociology* 29: 417–57.

Lopez, Nancy 2002. "Rewriting Race and Gender High School Lessons: Second Generation Dominicans in New York City." *Teachers College Record* 104(6): 1187–1203.

Major, Brenda, and Toni Schmader. 1998. "Coping with Stigma Through Psychological Disengagement." In *Prejudice: The Target's Perspective*, edited by Janet K. Swim and Charles Stangor. San Diego: Academic Press.

Mickelson, Roslyn A. 1990. "The Attitude-Achievement Paradox Among Black Adolescents." *Sociology of Education* 63(00): 44–61.

Mordkowitz, Eliott R., and Herbert P. Ginsburg. 1987. "Early Academic Socialization and Successful Asian American College Students." *Quarterly Newsletter of the Laboratory of Human Cognition* 9: 85–91.

Oakes, Jeannie, and Gretchen Guiton. 1995. "Matchmaking: The Dynamics of High School Tracking Decisions." *American Educational Research Journal* 32(1): 3–33

O'Connor, Carla. 1997. "Dispositions Toward Collective Struggle and Educational Resilience in the Inner City: A Case Analysis of Six African American High School Students." *American Educational Research Journal* 34(4): 593–629.

Ogbu, John. 1978. *Minority Education and Caste: The American System in Cross Cultural Perspective*. New York: Academic Press.

———. 2003. *Black American Students in an Affluent Suburb: A Study of Academic Disengagement*. Mahwah, N.J.: Lawrence Erlbaum.

Oyserman, Daphna, Larry Gant, and Joel Ager. 1995. "A Socially Contextualized Model of African American Identity: Possible Selves and School Persistence." *Journal of Personality and Social Psychology* 69(6): 1216–32.

Oyserman, Daphna, Kathy Harrison, and Deborah Bybee. 2001. "Can Racial Identity be Promotive of Academic Efficacy?" *International Journal of Behavioral Development* 25(4): 379–85.

Perez, Antonio. 2002. "Hispanics Must Raise the Bar." *Community College Week* 15: 4.

Phelan, Patricia, Ann L. Davidson, and Hahn T. Cao. 1991. "Students' Multiple Worlds: Negotiating the Boundaries of Family, Peer, and School Cultures." *Anthropology and Education Quarterly* 22(3): 224–50.

Phinney, Jean S. 1996. "Understanding Ethnic Diversity: The Role of Ethnic Identity." *American Behavioral Scientist* 40(2): 143–52.

Rosenthal, Robert, and Lenore Jacobson. 1968. *Pygmalion in the Classroom: Teacher Expectations and Student Intellectual Development*. New York: Holt, Rinehart, and Winston.

Ruble, Diane N. 1994. "A Phase Model of Transitions: Cognitive and Motivational Consequences." In *Advances in Experimental Social Psychology*, edited by Mark Zanna. Volume 26. San Diego: Academic Press.

Ruble, Diane N., Jeannette Alvarez, Meredith Bachman, Jessica Cameron, Andrew J. Fuligni, Cynthia Garcia-Coll, and Eun Rhee. 2004. "The Development of a Sense of 'We': The Emergence and Implications of Children's Collective Identity." In *The Development of the Social Self*, edited by Mark Bennett and Fabio Sani. Hove, England: Psychology Press.

Sellers, Robert M., Stephanie A. Rowley, Tabbye M. Chavous, J. Nicole Shelton, and Mia A. Smith. 1997. "Multidimensional Inventory of Black Identity: A Preliminary Investigation of Reliability and Construct Validity." *Journal of Personality and Social Psychology* 73(4): 805–15.

Spencer, Margaret B., Elizabeth Noll, Jill Stoltzfus, and Vinay Harpalani. 2001. "Identity and School Adjustment: Revisiting the 'Acting White' Assumption." *Educational Psychologist* 36(1): 21–30.

Steele, Claude M. 1997. "A Threat in the Air: How Stereotypes Shape the Intellectual Identities and Performance of Women and African Americans." *American Psychologist* 52(6): 613–29.

Steinberg, Laurence, Sanford M. Dornbusch, and B. Bradford Brown. 1992. "Ethnic Differences in Adolescent Achievement." *American Psychologist* 47(6): 723–29.

Steinberg, Laurence, B. Bradford Brown, and Sanford M. Dornbusch. 1996. *Beyond the Classroom: Why School Reform has Failed and What Parents Need to Do.* New York: Simon & Schuster.

Sue, Stanley, and Sumie Okazaki. 1990. "Asian American Educational Achievements: A Phenomenon in Search of an Explanation." *American Psychologist* 45(8): 913–20.

Taylor, Ronald D., Robin Casten, Susanne M. Flickinger, and Debra Roberts. 1994. "Explaining the School Performance of African-American Adolescents." *Journal of Research on Adolescence* 4(1): 21–44.

Thernstrom, Stephan, and Abigail Thernstrom. 2003. *No Excuses: Closing the Achievement Gap in Learning.* New York: Simon & Schuster.

Tyson, Karolyn. 2002. Weighing In: "Elementary-Age Students and the Debate on Attitudes Toward School Among Black Students." *Social Forces* 80(4): 1157–89.

Wise, Tim. 2004. "White Lies, Black Mimics." Think Piece. *The Black Commentator*, http://www.blackcommentator.com/193/193_white_lies_think_wise_pf.html.

Wong, A. Carol, Jacquelynne S. Eccles, and Arnold Sameroff. 2003. "The Influence of Ethnic Discrimination and Ethnic Identification on African American Adolescents' School and Socioemotional Adjustment." *Journal of Personality* 71(6): 1197–1232.

Chapter 7

Women of Color in College: Effects of Identity and Context on Contingent Self-Worth

Julie A. Garcia and Jennifer Crocker

The performance of women and minorities in secondary school has received considerable attention from social scientists, policymakers, and educators. Educational achievement predicts many life outcomes, including lifetime earnings and health. Consequently, social scientists, educators, and researchers want to understand factors that promote or prevent school achievement, particularly for minority students. At the postsecondary level, students of color graduate from college at lower rates than white students. For example, 66.4 percent of whites, 54.9 percent of blacks, and 60.2 percent of Latinos who enrolled in college in the 1995–1996 academic year had either completed their education or were still enrolled in college five years later (Horn and Berger 2004).

Women of Color in the Academy: Effects of Identity and Context on Contingent Self-Worth

A number of researchers have suggested that the value placed on school, or identification with schooling as an important personal goal, accounts for group differences in school achievement. Students who value education and identify with school persist more in academic environments (Vallerand and Bissonnette 1992). Consequently, researchers have suggested that disidentification with school contributes to the lower educational attainment of women in domains such as mathematics, science, and engineering, and students of color more generally (Crocker and Major 1989; Major and Schmader 1998).

Researchers have offered a number of reasons why students of color might value education less and disidentify with schooling. Signithia Fordham and John Ogbu (1986) offered the controversial hypothesis that African Americans view academic achievement as "white," and their peers pressure them not to "act white" by working hard and doing well in school. Claude Steele and his colleagues offered an alternative hypothesis, that negative stereotypes about their intellectual ability cause women and students of color to disidentify with school, or with certain domains of academic achievement, and this accounts for their underachievement (Steele 1992). Other researchers have suggested that people devalue or psychologically disengage from domains in which they personally perform worse than others (Tesser 1988) or in which their group fares worse than other groups, to protect their self-esteem from upward comparisons (Crocker and Major 1989; Rosenberg and Simmons 1972). Despite the persuasiveness of this line of reasoning, evidence that students of color do not value education or disidentify with school is scarce. Most research indicates that African American students value school as much as white Americans.

We suggest that school achievement among students of color is lower not because they care too little about school but because they care too much—specifically, that they identify with schooling in a way that undermines their achievement. We argue that students of color invest their self-esteem in school achievement, that they do so particularly in academic settings that activate negative stereotypes about their intellectual ability, that students who are more identified with their gender or ethnicity are especially likely to do so, and that investing self-esteem in academic achievement has counterproductive effects on stress, effort, and academic achievement.

Investing Self-Esteem in School Achievement

A number of researchers have argued that minority students invest their self-esteem less in school than white students. This conclusion is based on two types of evidence. First, despite the fact that black students on average perform worse in school than white students, their self-esteem is at least as high as that of white students (Demo and Parker 1987; Rosenberg 1965, 1979). Second, school achievement is a weaker predictor of self-esteem for black students than for white students (Osborne 1997). However, the weaker association between school achievement and global self-esteem could be due to disidentification with school or to increased valuing of other domains, such as religion, as a source of self-esteem (Crocker, Luhtanen et al. 2003). In a survey of 795 college freshman, Crocker and her colleagues found that African

American students based their self-esteem on academics just as much as white students (Crocker, Luhtanen et al. 2003).

Context, Identity, and Valuing of School

Although Jennifer Crocker, Riia K. Luhtanen et al.'s (2003) survey data suggest that black and white college students do not differ in how much they base their self-esteem on academic success, we suggest that these data actually underrepresent the degree to which students of color base their self-esteem on academics. Specifically, we argue that students of color actually base their self-esteem on academics more when they are in academic contexts than when they are in contexts unrelated to academics.

The meaning and value ascribed to social groups or identities can vary across contexts. Prior experience, shared cultural beliefs, and situational cues highlight the value of one's social identity in a particular context. The valence of these cues and messages influences whether or not a person perceives his social group as valued in that setting. Thus, any given social identity could be devalued in one context but carry little meaning in another.

The underrepresentation of female professors of color in the academy, coupled with negative stereotypes about women's and ethnic minorities' academic abilities, subtly connote the devalued nature of these identities. In the fall of 2003, women of color represented a tiny portion of the full-time instructional faculty in degree-granting institutions, a portion comprising only 2.7 percent black women, 2.1 percent Asian or Pacific Islander women, and 1.4 percent Latina (U.S. Department of Education, National Center for Education Statistics 2004). Moreover, academic environments can draw attention to negative expectations for women and ethnic-minority students. Stereotypes that women perform poorly in math and engineering (Spencer, Steele, and Quinn 1999; Steele 1997a) and that ethnic minorities generally perform poorly (Steele 1997b) remind female students of color of their devalued status.

School structures and teacher messages can also contribute to the negative perception of minority women's academic abilities. For example, Anne Galleta and William E. Cross, Jr. (chapter 1, this volume) offer a historical perspective on the development of school tracking and its influence on feelings of belonging in academic settings. Specifically, Galletta and Cross demonstrate that minority students question their right to belong in academic tracks if few other students of color are also tracked with them. Additionally, Meagan M. Patterson and Rebecca S. Bigler (chapter 3, this volume) suggest that classroom structures and teacher messages influence the salience of group differences. Namely, they contend that gendered language and segregation increase the salience of students' gender, which ultimately lead to the development and utilization of gender stereotypes. As these examples indicate, women and ethnic- minority students often learn the value and meaning of their identities from implicit and explicit contextual cues. When these cues suggest devaluation and difference, the academic environment becomes threatening for the self. As a consequence, women of color might worry about confirming negative expectations.

Previous research has investigated how social identity threats affect academic performance (Steele and Aronson 1995; Spencer, Steele, and Quinn 1999) and global self-esteem (Crocker and Major 1989). We add to this growing body of literature by examining how social-identity threat influences the domains in which women of color stake their self-worth. In academic settings negative stereotypes prevail for women and minorities. Stigmatized individuals are aware of the negative stereotypes others hold for their group and the settings in which these stereotypes are most prevalent. This awareness can increase concerns that they will confirm negative expectations of their group (Steele and Aronson 1995)—especially for those who highly identify with the devalued social group (Schmader 2002). We propose that women of color will stake their self-worth more on their academic performance in academic contexts compared to nonacademic contexts because in academic settings the value placed on academic competence is salient and the negative stereotypes pertaining to their academic abilities are relevant. We suggest that gender- and ethnic-identified women will be more likely to base their self-worth on academic performance in academic settings than women of color who are not so identified because the former group of women are more invested in debunking negative stereotypes for their group. In this chapter we explore these possibilities.

To that end, we first present background literature that fostered the development of our research ideas. Next, we present empirical research regarding the effects of context and identity on academically contingent self-worth for women of color, and the consequences of academically contingent self-worth. Finally, we suggest both institution- and individual-level strategies for altering level of academic contingent self-worth in women of color.

Basing Self-Esteem on Academic Competency

Over a century ago, William James (1890) noted that people stake their self-worth on their achievements in some domains but not others (see Crocker and Wolfe 2001, for a discussion). Contingent self-worth refers to the degree to which self-esteem depends on performance in a particular domain. For example, for people whose self-esteem is contingent on others' approval, state self-esteem increases when they receive approval or recognition and decreases when they receive criticism or rejection. Many college students stake their self-worth on their academic performance (Crocker, Luhtanen et al. 2003). In accordance with James's predictions, the more contingent self-esteem is on academics, the greater the shifts in self-esteem and affect in response to academic success or failure (Crocker, Karpinski et al. 2003; Crocker, Sommers, and Luhtanen 2002; Niiya, Crocker, and Bartmess 2004).

Previous research has exclusively investigated contingencies of self-worth as an individual-difference variable (for example, Crocker, Luhtanen et al. 2003; Crocker and Wolfe 2001), neglecting possible within-person variation. However, contingencies of self-worth may also vary in response to situational cues. Just as level of self-esteem has been conceptualized both as a personality trait (for example, Rosenberg 1979), and a psychological state (Heatherton and Polivy 1991), contingencies of self-worth may also vary both between and within people. We believe context predicts potential within-person variation.

Contexts and Contingent Self-Worth

We contend that academic contexts shape academically contingent self-worth for two reasons. First, academic contexts highlight the value placed on academic performance. Second, gender and ethnic-minority identities carry devalued meanings in this context. These propositions will be discussed in turn. Contingent self-worth should vary in response to situational cues that suggest that a person's worth depends on displaying a particular quality or behavior in that context. In specific contexts, some qualities are valued more than others. When on a date, people perceive charm and appearance as valued qualities. In athletic contexts, people recognize strength and endurance as esteemed traits. And in academic contexts, people identify academic competence as a valued characteristic. As these examples suggest, contexts shape perceptions of valued traits or behaviors. Contexts, then, may influence what traits people identify as important to possess or appear to possess to be worthy in their own and others' eyes. Contexts may shape contingencies of self-worth.

Furthermore, we propose that the devaluation that women of color experience in academic settings can further contribute to heightened academic contingency. Individuals who belong to stigmatized groups are often aware of the negative stereotypes that others hold of them (Devine 1989) and may fear confirming these stereotypes, even if they do not believe the stereotype applies to them (Steele and Aronson 1995). Consequently, stigmatized groups may use academic success to combat racial stereotypes (Cammarota 2004; Fordham 1996) and gender inequality (Cammarota 2004). In other words, women of color strive to prove their academic competence in order to debunk the negative stereotypes held for their group. Thus, others' negative expectations specific to educational settings may heighten academic contingent self-worth for women of color in academic contexts, but not elsewhere.

A daily-report study suggests that people with devalued social identities interpret their performance as validating or invalidating the self (Crocker, Karpinski et al. 2003). This study of male and female psychology and engineering majors found that academically contingent women in engineering—a group stereotyped as low in ability relative to men—experienced greater self-esteem decrements than academically contingent men in engineering when they received worse grades than expected (Crocker, Karpinski et al. 2003). Academically contingent women in psychology did not experience greater self-esteem decrements relative to men majoring in psychology when they received unexpectedly low grades. This finding suggests that women engineering majors perceived their gender identity as devalued and therefore were more likely to link their self-esteem to their academic competence. To them, good grades validated their ability and hence their self-worth, whereas bad grades invalidated their ability, and hence their self-worth.

However, basing self-esteem on academic performance should decrease in contexts where the stereotype is not applicable, such as at the gym. Thus, only settings associated with negative stereotypes should lead to more academically contingent self-worth.

Identification with Devalued Social Groups and Contingent Self-Worth

Members of social groups differ in the degree to which they identify with them. Some individuals do not perceive their group membership as an important self-aspect (Tajfel and Turner 1986), whereas others perceive it as self-defining. For example, a person might be African American, but may or may not view that social group as an important reflection of who they are. Highly ethnic- and gender-identified women of color may experience greater academic contingencies than less-identified women of color. Those who feel strongly identified often share a sense of common fate with their group (Gurin and Townsend 1986). Thus, highly identified people may view their behavior as consequential to both themselves and to those who share their social group. In particular, highly ethnic- and gender-identified women may perceive that being a good in-group member requires doing well academically (Oyserman, Brickman, and Rhodes, chapter 4, this volume). Consequently, highly gender- or ethnic-identified women of color may interpret their academic performance not only as a reflection of their own abilities but also as indicative of their group's general competency. Because they invest in doing well to have others perceive their in-group positively, more is at stake if they fail. Given the negative stereotypes associated with women of color in academic settings, gender- and ethnic-identified women may be more likely than low-identified participants to attempt to validate the academic competencies of their social group. This process ultimately leads to greater contingent self-worth.

To summarize, we propose that in academic contexts women of color base their self-worth on academic performance because of their knowledge of relevant negative stereotypes. Furthermore, we propose that this effect will be magnified for highly gender- and ethnic-identified women of color. Because their abilities are suspect, women of color may be particularly sensitive to the value that is placed on academic performance, resulting in greater academic contingent self-worth.

Women of Color and Contingent Self-Worth (CSW)

Using an experience-sampling methodology, we tested our predictions that context and identity strength influence moment-to-moment fluctuations of academic CSW in a sample of women of color. Experience-sampling methodology allows researchers to collect data from participants in multiple assessments over time in their natural setting. We implemented this methodology by asking women of color who were attending college to fill out questionnaires on a Palm Pilot over the course of two weeks. Participants filled out these questionnaires in specific contexts. These settings included academic contexts such as the classroom, when studying, or when talking about academics with others and nonacademic contexts such as during their morning routine, on a date, at the gym, during religious or spiritual activities, and when interacting with family. On average, participants filled out three questionnaires per day. Out of the contexts reported, participants were in academic contexts 49 percent of the time and in nonacademic contexts 51 percent of the time. In addition to the daily Palm Pilot assessments, participants completed an initial set of questionnaires that assessed chronic levels of CSW. This methodology allowed us to assess whether characteristics of the person, the context, or an interaction between the person and context lead to greater CSW in the moment.

The present study explores four main questions. First, among women of color in college, does academic CSW vary within-persons or is it stable across time and contexts? Second, if academic CSW varies within the person, does context influence these moment-to-moment variations in academic contingency? Third, how do chronic levels of academic contingent self-worth influence contingent self-worth in the moment? Fourth, does context more strongly influence momentary variations of academic contingency for women of color who have stronger ethnic or gender identities? A more detailed review of our methodology and analyses is presented elsewhere (Garcia and Crocker 2006); however, we summarize our findings below.

Variability of Academic CSW

To examine if academic contingency varied within persons, we analyzed the amount of the variance in academic contingency that could be accounted for by between-person and within-person variables. We found that 31 percent of the variance was accounted for by between-person variables, and the remaining 69 percent of the variance was accounted for by within-person variables. In other words, academic contingency did vary in the moment. Strikingly, the majority of the variance occurred within persons.

This finding has important implications for future research on CSW. Researchers who only rely on individual-difference measures of CSW might be missing a significant portion of the variance in this construct. For example, researchers might incorrectly conclude that people who do not chronically base their self-worth on academics will never experience the self-esteem concerns as those who chronically base their self-worth on academics.

We sought answers to our second question by seeing whether context could account for within-person variation in academic CSW. As predicted, women of color in our sample based their self-worth on academic competency more in academic contexts than in nonacademic contexts. Thus, context did account for within-person variation in academic CSW. In academic contexts, women of color recognize the value of academic performance and may also be aware of relevant negative stereotypes about their academic competencies. The high value of academic performance, coupled with the threat of confirming negative group stereotypes, might account for increases in academic CSW.

These results do not support the idea that women of color disidentify with school. On the contrary, when women of color enter academic contexts such as classrooms or other studying environments, academic achievements become an increasingly important basis of self-worth.

Chronic Academic Contingency as a Predictor of Academic Contingency in the Moment

We explored the influence of chronic levels of academic contingency by first examining its effect across contexts. We found that participants who based their self-worth on academic competence more chronically, as indicated by the global measure of contingencies of self-worth, tended to be more contingent on academics in both academic and nonacademic contexts. Though this effect was only marginally significant, it suggests that academic performance affected self-worth across many contexts, not just academic ones for chronically contingent women of color. Alternatively, the influence of academic performance on self-esteem may extend beyond academic contexts. That is, the effects of academic performance on self-worth may have spilled over from academic into nonacademic contexts. Third, academic performance may have affected self-worth in academic contexts only for non–chronically contingent women of color.

Furthermore, we examined whether the context effect differed by chronic levels of academic contingency. We found that chronic levels of academic contingency did not moderate the effect of context on academic contingency in the moment. Stated differently, the effect of context on academic contingency in the moment did not differ depending on one's chronic level of academic contingency. Self-worth depended on academic competency more in academic contexts than in nonacademic contexts, regardless of chronic levels of academic contingency.

Taken together, our results indicate that academic contingency depends both on one's chronic level of academic contingency and the context. Chronic levels of academic contingency predicted between-person reports of contingency across both academic and nonacademic contexts. The effect of context, on the other hand, accounted for within-person variation in contingency. Individuals based their self-worth on their academic performance in academic contexts, but not in nonacademic contexts. However, chronically contingent participants did not experience this context effect to a greater degree than non-contingent participants. That is, both chronically contingent and non-contingent participants experienced increases in academic CSW in academic contexts to similar degrees.

Identity as a Predictor of Academic Contingency in the Moment

Ethnic and, to a certain extent, gender identification moderated the effect of context such that highly identified individuals based their self-worth on academics in academic contexts to a greater degree than those who were less identified (see figures 7.1 and 7.2). Contrary to the notion that identification with school is incompatible with identification with one's race or ethnicity, more-identified students were more likely to base their self-worth on academics when they were in academic contexts. Gender- and ethnic-identified women of color may view their individual academic performance as consequential to the group as a whole. Thus, highly identified women may seek to prove not only their own academic competency but also the competency of their group. As

Figure 7.1   Predicted Values for Ethnic Identity as a Moderator of the Effect of Context on State Academic Contingency at One Standard Deviation Above and Below the Mean of Ethnic Identification

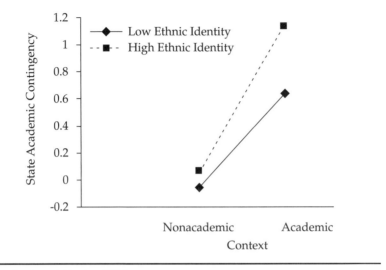

Source: Garcia and Crocker (2006).

Figure 7.2   Predicted Values for Gender Identity as a Moderator of the Effect of Context on State Academic Contingency at One Standard Deviation Above and Below the Mean of Gender Identification

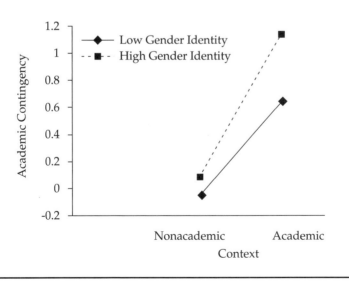

Source: Garcia and Crocker (2006).

these women become so invested in proving themselves, the influence of their performance on their self-worth is heightened, especially in academic settings.

We believe the moderating effects of gender identity would have been stronger if we had examined exclusively math and hard-science contexts, instead of all academic contexts. Negative stereotypes about women's academic ability are typically confined to poorer performance in math and hard-science courses. Thus, the threat of confirming negative gender stereotypes is only applicable within these domains and not within all academic contexts. The level of one's gender identity may more strongly moderate the context effect if we were to restrict our analyses to math and hard-sciences context. We are currently conducting another study to investigate this possibility.

In sum, our research shows that women of color base their self-esteem on their academic achievements, and they do so more in academic settings than nonacademic settings, and women of color who are ethnically identified or gender-identified are especially likely to do so. We next consider the consequences of this form of valuing of academics.

Costs of Basing Self-Esteem on Academic Performance

When self-esteem is academically contingent, success and failure reflect not only on one's ability but also on the worth and value of the self. Students who base their self-esteem on academics experience boosts to self-esteem when they succeed academically and drops in self-esteem when they fail or perform worse than expected. Students whose self-worth is not contingent on academics (or is less invested in this domain) are not as susceptible to these boosts and drops in self-esteem, even if they care deeply about the domain for other reasons (Crocker, Sommers, and Luhtanen 2002; Crocker, Karpinski et al. 2003; Niiya, Crocker, and Bartmess 2004). This linking of performance to self-worth is highly motivating; when self-esteem is contingent, people want to succeed and experience the positive emotions and high self-esteem that accompany success, and avoid the painful emotions and low self-esteem that accompany failure (Crocker and Wolfe 2001; Crocker et al., 2006). Academic CSW can motivate students to invest effort to accomplish their goals. Because of its link to motivation, researchers have suggested that disengagement of self-esteem from academics is problematic, particularly for minority students (see Crocker and Major 1989; Major and Schmader 1998; Marx, Brown, and Steele 1999; Osborne 1995, 1997; Schmader, Major, and Gramzow 2001; Steele 1997b).

Despite its unquestioned motivational force, academic contingent self-esteem has downsides both for academic achievement and well-being (Crocker and Park 2004). In terms of achievement, accumulating evidence suggests that basing self-esteem on academics (1) fosters problematic achievement goals, which undermine interest and achievement, (2) provides a fragile source of motivation that quickly dissipates following failure or setbacks, (3) creates stress and anxiety, and (4) undermines performance on difficult tasks. In terms of well-being, students who base their self-esteem on academics have vulnerable self-esteem, respond to setbacks such as disappointing grades by deciding they do not belong in their major, and are vulnerable to depression.

Achievement Goals: Learning and Performance Goals

Achievement researchers have long recognized that students' goals shape their academic experiences and outcomes—their intrinsic interest, persistence in the face of difficulty, and grades. Achievement research focuses on two general classes of achievement goals thought to shape academic experience: performance goals, those geared toward demonstrating ability by achieving successful outcomes or avoiding unsuccessful outcomes, and learning goals, geared toward acquiring new knowledge or skills (see Grant and Dweck 2003, for a discussion). Performance goals are detrimental, especially on challenging tasks. For example, when students with performance goals encounter difficulty, they may experience learned helplessness or loss of interest. Learning goals are widely agreed to be superior to performance goals for sustaining intrinsic interest and fostering deeper learning strategies in the face of challenges and, in many studies, improved performance outcomes (see Grant and Dweck 2003, for a review).

The more students base their self-worth on academics, the more they tend to have performance goals. We examined the association between three performance goals (outperform others, avoid failure, demonstrate competence) and three learning goals (acquire knowledge, acquire mastery of material, and learn from failure) with academic CSW by entering all six achievement goals simultaneously into a regression equation as predictors of academic contingency (Crocker et al. 2006) to examine the unique associations of achievement goals with academic contingency. Two achievement goals were strongly related to basing self-esteem on academics: avoiding failure and demonstrating competence. Not coincidentally, these two achievement goals have been shown to have the most negative effects on motivation, persistence, and grades (see Grant and Dweck 2003). In this analysis, none of the learning goals were significantly related to basing self-worth on academics. In sum, basing self-esteem on academics fosters achievement goals focused on performance rather than learning.

Performance Goals Provide a Fragile Source of Motivation

In the face of difficulty, students with performance goals tend to lose motivation, withdraw effort, and spend less time on achieving their goals (Grant and Dweck 2003). Amara T. Brook (2005, study 2) had students complete a measure of basing self-esteem on academics, then do either an easy or difficult academic task. After they completed the task, participants completed a measure of academic self-validation goals consisting of items such as "It is important for me to confirm my intelligence through my schoolwork" (Grant and Dweck 2003). For students in the easy condition, the academic contingency of self-worth was strongly and significantly related to academic self-validation goals after the task, consistent with other research. However, after the difficult task, there was no significant association between academic contingency and academic self-validation goals, because highly contingent students no longer had the goal of validating their ability. Letting go of one's goal as soon as a task becomes difficult is a hallmark of poor self-regulation; thus, self-validation goals associated with CSW seem to be ineffective guides to self-regulation in the face of obstacles.

Motivation Based on CSW Can Lead to Stress

Although contingencies of self-worth can be motivating, they also create stress. At the start of their freshman year, six hundred fifty students completed a measure of how much they based their self-esteem on academic success; at the end of the year, they completed a measure of daily hassles of college students (Crocker and Luhtanen 2003). The more students based their self-esteem on academics at the start of the year, the more daily hassles they reported at the end of the year, including more time pressure, dissatisfaction with their abilities, conflicts with professors and teaching assistants, and loss of interest in their courses.

Academic CSW Undermines Performance on Challenging Tasks.

A number of studies provide indirect evidence that basing self-esteem on academics undermines performance. Academic CSW strongly predicts performance goals, which in turn undermine performance on difficult tasks (Elliot and McGregor 1999; Grant and Dweck 2003). More direct evidence of the effects of academic contingency on performance was provided by two laboratory experiments in which students completed a difficult task that was defined as either diagnostic or nondiagnostic of ability (Lawrence, Crocker, and Dweck 2006). When the test was described as diagnostic, the more students based their self-esteem on academics, the worse they performed on the task; this effect of CSW was not observed on the nondiagnostic tasks. Furthermore, this negative effect of contingency on performance was observed for both men and women, on both a verbal and a mathematical task. In other words, academic CSW undermines performance on tasks that students believe reflect their ability, and they do so both for students stereotyped as low in ability on the task (women on the mathematical task), and for students not stereotyped as low in ability (women on the verbal task, men on both tasks).

Together, these studies suggest that basing self-esteem on academics creates obstacles and barriers to academic achievement by fostering the development of unhelpful achievement goals, creating fragile motivation, increasing stress, and undermining performance.

Lower Psychological Well-Being

External contingencies of self-worth, including basing self-esteem on academics, lead to increased symptoms of depression. As noted, students with academic CSW experience increases in self-esteem in response to academic successes and drops in self-esteem in response to academic setbacks (Crocker, Sommers, and Luhtanen 2002). The resulting instability of self-esteem predicts increases in symptoms of depression over time for these students (Crocker, Karpinski et al. 2003).

In sum, although academic CSW motivates students, it provides a problematic source of motivation that can foster performance rather than learning goals, increase stress, undermine performance on challenging tasks, and increase vulnerability to depression.

Strategies to Improve the Experiences of Women of Color in College

As we have shown, those who are both highly contingent and highly identified with their group membership were more susceptible to fluctuations in academic CSW. Some might conclude that to buffer against the costly pursuit of self-esteem, women of color should avoid having very strong gender or ethnic identities. As Catherine Good, Carol S. Dweck and Joshua Aronson (chapter 5, this volume) note, research has shown that individuals highly identified with devalued groups can be both more and less susceptible to social-identity threats. For example, highly identified people experience greater stereotype-threat effects

(Schmader 2002), but can also feel greater achievement efficacy (Oyserman, Harrison, and Bybee 2001). Do our findings contribute to this body of literature that suggests that identifying with devalued social groups is "bad"? We argue that identifying is not "bad" per se. Rather, our findings merely indicate that the negative stereotypes associated with women of color's academic abilities can lead them to value academics in an ego-involved way. This ultimately detracts from true learning.

We must also emphasize that the effect of identification on academic contingencies depended on the context. Highly identified women of color did not perpetually base their self-worth more on academics. To be more precise, they experienced heightened state academic only when they were in contexts that suggested devaluation. As such, women of color's state academic contingency should be viewed as a function of both their environment and their social identity.

Thus, we do not suggest that disidentifying with one's group members is the best solution. Instead, we propose returning to the heart of the problem by asking, "What can be done to improve the experience of women of color in college?" To answer this question, one must first address two issues: the devaluation experienced by women of color in academic settings and the ways women of color cope with this devaluation. Using both a top-down and a bottom-up approach can be effective in assessing these issues. We offer both institution- and individual-level strategies to address these issues.

Institution-Level Strategies

College environments should work toward reducing the negative association between being a woman or ethnic minority and the expectation that these groups will underperform in certain academic domains. The academy can highlight the importance of having both women and ethnic minorities as members of the intellectual community. Increased minority representation in prestigious academic positions can connote a positive value for the minority member's social identity. Thus, female students of color can learn that their membership is valued if they feel that their social groups are adequately represented on university faculty and administration.

Teachers should avoid using social groups in ways that create divisive environments. Patterson and Bigler (chapter 3, this volume) demonstrate how teachers can subtly increase the salience of group differences, ultimately leading to the development and utilization of gender stereotypes. Notably, Patterson and Bigler highlight that seemingly benign actions can foster the development of gender stereotypes. For example, sitting students in alternating seating boy, girl, boy, girl can implicitly teach students that gender is important. Thus, teachers should be mindful to not inflate perceptions of group differences.

In addition to lowering perceptions of difference, teachers could also provide feedback in a way that does not foster the development of CSW. Feedback can differ in the degree to which it emphasizes global assessments of the person or strategies and effort. Feedback that emphasizes global assessments is referred to as person feedback, whereas feedback that emphasizes effort is referred to as process feedback (Kamins and Dweck 1999). Research has suggested that person rather than process feedback leads to greater CSW (see Kamins and Dweck 1999; Mueller and Dweck 1998) and feelings of helplessness (Burhans, Klein, and Dweck 1995). Specifically, when both criticism and praise were attributed to the individual, rather than the process, children experienced greater negative affect and persisted less on a task (Kamins and Dweck 1999). Melissa L. Kamins and Carol S. Dweck (1999) suggested that person-based feedback fosters the development of a performance-based sense of self-worth, which leads students to develop CSW. Thus, professors could make sure that they provide feedback that is more process oriented (for example, "You worked hard") rather than person-oriented (for example, "You are smart") to ensure that students do not link their performance to global assessments of their self-worth. Process- instead of person-based feedback may be one way to lower CSW, thereby positively influencing the experiences of women of color in college.

Individual-Level Strategies

Individual-level strategies for lowering CSW could increase how efficacious women of color feel in dealing with potentially threatening environments. For example, developing a learning orientation toward academic achievement can help buffer against the negative consequences that CSW can have on self-esteem and affect (Niiya, Crocker, and Bartmess 2004). In other words, when individuals believe their academic abilities are pliable rather than fixed, their self-worth becomes less tied to their academic performance. Thus, even though negative feedback still stings, they are able to bounce back because they feel as though they can improve. Good, Dweck and Aronson (chapter 5, this volume) also highlight that incremental-learning orientations can increase performance and that this effect holds even when people continue to perceive negative stereotypes for their social groups.

Therefore, encouraging learning goals instead of performance goals could be a powerful strategy to improve the experiences of women of color in college. if women of color focus on learning and believe that their abilities are pliable, they will be able to let go of perceiving academic performance as an indicator of self-worth. Rather than worrying about what their academic performance says about them or their in-group, women of color can focus on what they want to learn or what they hope their education can help them achieve and contribute.

Conclusions

In academic environments, women of color must contend with nega-tive stereotypes about their social groups' academic abilities. Conse-quently, women of color feel as though they need to dispel these nega-tive perceptions via strong academic performance. Succumbing to this pressure can lead to greater shifts in self-worth as a function of their ac-ademic performance, especially for highly gender- or ethnic-identified women. Research has shown that trying to validate the self can lead to greater depression (Dykman 1998), lower self-esteem and affect, (Crocker, Karpinski et al. 2003), and impede learning goals (Niiya, Crocker, and Bartmess 2004).

Academic contexts do not necessarily have to be associated with greater CSW for women of color. Academic structures, teachers, and students can all do their part to improve the experiences of women of color in college. Specifically, academic structures can be more deliberate in fostering cues that create identity safety. Teachers could ensure that they do not inflate perceptions of difference and provide feedback that does not increase CSW. Women of color must re-frame the reasons for doing well academically. They should learn to concentrate on learning for inherent reasons, and less on trying to prove something to them-selves or others. If they let go of perceiving their value as dependent on academic success, they will likely experience less stress and anxiety, which takes away from their ability to both enjoy and perform well in an academic environment.

The research reported in this article was supported by National Institute of Mental Health grant R01 MH58869-01. Julie A. Garcia was supported by a National Science Foundation postdoctoral fellowship, and Jennifer Crocker was supported by National Institute of Mental Health grant K02 MH01747-01 during the preparation of this manuscript. The authors would like thank Riia Luhtanen, Diana Sanchez, Laura Naumann, Daryl Wout, and Tiffany Yip for comments they made on an earlier version of this manuscript.

References

Brook, Amara T. 2005. "Effects of Contingencies of Self-Worth on Self-Regula-tion of Behavior." Ph.D. diss., University of Michigan.

Burhans, Karen Klein, and Carol S. Dweck. 1995. "Helplessness in Early Childhood: The Role of Contingent Worth." *Child Development* 66(6): 1719–38.

Cammarota, Julio. 2004. "The Gendered and Racialized Pathways of Latina and Latino Youth: Different Struggles, Different Resistances in the Urban Context." *Anthropology and Education Quarterly* 35(1): 53–74.

Crocker, Jennifer. 1999. "Social Stigma and Self-Esteem: Situational Construction of Self-Worth." *Journal of Experimental Social Psychology* 35(1): 89–107.

Crocker, Jennifer, Andrew Karpinski, Diane M. Quinn, and Sara K. Chase. 2003. "When Grades Determine Self-Worth: Consequences of Contingent Self-Worth for Male and Female Engineering and Psychology Majors." *Journal of Personality and Social Psychology* 85(3): 507–16.

Crocker, Jennifer, and Riia K. Luhtanen. 2003. "Level of Self-Esteem and Contingencies of Self-Worth: Unique Effects on Academic, Social, and Financial Problems in College Students." *Personality and Social Psychology Bulletin* 29(6): 701–12.

Crocker, Jennifer, Riia K. Luhtanen, M. Lynne Cooper, and Alexandra Bouvrette. 2003. "Contingencies of Self-Worth in College Students: Measurement and Theory." *Journal of Personality and Social Psychology* 85(5): 894–908.

Crocker, Jennifer, Riia K. Luhtanen, Paul Denning, and Yu Niiya. 2006. "Egosystem and Ecosystem Goals: Links to Performance and Learning Goals and Academic Experiences in the First semester of College." Unpublished paper. Ann Arbor: University of Michigan.

Crocker, Jennifer, and Brenda M. Major. 1989. "Social Stigma and Self-Esteem: The Self-Protective Properties of Stigma." *Psychological Review* 96(4): 608–30.

Crocker, Jennifer, and Lora E. Park. 2004. "The Costly Pursuit of Self-Esteem." *Psychological Bulletin* 130(13): 392–414.

Crocker, Jennifer, and Diane M. Quinn. 2000. "Social Stigma and the Self: Meanings, Situations, and Self-Esteem." In *Social Stigma*, edited by T. F. Heatherton, R. E. Kleck, M. R. Hebl, and J. G. Hull. New York: Guilford.

Crocker, Jennifer, Samuel R. Sommers, and Riia K. Luhtanen. 2002. "Hopes Dashed and Dreams Fulfilled: Contingencies of Self-Worth and Admissions to Graduate School." *Personality and Social Psychology Bulletin* 28(9): 1275–86.

Crocker, Jennifer, and Connie T. Wolfe. 2001. "Contingencies of Self-Worth." *Psychological Review* 108(3): 593–623.

Demo, David H., and Keith D. Parker. 1987. "Academic Achievement and Self-Esteem Among Black and White College Students." *Journal of Social Psychology* 127(4): 345–55.

Devine, Patricia G. 1989. "Stereotypes and Prejudice: Their Automatic and Controlled Components." *Journal of Personality and Social Psychology* 56(1): 5–18.

Dykman, Benjamin M. 1998. "Integrating Cognitive and Motivational Factors in Depression: Initial Tests of a Goal Orientation Approach." *Journal of Personality and Social Psychology* 74(1): 139–58.

Elliot, Andrew J., and Holly A. McGregor. 1999. "Test Anxiety and the Hierarchical Model of Approach and Avoidance Achievement Motivation." *Journal of Personality and Social Psychology* 76(4): 628–44.

Fordham, Signithia. 1996. *Blacked Out: Dilemmas of Race, Identity, and Success at Capital High*. Chicago: University of Chicago Press.

Fordham, Signithia, and John U. Ogbu. 1986. "Black Students' School Success:

Coping with the 'Burden of "Acting White."'" *The Urban Review* 18(3): 176–206.

Garcia, Julie A., and Jennifer Crocker. 2006. "Women of Color in College: Identity and Context Affect Contingent Self-Worth." Unpublished manuscript. Ann Arbor: University of Michigan.

Grant, Heidi, and Carol S. Dweck. 2003. "Clarifying Achievement Goals and Their Impact." *Journal of Personality and Social Psychology* 85(3): 541–53.

Gurin, Patricia, and Aloen Townsend. 1986. "Properties of Gender Identity and Their Implications for Gender Consciousness." *British Journal of Social Psychology* 25(2): 139–48.

Heatherton, Todd F., and Janet Polivy. 1991. "Development and Validation of a Scale for Measuring State Self-Esteem." *Journal of Personality and Social Psychology* 60(6): 895–910.

Horn, Laura, and Rachael Berger. 2004. *College Persistence on the Rise? Changes in 5-Year Degree Completion and Postsecondary Persistence Rates Between 1994 and 2000.* NCES publication no. 2005-156. Washington: U.S. Government Printing Office, for U.S. Department of Education, National Center for Education Statistics.

James, William. 1890. *The Principles of Psychology.* Volume 1. Cambridge, Mass.: Harvard University Press.

Kamins, Melissa L., and Carol S. Dweck. 1999. "Person Versus Process Praise and Criticism: Implications for Contingent Self-Worth and Coping." *Developmental Psychology* 35 (3):835–847.

Lawrence, Jason S. L., Jennifer Crocker, and Carol S. Dweck. 2006. "Stereotypes Negatively Influence the Meaning Students Give to Academic Settings." In *Navigating the Future: Social Identity, Coping, and Life Tasks,* edited by Geraldine Downey, Jacquelynne Eccles, and Celina M. Chatman. New York: Russell Sage Foundation.

Major, Brenda, and Toni Schmader. 1998. "Coping with Stigma Through Psychological Disengagement." In *Prejudice: The Target's Perspective,* edited by Janet K. Swim and Charles Stangor. San Diego: Academic Press.

Marx, David M., Joseph L. Brown, and Claude M. Steele. 1999. "Allport's Legacy and the Situational Press of Stereotypes." *Journal of Social Issues* (special issue: Prejudice and Intergroup Relations: Papers in Honor of Gordon W. Allport's Centennial) 55(3): 491–502.

Mueller, Claudia M., and Carol S. Dweck. 1998. "Praise for Intelligence Can Undermine Children's Motivation for Performance." *Journal of Personality and Social Psychology* 75(1): 33–52.

Niiya, Yu, Jennifer Crocker, and Elizabeth N. Bartmess. 2004. "From Vulnerability to Resilience: Learning Orientations Buffer Contingent Self-Esteem from Failure." *Psychological Science* 15(12): 801–5.

Osborne, Jason W. 1995. "Academics, Self-Esteem, and Race: A Look at the Underlying Assumption of the Disidentification Hypothesis." *Personality and Social Psychology Bulletin* 21(5): 449–55.

———. 1997. "Race and Academic Disidentification." *Journal of Educational Psychology* 89(4): 728–35.

Oyserman, Daphna, Kathy Harrison, and Deborah Bybee. 2001. "Can Racial

Identity be Promotive of Academic Efficacy?" *International Journal of Behavioral Development* 25(4): 379–85.

Rosenberg, Morris. 1965. *Society and the Adolescent Self-Image*. Princeton: Princeton University Press.

———. 1979. *Conceiving the Self*. New York: Basic Books.

Rosenberg, Morris, and Roberta G. Simmons. 1972. *Black and White Self-Esteem: The Urban School Child*. Washington, D.C.: American Sociological Association.

Schmader, Toni. 2002. "Gender Identification Moderates Stereotype Threat Effects on Women's Math Performance." *Journal of Experimental Social Psychology* 38(2): 194–201.

Schmader, Toni, Brenda Major, and Richard H Gramzow. 2001. "Coping with Ethnic Stereotypes in the Academic Domain: Perceived Injustice and Psychological Disengagement." *Journal of Social Issues* 57(1): 93–112.

Spencer, Steven J., Claude M. Steele, and Diane M. Quinn. 1999. "Stereotype Threat and Women's Math Performance." *Journal of Experimental Social Psychology* 35(1): 4–28.

Steele, Claude M. 1992. "Race and the Schooling of Black Americans." *The Atlantic*, April, 68–78.

———. 1997a. *Race and the Schooling of Black Americans*. Upper Saddle River, N.J.: Prentice-Hall.

———. 1997b. "A Threat in the Air: How Stereotypes Shape Intellectual Identity and Performance." *American Psychologist* 52(6): 613–29.

Steele, Claude M., and Joshua Aronson. 1995. "Stereotype Threat and the Intellectual Test Performance of African Americans." *Journal of Personality and Social Psychology* 69(5): 797–811.

Tajfel, Henri, and John C. Turner. 1986. "The Social Identity Theory of Intergroup Behavior." In *The Social Psychology of Intergroup Relations*, edited by W. Austin and S. Worchel. Monterey, Calif.: Brooks/Cole.

Tesser, Abraham. 1988. "Toward a Self-Evaluation Maintenance Model of Social Behavior." In *Advances in Experimental Social Psychology*, edited by L. Berkowitz. San Diego: Academic Press.

U.S. Department of Education, National Center for Education Statistics. 2004. "Full-Time Instructional Faculty in Degree-Granting Institutions, by Race/Ethnicity, Academic Rank, and Sex: Fall 2003." Digest of Education Statistics, chapter 3, table 228, available at http://nces.ed.gov/programs/digest/d04/tables/dt04_228.asp.

Vallerand, Robert J., and Robert Bissonnette. 1992. "Intrinsic, Extrinsic, and Amotivational Styles as Predictors of Behavior: A Prospective Study." *Journal of Personality* 60(3): 599–620.

PART III

How Social Relationships Mediate the Effects of Social Categories and Identities

Chapter 8

The Meaning of "Blackness": How Black Students Differentially Align Race and Achievement Across Time and Space

Carla O'Connor, Sonia DeLuca Fernández, and Brian Girard

T his chapter explores the ways African American students differentially align race and achievement in moving from a predominantly white high school to historically black colleges and universities (HBCUs). In contrast to popular and academic discourse, which suggest that black students enter school with racialized conceptions of achievement performance and the concomitant notion that being black is in conflict with doing well academically, we show how the racial character and organization of educational institutions play a role in the process whereby students come to construct blackness and whiteness in relation to schooling. We begin by summarizing the birthplace and logic of the articulated conflict between being black and doing well in school. We subsequently discuss how our findings complicate this perspective.

The Conflict Between Being Black and Doing Well in School

The notion that being black is in conflict with doing well in school is rooted in John Ogbu's cultural ecological theory (hereafter referred to as CET), which has assumed a prominent place in the discourse on black underachievement. A significant number and variety of theories have been advanced to explain black underperformance in school, including theories of innate intelligence, cultural difference, and cultural reproduction, but these explanations have had significantly less impact than CET (Horvat and O'Connor 2006). The theory is, however, rarely taken up in its entirety. This is due in part to its complexity and comprehensiveness.

The theory not only distinguishes between two types of minorities (voluntary and involuntary) but conceptualizes how their differential accommodation to the norms and expectations of school represent distinct cultural adaptations to the way each type of immigrant was incorporated into and subsequently treated in the United States. In the case of African Americans, who are included among the involuntary minorities, their less successful accommodation to the norms and expectations of schools presumably represents a cultural adaptation to a history of systemic racial discrimination that is manifest as an oppositional cultural frame of reference.

More specifically, John U. Ogbu (1987, 1991, 2006) argues that African Americans and other involuntary minorities—including Native Americans, Mexican Americans, and Puerto Ricans, who were incorporated into the United States through slavery, conquest, or colonization—situate whites as their reference for interpreting their life chances and experiences. In doing so, they "often conclude that they are far worse off than they ought to be because of white treatment" (Ogbu 1987, 331). Furthermore, "They know from generations of experiences that the barriers facing them in the opportunity structure are not temporary" but systemic and enduring (Ogbu 1987, 325). They are aware not only of how historical and contemporary expressions of subjugation and exploitation limit their access to social and economic rewards upon their completion of school, but also of how schools' structural inequities—including "biased testing, misclassification, tracking, biased textbooks, and biased counseling"—already circumscribe their potential to be viable competitors in the contest for social and economic rewards (Ogbu 1990, 127).

According to CET, it is involuntary minorities' knowledge of and experience with structural barriers to upward mobility that cause them to question the instrumental value of school and to develop a deep distrust of whites and the institutions they control, notably, schools. Consequently, they come to privilege their collective identity and favor collective struggle in the effort to cope with their oppression (Ogbu 1989). Collective identity buffers involuntary minorities psychologically and enables them to "maintain their sense of self worth and integrity" despite their subjugation (Ogbu 1990, 62). Their engagement with collective struggle provides an instrumental means for reducing or eliminating barriers to mobility (Ogbu 1987, 1990). Although Ogbu contends that involuntary minorities' collective orientation may help them maintain their mental health, and may improve their likelihood of experiencing greater social justice, he (1987) indicates that it also produces maladaptive educational consequences.

Unlike immigrant minorities, involuntary minorities perceive the cultural differences they encounter in school as "markers of identity to be maintained," not "barriers to be overcome," and they develop an oppositional stance and identity vis-à-vis white Americans and what they see as indices of white culture (Ogbu 1987, 327). They consequently "equate following the standard practices and related activities of the school that enhance academic success with 'acting white'" (Ogbu 1987, 330). With little evidence that they will be appropriately rewarded for their efforts in school and the accordant notion that schooling is the province of white Americans and threatens their own cultural identity, involuntary minorities are said to have little reason to work hard in school and consequently experience poor or underachievement.

Researchers have been enamored by the way in which CET effectively links structure, culture, and agency in explaining black achievement performance. But the intricacy and expansiveness of the theory prevent it from being interrogated in total. Methodological, funding, and time constraints have prevented researchers from designing and implementing empirical studies that account simultaneously for each facet of this multidimensional theory. Instead, researchers have selected particular aspects of CET for further exploration. Of special concern has been how an oppositional cultural frame of reference, accordant oppositional identity, and the presumed "fear of acting white" are implicated (or not) in the poor school performance of black youths. This last aspect of the theory was foreshadowed by Ogbu's (1974) independent research. However, the elaborated conception of an "acting white hypothesis" and the "burden of 'acting white'" was founded and articulated in the research of Signithia Fordham (1988, 1991, 1996) and Ogbu's collaborations with her (Fordham and Ogbu 1986).

The notion that blacks do poorly in school out of fear of "acting white" has been popular outside as well as inside academia. Articles in major newspapers, news magazines, and journals regularly attribute blacks' underachievement to black students' defining their identities in opposition to whites and to their fear of (being accused of) "acting white" if they do well in school (O'Connor, Horvat, and Lewis 2006). In the midst of this mainstream reference to and acceptance of the "acting white" hypothesis, researchers have debated the influence and generalizability of this phenomenon as well what is being signified when black students accuse each other of "acting white."

Prudence Carter (2006) discussed the extent to which this accusation is gendered. She "found that African American and Latino youth tended to feminize certain dimensions of 'acting white,' particularly speech codes and personal styles associated with whites, especially the white characters on TV programs" (Carter 2006, 29). Consequently, "[m]ales were more likely to shy away from feminine behaviors that might allow others to attribute to them a (stigmatized) gay identity" and in the process avoided academically related behaviors that might have made them appear "soft" (Carter 2006, 29–30). Annette Hemmings (1996) demonstrated that black peer culture varies from one school context to the next and differentially frames how blackness is defined in relation to excelling in school and to the question of whether an oppositional frame of reference is constructed in relation to whiteness.

Although James W. Ainsworth-Darnell and Douglas B. Downey (1998) and Philip J. Cook and Jens Ludwig (1998) did not specifically address themselves to the ways accusations of "acting white" play out in the school experience of black students, their studies provided evidence that black students demonstrate positive attitudes toward school and are no more vulnerable than white students to negative peer sanctions for high performance. More specifically, Ainsworth-Darnell and Downey (1998, 547) found that "African American students have more pro-school attitudes than do whites" and Cook and Ludwig (1998) found that "black and white students who excel in school are no more likely to be unpopular than other students and that in the case of black students participation in an honor society provides a social advantage" (391). Jason S. Lawrence, Meredith Bachman, and Diane N. Ruble (chapter 6, this volume) demonstrate that in comparison to whites and voluntary immigrants, blacks similarly demonstrated a high valuation of schooling and were more likely to report that their parents expected them to achieve in school, that they wanted to achieve in school for intrinsic reasons, that they were more engaged in school, and that their same-race peers believed that school achievement was important.

Ogbu himself argued in his last work (published posthumously, in 2004) that "there are relatively few students who reject good grades because it is White[;] on the contrary they want to make good grades and many report that they are well received by their close friends when they get good grades" (28). Nevertheless, he maintained that "what [black] students reject that hurt their academic performance are 'white' attitudes and behaviors conducive to making good grades." Included among these supposed "white" attitudes and behaviors conducive to making good grades were "speaking standard English, enrollment in Honors and AP classes, being smart during lessons, having too many White friends," "studying a lot or doing homework everyday," "acting like a nerd," "taking mathematics and science classes," "spending a lot of time in the library," and "reading a lot" (Ogbu 2004, 28). In turn, black students "experience peer pressures from other black students to discourage them from adopting such white attitudes and behaviors" (Ogbu 2004, 28–29).

Having directed our attention to black students' opposition to "'white' attitudes and behaviors conducive to making good grades" (Ogbu 2004, 29), Ogbu nevertheless forwarded essentialized conceptions of whiteness (and, by implication, blackness) and continued to convey that black underperformance in school derives in part from black students' opposition to whiteness. Here the analytical emphasis was on how blacks conflate whiteness not with competitive educational outcomes such as "good grades" but with "behaviors" and "attitudes" that produce these competitive outcomes or good grades. By implication, blackness or conceptions of what it means to act black are then aligned with behaviors and attitudes likely to produce poor achievement outcomes.

Defining the Limits of "the Conflict"

In this chapter we challenge the manner in which the debates over conceptions of acting white and acting black and their salience to black student performance are usually taken up: as if these conceptions were static constructs. We argue that the logic of these debates often operates on the assumption that black students enter school with these intractable notions of what it means to be black instead of white. Little attention is paid to whether and how constructions of blackness and whiteness change as a consequence of space and time and to the academic meaning and impact of these more local and context-dependent influences. Thus we observe little variation in how researchers report on conceptualizations of whiteness and blackness across different contexts. For example, Fordham's (1988, 1991) account of how students conceived of blackness in a low-income African American school in Washington, D.C., varied little from Ogbu's (2003) account of how students conceived of blackness in a middle-class racially integrated school in Shaker Heights, Ohio.

Where researchers have been attentive to how local contingencies impact students' conceptualizations of whiteness and blackness and the consequent impact on schooling orientation, they have focused either exclusively on macrostructural contingencies or have stopped short of providing us with empirical evidence of the dynamic impact of micro-contingencies. As an example of the first scenario, Ogbu (2004) conceptualized changing constructions of whiteness and blackness across different eras. Dividing the history of black-white relations in the United States into three historical periods—pre-emancipation, post-emancipation, and post–civil rights era—Ogbu claimed that evolving historical racial constraints on black status reinforce collective identity and provide the "context for understanding why black students label and avoid some attitudes and behaviors as 'White'" (Ogbu 2004, 18). According to Ogbu, the evolution of racial constraints reflected changing notions of how whites expected blacks to act and react or risk punishment. In response, blacks developed ways of being that were articulated in opposition to these white expectations.

A framework such as this one privileges how whites conceived of and imposed these racialized expectations over different historical periods and suggests strong trends in how blacks responded to and redefined the imposition of such racialization. This macrostructural framework ignores the local and micro-contingencies that affect black people's conceptualization of and response to these constructs. Moreover, Ogbu's (2004) focus on macro-historical contingencies would lead us to believe that black students necessarily enter into schools with conceptions of racial identity and allegiance that align blackness with underachievement, or at the very best, with attitudes and behaviors that produce underachievement. Furthermore, the logic of his analysis suggests that black students have always entered school with these notions. That is, having received access to education post-emancipation but remaining subject to white domination and racialized expectations, blacks have presumably articulated these notions and corresponding oppositions for as long as they have had the "opportunity" (however limited) to attend school. There is no consideration whether the practice and organizations of school (as they might shift in relation to historical periods or be evidenced differentially from one context to the other) may in part shape black students' understanding of blackness and whiteness and whether and how these identity constructs are aligned with high- versus low-achievement performance and accommodation to versus resistance to the norms and expectations of school.

Some researchers have offered insights into and speculations about how local and historical contingencies may impact the ways students align race and achievement. For example, Karolyn Tyson (2002, 1184) advanced the importance of focusing in on local and micro-contingencies across the life course after she found that although black elementary school students were on average enthusiastic about school, those who experienced academic failure "were more likely to express negative school-related attitudes than [those who experienced academic success] and those attitudes were directly related to their achievement experiences." She concluded that these findings "suggest that the schooling experience, particularly achievement outcomes, plays a central role in at least the *development* of attitudes toward school" (Tyson 2002, 1184, original emphasis). Later, Tyson (2006, 84) directed us to examine how "schools create and sustain structures including racially stratified academic hierarchies that conflate race and achievement" and to more precisely explore how and why "that fusion [of experiences and attitudes] has little salience for students until they reach adolescence." Tyson's work was not longitudinal, and stopped short of providing us with an empirical account of how local and micro-contingencies shifted across space and time to understand how students come to align race and achievement differentially in their constructions of black and white identity.

Anne Galletta and William E. Cross (chapter 1, this volume) demonstrate the importance of examining the influence of such contingencies, particularly as they might be framed by historical time. Their work indicates that evidence of the tension between being black and doing well in school is "readily traceable to structural elements and educational policies that defined integrated schooling" following the civil rights era (Galletta and Cross, chapter 1, this volume). Using Shaker Heights, Ohio, as an illustrative case, they show how, in response to desegregation, the common curriculum of the high school, which "provided a rigorous college preparatory program" for most of its students, was abandoned in favor of a comprehensive and academically stratified "levels" curriculum. Black secondary school students in Shaker Heights (and often elsewhere) found themselves disproportionately relegated to the least rigorous courses in the school and were subject to racial isolation and stigmatization if they transgressed these racialized patterns by enrolling in the more rigorous academic courses. Galletta and Cross demonstrated how the contemporary phenomenon of the racially stratified academic hierarchy contributed to "displays of oppositionalism and muted achievement by black students."

Their historical analysis is confirmed and amplified in light of Roslyn Arlin Mickelson and A. E. Velasco's (2006) finding that black students' interactions around and attitudes about the relationship between racial identity and achievement varied in relationship to whether the school evidenced a racially stratified academic hierarchy or not. They found that although students demonstrated and articulated tensions between being black and doing well in school in high schools characterized by a racially stratified academic hierarchy, these tensions were not demonstrated or articulated in high schools where blacks were proportionately represented throughout the school's academic hierarchy. Mickelson and Velasco's work was cross-sectional, however, and did not allow us to examine how specific individuals may alter their interpretations of the alignment between race and achievement as a consequence of operating under dramatically different racial and academic contexts.

In the effort to more precisely explore the dynamic nature of black students' understanding of what it means to "act white" and to "act black" in relation to achievement performance and how these understandings are shaped in part by the racial character and organization of local contexts, this paper will examine how five black students differentially align race and achievement in transitioning from a predominantly white high school to an HBCU.

The demographic contrasts between a predominantly white high school and an HBCU (historically black college or university) are evident. In the first context, African Americans are the numerical minority, and in the second, they are the majority. In the latter case, moreover, HBCUs, as sites for higher learning, are in part indicative of academic success because they capture a segment of the American public privileged enough to attend college. In this context, then, blackness is consistent with indices of high achievement because black people predominate in an academic space that signals privileged educational access and competitive educational outcomes. In contrast, there is extensive evidence that blacks are often relegated to the least rigorous academic spaces in predominantly white high schools (Hallinan 2001; Oakes 1995; Wells and Crain 1997), and the high school we studied was no exception to this pattern. In this high school, then, as in many others, the institutionalized "link" between black people and academic success was more tenuous. By comparing the experiences of students who transition from this predominantly white high school to an HBCU, we are afforded a vantage point for studying how the racial character and organization of institutions can racialize achievement performance and how this impact must be accounted for in further efforts to conceptualize the interface of identity and achievement.

Towards this end, we begin by reporting on our methods of data collection and analysis and on how we selected focal participants for the purposes of this paper. We subsequently share our findings and conclusions.

Methods: Data Collection, Study Participants, and Analysis

We drew the data pertaining to the focal participants in this paper from a larger longitudinal study. This study of black students investigated in part how conceptions and expressions of black racial identity change over time and in response to social context as well as the ways students came to cope with the challenges and demands of these contexts in light of these conceptions and expressions. This longitudinal study included three waves of data collection. The first wave of data collection occurred during the students' sophomore year (the 2000–2001 academic year) in the predominantly white high school we will refer to as Hillside High. This first wave of data collection relied extensively on semi-structured individual interviews that were designed to capture information on a wide variety of issues, including students' social-background characteristics, school engagement, peer networks and interactions, assessment of how race operated (or not) in their high school or in society at large, interpretations and evaluations of "acting white" versus "acting black," and beliefs regarding how these "acts" were represented (if at all) in their own practices.

As part of this first wave of data collection we also captured the broader culture of Hillside High. Consequently, throughout the academic year we observed a variety of school-based activities, including sporting events, lunch time in the cafeteria, passing in the hallways, dances, assemblies, and graduation. We also collected artifacts such as school newspapers, printed policies, public relations documents, and announcements of special school events, that afforded further insight into the culture of Hillside High and served as supplements to our observations.

During the second wave of data collection, which occurred during the students' senior year (the 2002–2003 academic year), we relied in part on an interview protocol that featured both closed and open-ended items aimed at exploring various dimensions of students' racial identities. As part of this exploration we examined how students assessed "acting black" and "acting white," and under what conditions they imagined themselves or others as acting white or black or acting differently in their interactions with whites as compared to their interactions with blacks.

During the third wave of data collection, which occurred during the first year after high school graduation (the 2003–2004 academic year), we again administered the aforementioned interview from the 2002–2003 academic year, which explored the multidimensional character of students' racial identity. We also visited with the students in both the fall and spring of that post-graduation year not only to develop "snapshots" of their post-high-school cultural context but also to shadow them as they moved through their everyday activities. During these visits we conducted both individual and group interviews, the latter with the participant under study and his or her close friends. These interviews were designed to explore how the participants' peer networks had changed since high school. In addition, we used these interviews to explore how the participants and their peers assessed the post-high-school context, how race figured in their assessment, and how they interpreted race as a social phenomenon—including how they understood what it meant to be black and how they interpreted themselves and others as racial beings.

For the purposes of this paper, five students serve as focal participants: Sheila, Deanne, Allyson, Khenedi, and Tandy. These students were selected for study because they participated in all three waves of data collection and had all entered an HBCU after completing high school, as opposed to working or attending a junior college or predominantly white college or university, as was the case for the other respondents.

In order to assess more specifically how the students' constructions of race, particularly whiteness or blackness, coincided or did not coincide with their interpretations of what it meant to do well in school or to accommodate to the norms and expectations of school, we began by analyzing all interview data (including semi-structured, informal, and focus-group interviews) we had coded as either "constructions of whiteness" or "constructions of blackness." These coding categories captured students' beliefs regarding what it meant to be black versus white, including how these meanings may have reflected distinctions, if any, in practices, attitudes, worldviews, preferences, language, styles of interactions, and orientations. In analyzing the content of these categories we sub-coded for instances when the students invoked schooling- or achievement-related factors in relation to these constructs.

Beginning with time-ordered within-case analyses, we analyzed not only how the students' constructions of blackness and whiteness changed over time, but also—given the specific interest of this chapter—if, when, and how these constructions were aligned (if at all) with schooling- and achievement-related considerations. In conducting subsequent across-case analyses we sought to determine whether substantive patterns emerged across the cases with regards to when and how the students aligned or did not align the constructs of race and schooling or achievement over the three waves of data collection. We were especially attentive to whether there were distinctions in how the students discussed these alignments during their high school years (captured by waves 1 and 2 of data collection) as compared to their first year of college (captured by wave 3 of data collection).

In order to situate the findings that emerged from this analytical procedure, we begin by describing the context of Hillside High School. We specifically document how the high school was organized spatially and academically and where black students were situated within this academic space as a basis for understanding how the character and organization of the high school "linked" blackness and achievement. We then describe in brief the social and academic backgrounds of our focal participants and offer insight into the colleges they attended. We subsequently discuss how the students (re)aligned race in relation to schooling and achievement when they transitioned from Hillside High to a historically black college or university.

Hillside High School

Hillside High School is one of four public high schools included in the Hillside School District, which is nested in a small affluent city that is also home to a major university. HSD is predominantly white (65 percent white; 14 percent African American; 17 percent Asian; 9 percent Hispanic; 2 percent Arabic; 3 percent other) with only 14 percent of the student population qualifying for free or reduced lunch.[1]

Hillside High is a comprehensive and overcrowded high school that is set on a sprawling campus. The current structure, including building extensions, was designed to house eighteen hundred students. Approximately twenty-seven hundred students are now in attendance at Hillside High. Fifteen portable classrooms have been erected on the campus to ease overcrowding. The campus also features four tennis courts, a field hockey field, football field, a soccer practice field, and three parking lots. One lot is designated for staff with a select number of spots for visitors. The main building houses a garage for an automotive shop, a small theater, and a large auditorium with balcony seating. There are fifteen science labs and four computer labs. There are twenty-five additional computers available in the school library, which houses nearly thirty thousand volumes.

The campus grounds and building accommodations only hint at the extracurricular activities that are offered by the school. The school features more than thirty student clubs and a competitive sports program encompassing more than twenty-five interscholastic sports. It is not uncommon for the Hillside athletic program to earn as many as five state championships in a given year. The music program is nationally recognized and the theater program produces a number of elaborate theatrical productions each year.

The academic offerings are similarly impressive. Advanced placement (AP) courses are provided in over fifteen subjects, including calculus, physics, chemistry, German, French, Spanish, Latin, English, and U.S. history. A series of accelerated, or intensive, courses is offered in the primary subject areas of math, English, science, and social studies. These courses move more rapidly and are more challenging than the core courses in these subject areas, but are not as demanding as the AP courses. Finally, remedial course offerings are provided in both math and science.

Nearly three quarters of the student body is white, and black students make up about 15 percent of the student body. Asian American students, approximately 6 percent of the student body, are the next largest minority group, followed by Latino students, around 3 percent of the population. Middle Eastern, Native American, and multi-ethnic students combined constitute 3 percent of the student body. In the next section we elaborate upon the inequitable distribution of these racial groups across this academic hierarchy.

School Organization and the Creation of Black (Non-Academic) and White (Academically Rigorous) Spaces

Hillside is organized according to instructional wings. In the athletic wing the gymnasiums and physical education classrooms are clustered. The music wing has a band room, choral rooms, and an orchestra-practice room. There is also a vocational wing, where auto shop, health sciences, drafting, and other vocational courses are offered. The yearbook office and the student newspaper headquarters are also housed in this wing. The central part of the building, the main hall, houses classrooms for most of the academic courses. The first floor is designated primarily for physical science classes, both upper-level courses such as chemistry and physics and lower-level courses such as "physical" science. The second floor is designated primarily for language and history courses, and the third floor is designated primarily for English and math courses, though some of the math classrooms can be found on the first floor next to the vocational education wing. Teachers in these classrooms teach advanced math courses such as calculus and algebra 3-4, and most of the lower-level remedial math courses are also taught within this cluster of classrooms.[2]

Students are not distributed equally across these instructional wings, and we were able to observe and document the racial stratification that occurs within the school academic hierarchy. Although we observed remedial math courses and vocational courses in which black students made up anywhere from 20 percent to 40 percent of the students in the class, the AP and accelerated (AC) courses we observed generally had one or sometimes two blacks enrolled, representing 3 to 8 percent of the students in the class.[3] The college prep courses we visited that were neither AP nor AC usually had between two and four blacks, or 7 to 15 percent of the class. In contrast, sections of the African American literature course, an elective in English, was populated almost wholly by blacks, who constituted between 82 and 90 percent of the class.

This racially stratified placement system and the wing organization of the school produce noticeably black spaces and movement in the building. For example, because what is referred to as North hall is housed in the vocational wing of the school and was where the preponderance of remedial math courses are taught, a disproportionately high number of black students were found moving around North Hall between classes. Additionally, because only two years of math are required for graduation and black students are underenrolled in more-advanced math and science courses, they are less likely to be found on the third floor of the building, where sections of algebra 3-4 are taught.

Because the first floor houses courses in which blacks are overenrolled and is the gateway by which students enter and exit the building, black students have a greater likelihood of encountering each other on the first floor, and so they often congregate informally on this floor. Their preference is to cluster just inside the main entrance, several yards away from the cafeteria. Such clusters are especially identifiable just before the first bell rings and around lunch time. Black students also cluster near a second entrance near the physical education wing. During lunch hour black males dominate the basketball courts in this wing.

As conveyed by the following exchange with Deanne and Sharon, one of whom, Deanne, is also a focal participant in this paper, black students were acutely aware of how the organization of the school and the racialized patterns of course taking determine how black bodies move through Hillside and come together to produce identifiably black spaces:

> Carla O'Connor: What do you think we [my graduate students and I] should pay attention to? What do you think would give us insight into black life at [Hillside]?
> Deanne: The hallways.
> Sharon: Yup.
> Deanne: All the black people are on the first floor, particularly down like [North hall]. And then you see some of them on the second floor and even less on the third floor. Except during second and third hour, when they're all on the third floor. . . .
> Sharon: Because they're all taking African American literature. [Both Sharon and Deanne, who were enrolled in the course, laugh enthusiastically] . . .

The predominantly black spaces at Hillside did not coincide with spaces where rigorous academic courses were being taught, so a divide was institutionalized between the black academic elite and the other black students in the school. This paper shows how these racialized academic spaces influenced students' interpretations of the relationship between race and achievement. We also show how those interpretations shifted in a dramatically different racial context: attendance at an HBCU.

The Focal Participants

All five of the focal participants in the study are female and identify as "African American" or "black"; and all completed their first year of college at an HBCU.

Deanne was born in Hillside and attended private schools until mid-way through the seventh grade. She described this year as significant; after experiencing "some racial problems," she transferred to a public middle school. She has a younger brother and was raised primarily by her mother. Deanne's parents identify as black. They divorced during her sophomore year in high school. Of this time in her life Deanne said "It wasn't anything" because for as long as she can remember her father regularly commuted out of state for work, and as a result she didn't spend much time with him. Deanne's mother received a bachelor's degree from a regional state university, and is employed as a lead teacher in a Jewish day school. Despite the fact that Deanne's father received a medical degree from a prestigious medical school and was employed as a physician, she received "free or reduced lunch" benefits while attending public schools.

Deanne completed a traditional college preparatory curriculum while attending Hillside, including four years of math, science, and English. She completed AP English during her senior year. Deanne reported receiving a 2.7 GPA during her sophomore year.

Deanne is attending a selective, private, independent university in the South that has roots as a normal school founded in 1868. Currently this school has a combined undergraduate and graduate enrollment of just under six thousand students, and over 90 percent of them are African American. Deanne is hoping to be a pre-law major.

Sheila was raised in a household with her mother, stepfather, and four siblings. Sheila's father identifies as black, and her mother identifies as biracial and black. Both of her parents completed some college at regional state universities, though neither received a degree. Her mother is employed as a custodian in the residence hall system of the state university in town. Her family moved to Hillside when she was in the second grade, and she attended traditional public schools for all but the eighth and ninth grades. During this time she attended a predominately black, alternative public school known for its unique approach to instruction and student assistance. While at Hillside she completed a traditional college preparatory curriculum, and reported a 3.7 GPA. Sheila is attending the same university as Deanne.

Allyson was born in a neighboring city and was raised in a household with her mother, father, and younger brother. Both of her parents identify as African American. Her father completed some college at a regional state university, but did not receive a degree. Her mother finished an associate's degree at the local community college. Both of Allyson's parents are employed in administrative capacities at a private hospital. Her parents moved from a neighboring community to Hillside when Allyson was in fifth grade in order to take advantage of the quality public school system. Allyson reported having a 3.4 GPA during her sophomore year. During her high school career she took traditional college preparatory courses, including three years each of math and science.

Allyson is attending a comprehensive doctorate-granting, land-grant university located in an urban area in the South. This university, founded in 1912, began as a "normal school for Negroes," received land-grant status in 1958, and in 1979 merged with another state university located in the same city to form the current institution. In the fall of 2003 the enrollment was over nine thousand students, 75 percent of them African Americans and 21 percent whites. Allyson hopes to be admitted to the nursing college during her sophomore year.

Khenedi was born in a large urban center, but in the early 1990s, her family moved to Hillside to take advantage of the "better schools." Khenedi lived with her mother, father, and an older brother. Both of Khenedi's parents identify as African American, and both completed graduate degrees—her mother earned a master's degree in education and her father, a Ph.D. in psychology. Her mother is employed by the state department of education, and her father had been a psychologist at a regional state university. While at Hillside, Khenedi took a traditional college preparatory curriculum and achieved a GPA of 3.0.

Khenedi is attending a comprehensive land-grant university in the South with an enrollment of more than ten thousand students. Ninety-one percent of the undergraduates are African American and 6 percent are white. This university was founded in 1891 as an "agricultural and mechanical college for Negroes." In 1915, the name was changed to "State Agricultural and Technical College"; it became a university in 1967, merged into the state university system in 1972, and began offering doctoral programs in 1993. Khenedi is studying psychology.

Tandy, the youngest of four children (she has three older brothers), was raised by her mother, father, and grandmother. All of Tandy's family is originally from Nigeria. Her parents consider themselves African or Nigerian, and explain how a strong ethnic identity is important to them in the raising of their children. Both of Tandy's parents received graduate degrees, her father, a Ph.D. in engineering, and her mother, a master's in education. Tandy's father is a professional engineer and teaches at an urban university and her mother is a technician at the university library in town.

Tandy attended public schools in Hillside starting with kindergarten. While at Hillside High she completed a college preparatory curriculum that included numerous accelerated and AP courses (Spanish, biology, English, geometry, physical science, algebra, calculus, and government). During her sophomore year, Tandy reported having a 3.53

GPA. Throughout her four years at Hillside High School, Tandy was involved in several student organizations and activities, and assumed leadership roles during her junior and senior years.

Tandy is attending a selective private university with a total enrollment of just over ten thousand, located in a large southern city. It was founded in 1867 as a university "for the education of youth in the liberal arts and sciences." Tandy is majoring in pharmacology.

Realigning Race and Achievement

When these students were asked to define what it means to "act white" or to "act black," they did not directly reference schooling or achievement-related indices in their responses. In fact, in most instances the students responded to such questions with hesitancy and conveyed via a variety of speech practices that "acting white" and "acting black" were not viable, verifiable, or readily tangible constructs. Despite student hesitancy to accord these constructs wholesale legitimacy, they offered their interpretations of how these constructs were conceived of by those who operated in their immediate social world or society at large and how they had developed their own shorthand measures for distinguishing the ways whites and blacks "acted." Consistent with Carter's (2005) findings, students most often offered that acting white versus black was distinguished via speech, dress, style, and the company you keep. For example, during her sophomore year, Deanne explained:

> I think acting white is—well people tell you you act white when you talk like, "Oh, my god." [Impersonating the voice of a "Valley girl".] And when—sometimes when you act stuck up. But everybody can act stuck up sometimes—that's not really. But, like, I guess it's like the people you hang out with and how you . . . It's different things, like maybe how you dress. 'Cuz at Hillside, most of the white people wear Abercrombie and Fitch and that's like this store in the mall. That's all they buy. That's all you'll see them wearing. And . . . then the black people say they [whites] do their hair in these knot balls. They like take their hair, and they . . . put it in a pony tail, and they wrap it around like a couple of times, then they scatter it out. I don't know.

In response to the same request to define what it means to act white or black, Sheila similarly responded with hesitancy, false starts, and qualifiers. She too relied on "I don't knows" and "guesses" and what "people" say versus what "she thinks" to convey her discomfort with these two constructs. Nevertheless, she introduced indices of speech, dress, personal style, and social relations that would distinguish acting white from acting black. She began by stating:

Dang, that's a hard one. I don't know. To be like kind of like more on the proper side. Like a lot of people . . . would say, that I sound white, but I don't act white 'cuz I have like a proper voice, I guess, but like I don't know, it could be like, I don't know. Like you gotta sound like them, and act like them, and dress like them.

In response to follow-up questions Sheila elaborated upon why she was not perceived as "acting white" and what it "meant" to sound like whites, act like whites, and dress like whites:

[People don't think I act white] because the majority of my friends are black, and just we're like alike. Like all my friends like here at Hillside, like all, the majority of the black people sound white, basically. Like, I mean like my friends, like, I don't know of any of them that sound like all like, I don't know. It shouldn't really be like you sound white or you sound black but, I don't know. . . . Well it shouldn't be even be like you act white. You act who you are. Whatever. But then there's a certain way that whites tend to act and there's a certain ways that blacks tend to act. . . . I guess since we were like segregated and like we listen to different music and we do different things and we dress—we like have different tastes in clothes. That if you're like the total opposite of that, then you act white, I guess. . . . [At Hillside white girls] wear really big flares and they'll have them ripped at the bottom and looking dirty. I don't play that. They wear, like, little skirts that come down to their knees and little shirts like this (pointing to the fitted cropped T-shirt that she was wearing) . . . I mean I wear GUESS and stuff [but one of my neighbors was saying] like you dress white but you do it with soul. . . . [Black] people make fun of me because my favorite store is The Gap.

As the excerpts above reveal, the students indicated that for others and often for themselves acting white was signified by standard English, mainstream intonation, and "Valley girl" talk. Further distinguishing aspects of "acting white" were when blacks opted to associate primarily or exclusively with whites, when they wore clothing from stores that feature attire that had been either popularized by boy bands such as N'Sync or were consistent with the dress styles displayed in television shows and movies such as *Dawson's Creek* and *Clueless*, which are targeted to young (white) teens. For the most part these findings were consistent with those reported by Carter (2005, 2006).

In contrast to Carter's findings, however, the students in this study also aligned whiteness with being academically inclined. That is, despite their heightened (even if usually hesitant or qualified) account of how speech, dress, personal style, and the company one keeps were racialized in the social world, in their own everyday experiences, and in the conceptions they took for granted, all of them with the exception of Allyson indicated that as high school students they had also aligned race and achievement in ways that were consistent with the logic of CET. For them, "acting white" or whiteness was aligned with being smart and doing well in school and "acting black" or blackness (usually by implication) was aligned with being less than smart and doing poorly in school. Tandy provides our first case illustration of this alignment.

While in high school, Tandy, like Sheila and Deanne, initially offered qualified and hesitant indices of what it meant to act black versus white and her interpretation of what distinguished these constructs were centered on personal style and orientations. She stated:

> I guess [acting white is] preppiness. I don't—I don't know. I don't see any acting white. A lot of people think that acting white may be acting mature, because a lot of black people are not mature. Or people see it that way. It's like, "Oh you're trying to act mature." No, I'm just being mature. . . . And then a lot of white people are, like, "Oh, you're trying to act black and be ghetto." No, you just like how some black people are and you want to be that way.

When the interviewer subsequently asked Tandy whether she perceived herself as acting white or acting black, she responded by extending her definition of acting white versus black to include indices of dress and achievement performance:

> I would say I'm in the middle [with regard to acting white or acting black]. I'm a little mix, because . . . my . . . immediate older brother, he was just a bad kid. He was—he was the little ghetto end of the family. And then my [oldest brother], he was, as you would say, he was acting white because he was really really smart and people were, like, "Oh you're trying to be smart and act white.' But then my [middle] brother . . . everyone loved him. Like he was homecoming king. . . . Like everyone loved him. And he didn't dress preppy, or dress, like, you know, like FUBU and stuff.[4] He wore what was comfortable. So his favorite store was not, you know, The Gap or whatever, it was the thrift shop. . . . So I try and put that mix into things, because I don't want to be categorized as "Oh wearing Abercrombie and Fitch. Trying to be white."

In the excerpt above, Tandy's understanding of whiteness is not limited to speech, dress, personal style, or the company one keeps. It is embodied in her immediate older brother and is offered as shorthand for being "really really smart." Blackness, in contrast, embodied in her oldest brother, is commensurate with being "bad" and being "ghetto." Although Tandy does not specifically state that blackness is in conflict with being "really really smart" by situating her oldest brother (representing blackness) and her immediate older brother (representing whiteness and being really really smart) as polar opposites , she clearly aligns blackness with being other than smart.

The question that arises is how and why did acting white become Tandy's shorthand for being "really really smart." Tandy directed us toward an answer when she offered the following in an individual interview during her first year in college:

> In all my precollege—like middle school, high school, elementary school—a lot of time I was the only black person in my class. A lot of times. And I thought that in that way I was different from black people as a whole. That I was something they were not. And if I was smart then well—you know.

Through this comment we learn how Tandy's racial isolation in school contributed to the way she came to align race and achievement. She recalled that she was often the only black person in her class. When she entered middle school, and to a greater extent when she entered high school, courses were hierarchically organized, and being the only black person in her class coincided with being in the more demanding classes. As the black exception in the classes for the smart kids she came to perceive herself not only as smart but also as different from black people along this dimension. Upon attending an HBCU, however, Tandy had reason to question how she came to understand herself against what she believed constituted blackness.

In a group interview with friends Tandy had made in college, which was conducted shortly after the completion of this individual interview, Tandy sought to explain the impact of the way she and her friends had come together in college. All of them had also attended predominantly white high schools. She began by saying, "We were all the little token 'white people' [in our classes in high school] or the people that everyone called white, and now we're coming together [in college]." As a consequence of coming together with these other girls, Tandy reevaluated her understanding of what it meant to be black. Finding herself among others who also previously had been racially isolated in rigorous academic spaces, she no longer perceived that she was "different from black people as whole." Instead, she came to believe that there were many other blacks like her. Consequently, she conceived of blackness in a much more variegated way than previously. Blackness was no longer relegated to the ghetto, or to speaking nonstandard English, or to being disengaged from school. More specifically, she explained, "Now I see that everybody's not the same and everybody's not trying to be ghetto fabulous. Everybody's not speaking Ebonics or whatever. Everybody's not not caring about school or education. I learned I'm not all that different and if I am, there are a lot of black people that are different like me."

A similar reconceptualization occurred in the case of Khenedi. During her senior year, Khenedi, in her effort to explain why she only "kind of agreed" with the statement that she had a strong belonging to other black people, stated that although she "can't generally relate to whites"—particularly white males—she feels "apart" from blacks "when it comes to school and education," and added that "some of them just don't feel like doing [school] work, and I do." She subsequently noted that her sense of belonging was especially compromised when she was the only black or one of two blacks in her class. Since attending an HBCU, however, Khenedi offered the following in her effort to explain why she would not choose to be a member of another race:

> I'm proud of our achievements and how far we've come cause I know—
> I do believe—that we are the strongest race. We were here first. It's in history. They [whites] don't want to admit it, but we were. So I just think we're the strongest race, and we're just beautiful. Look at our bodies. . . .
> When I came here—I mean I always appreciated it—us—but I really came in full force when I came to [HBCU] cause I was surrounded by so many beautiful aspiring black people that's smart.

Khenedi aligned race and achievement in far more subtle ways than Tandy did. She did not convey that she thought blackness was inconsistent with being smart. However, like Tandy, she felt "apart" from other blacks when it came to school and education. And like Tandy, the racial stratification of Hillside also contributed to Khenedi feeling set apart in this way. Although Khenedi began by explaining that she felt set apart because of how her academic orientations seemed to contrast with those of other blacks in the school when she pointed out that "some of them just don't feel like doing work and I do," it is telling that her sense of being different along this dimension was magnified when she found herself as the only black or one of two blacks in her classes. Thus, the racially stratified academic hierarchy of her high school contributed to her ambivalent connection to other blacks—her sense that she could only "kind of" (and not "really agree") that she had a really strong sense of belonging to other black people.

Having enrolled in an HBCU, Khenedi could now "really agree" that she had a strong sense of belonging to other black people. Although she explained that her ability to really agree with this statement was rooted in her understanding of how blacks have had to struggle with racial discrimination,[5] it was evident from her comments that it was also bound to her finding herself "surrounded by so many black people" whom she perceived as "aspiring" and "smart." In high school she had been both figuratively (and therefore emotionally) and literally (and therefore structurally) "set apart" from other blacks "when it [came] to school and education."

The way the racial character and structure of an educational institution can affect students' interpretation of the alignment of race and achievement was probably most poignantly articulated in the next exchange, which occurred during our spring visit with Sheila during her first year in college. As part of this spring visit the research team member assigned to Sheila had conducted a group interview with Sheila and three of her close friends in college. Included in the interview was Deanne, the focal participant who had told us to examine "the hallways" if we wanted to gain insight into black life at Hillside High. Also included in this interview were Mona and Terry, who, in contrast to Sheila and Deanne, had grown up in the South and had attended only all-black schools before enrolling in college. The interviewer prompted the exchange by asking Sheila and Deanne whether attending an HBCU had "changed their perceptions" or "created any new perceptions" for them. Sheila was the first to respond:

Sheila: I definitely feel bad for the way I judged people. But when I came to [HBCU] I thought like I was going to be "it" in class. And I just thought I was going to be like the smart person in all the classes and that people are going to be dumb. I mean to be honest, that's what I thought. I didn't necessarily think they were dumb, but I was used to being a smart girl with all the white kids so I figured that the black kids just from my own ignorance, I just figured they would all just be not so smart because I was smarter than white kids in some of my classes back at home. . . .

Deanne: I agree totally with Sheila, 'cause when I came here, I judged the black boys. I ain't going to lie. I was thinking to myself, the boys are not smart just going on what I had seen at home and the stuff I was exposed to at home. . . . But when I came to [HBCU] some people showed me up.

Terry: I went to an all-black high school, [all-black] elementary school, so I was used to intelligent African American people and that was all I was used to. I mean, I know there's some smart white kids, but I was used to it [seeing intelligent black people]. So coming to [HBCU] didn't make a big change in my thought process. It just made me learn things of course, higher, you know, higher classes and harder classes.

Mona: I went to an all-black high school too—and middle school. So there wasn't much difference there [when I got to HBCU]. Only difference was like the difference between the North and the South people and people from the Bahamas and stuff like that. It was different. And that was the only thing that was like different, even though it's all black people.

Sheila and Deanne's pre-high-school perspectives on the alignment of race and achievement, like those of Tandy and Khenedi, not only change substantially upon their transition to an HBCU but stand in stark contrast to that of Terry and Mona, who had attended predominantly black high schools. Sheila begins by pointing out that having been the "smart [black] girl with all the white kids" in high school she had arrived at the conclusion that black people in general "were not so smart." Having chosen to attend an HBCU, she expected that she would continue to be the academic exception and that her black classmates would be "dumb." Deanne confirmed that she had arrived at college with similar presumptions and that these presumptions were especially salient when it came to how she conceived of the academic potential of black males.

In contrast to Sheila and Deanne, Terry responded that having attended an all-black high school, she "was used to intelligent African American people." Mona concurred. It is important to emphasize that Terry and Mona, like Sheila and Deanne, had attended comprehensive high schools where the academic courses were hierarchically organized. Within these academic hierarchies they also found themselves in the college preparatory classes. However, because their high schools were all- black, the academic hierarchy did not coincide with a racial hierarchy in which few blacks were found in the most rigorous courses and most blacks were found in the least rigorous courses. Consequently, where the racial character and organization of Hillside High School reinforced the notion that blackness was in conflict with doing well in school, Mona and Terry found themselves in academic settings where they did "not have to change [their] thought process" about the academic potential and ability of black people. In contrast to Sheila and Deanne, Tandy and Khenedi never found themselves in schools where they were physically situated as if they were exceptions to black people's limited academic capacity and inclination.

Conclusion

While in high school four of the five women featured in this paper initially aligned race and achievement in ways that would be predicted from Ogbu's CET. In addition to drawing distinctions between acting white and acting black that were marked by speech, dress, personal style, and the company one keeps, they also racialized achievement. They imagined that acting white or whiteness coincided with being smart and being academically inclined. In contrast, acting black or blackness coincided with being less than smart (or even being dumb) and being disinclined to do well in school. Much of contemporary educational research would lead us to believe that these students entered into school having aligned race and achievement in these ways and that such a priori alignments are what suppress black students' academic engagement. However, this paper adds to growing evidence that the very structure and organizations of schools contributes to students' understanding of how race and achievement are aligned.

When they moved from a predominantly white high school with a racially stratified academic hierarchy to an HBCU, all four of these women came to reconceptualize this alignment such that they no longer perceived blackness to be in conflict with intelligence and high-achievement performance. Although these young women's voices and experiences revealed the ways the racial character and organization of educational institutions racializes achievement performance and constructs material divides between black identity and academic excellence, it was also evident that these divides did not in and of themselves explain why some black youths arrive at the conclusion that being black is in conflict with doing well in school. After all, one of these five students, Allyson, never aligned race and achievement. Her discussions of what it meant to be black versus white not only remained hesitant and qualified but were only limited to indices of speech, dress, personal style, and social relations. Although the substantive patterns that mark the voices and experiences of Khenedi, Sheila, Deanne, and Tandy confirm how schools can mark black identity in ways that situate it in conflict with doing well in school, Allyson's voice and experience indicates that black students are not similarly susceptible to this marking.

These findings further substantiate the call issued by Elizabeth Birr Moje and Magdalena Martinez (chapter 9, this volume) to researchers examining how identities are enacted in relation to schooling: they must elucidate not only how the character and demands of the schooling context under study contribute to these enactments but also how these enactments are simultaneously a function of "histories of participation." Such histories of participation are manifest not just at the individual level, where they account for the departures we documented between Allyson and that of the four other young women featured in this study. They are also a function of how identities (in this case blackness) are articulated differently from one school to the next as a consequence of how schools vary in their demographics, organization, and culture and, conversely, shape but do not wholly determine how (black) individuals participate in and experience school. In addition, Galletta and Cross (chapter 1, this volume), remind us that these individual- and school-specific histories of participation are also simultaneously framed at the macro-historical level because the very variation we see (or don't see) in the demographics, organization, and culture of schools is a function of social phenomena that arise in specific historical moments and in relation to historically defined social conflicts. In this case, both the phenomenon of racially stratified integrated settings and the legacy of HBCUs are emblematic of historical racial struggles over social and educational opportunity.

In light of this individual variation and the local and historical contingencies that surround and inform it, future research should be directed toward further unpacking the ecology of black students' experience in school across these multiple levels of influence. In doing so, we will continue to make better sense of how schools and institutions differentially racialize black bodies across space and time, in ways that may work against black students' academic engagement. Furthermore, we will better understand which black children find themselves more vulnerable and which are especially resilient in these racialized contexts, and why.

Notes

1. In order to maintain the anonymity of both the district and the school under study, the demographic data we offer are approximations.
2. Two levels of remedial math courses are taught in the school. The more challenging remedial math courses are consistent with traditional high school math courses such as algebra and geometry, but are watered down and provide students with "extra help." For example the remedial geometry course does not require students to solve proofs and otherwise covers less course material than the regular geometry course. The less challenging remedial math courses either offer instruction in "core" (that is, basic) mathematical skills or "integrate" the study of computation, algebra, geometry, and analysis in a special math program. It is important to note that the designers of the integrated math program did not intend it for remedial study, but both teachers and students relate their impression that these classes are used to house students who presumably struggle the most with mathematics. I use the word "presumably" because several faculty and students conveyed their impression that African American students are more likely than others students to be improperly placed in this program, even when they are capable of completing the work in more challenging mathematics courses.
3. Since we were only visiting the classrooms of black students who were participating in the study, each classroom we visited was guaranteed to have at least one black student enrolled. By student and teacher accounts and our own casual glimpses into classrooms, it was clear that there were other advanced courses or sections of courses in which no black students were present or enrolled.
4. FUBU is a clothing line owned by blacks. The acronym stands for "For Us By Us."
5. She explained, "I mean we've gone through a lot of the same things, like with discrimination. . . . What it's like to sort of have to struggle. . . . Opportunities aren't always given to us as it is to whites. I mean, you have to work a little bit harder for those certain opportunities."

References

Ainsworth-Darnell, James W., and Douglas B. Downey. 1998. "Assessing the Oppositional Culture Explanation for Racial/Ethnic Differences in School Performance." *American Sociological Review* 63(4): 536–53.

Carter, Prudence. 2005. *Keepin' It Real: School Success Beyond Black and White*. Oxford: Oxford University Press.

———. 2006. "Intersecting Identities: Acting White," Gender, and Academic Achievement." In *Beyond Acting White: Reframing the Debate on Black Student Achievement*, edited by Erin MacNamara Horvat and Carla O'Connor. New York: Rowman & Littlefield.

Cook, Philip J., and Jens Ludwig. 1998. "The Burden of Acting White: Do Black Adolescents Disparage Academic Achievement?" In *The Black-White Test Score Gap*, edited by Christopher C. Jenks and Meredith Phillips. Washington, D.C.: Brookings Institution Press.

Fordham, Signithia. 1988. "Racelessness in Black Students' School Success: Pragmatic Strategy or Pyrrhic Victory?" *Harvard Educational Review* 58(1): 54–84.

———. 1991. "Racelessness in Private Schools: Should We Deconstruct the Racial and Cultural Identity of African-American Adolescents?" *Teachers College Record* 92(3): 470–84.

———. 1996. *Blacked Out: Dilemmas of Race, Identity, and Success at Capital High*. Chicago: University of Chicago Press.

Fordham, Signithia, and John U. Ogbu. 1986. "Black Students and School Success: Coping with the 'Burden of "Acting White."'" *Urban Review* 18(3): 176–206.

Hallinan, Maureen. T. 2001. "Sociological Perspectives on Black–White Inequalities in American Schooling." *Sociology of Education* (extra issue): 50–70.

Hemmings, Annette. 1996. "Conflicting Images? Being Black and a Model High School Student." *Anthropology and Education Quarterly* 27(1): 20–50.

Horvat, Erin MacNamara, and Carla O'Connor. 2006. *Beyond Acting White: Reframing the Debate on Black Student Achievement*. New York: Rowman & Littlefield.

Mickelson, Roslyn Arlin, and A. E. Velasco. 2006. "Bring It On! Diverse Responses to 'Acting White' Among Academically Able Black Students." In *Beyond Acting White: Reframing the Debate on Black Student Achievement*, edited by Erin M. Horvat and Carla O'Connor. New York: Rowman & Littlefield.

Oakes, Jeannie. 1995. "Two Cities' Tracking and Within-School Segregation." *Teachers College Record* 96(4): 681–90.

O'Connor, Carla, Erin MacNamara Horvat, and Amanda E. Lewis. 2006. "Framing the Field: Past and Future Research on the Historic Underachievement of Black Students." In *Beyond Acting White: Reframing the Debate on Black Student Achievement*, edited by Erin MacNamara Horvat and Carla O'Connor. New York: Rowman & Littlefield.

Ogbu, John U. 1974. *The Next Generation: An Ethnography of Education in an Urban Neighborhood*. New York: Academic Press.

———. 1987. "Variability in Minority School Performance: A Problem in Search of an Explanation." *Anthropology and Education Quarterly* 18(4): 312–34.

————. 1989. "The Individual in Collective Adaptation: A Framework for Focusing on Academic Under-performance and Dropping Out Among Involuntary Minorities." In *Dropouts from School*, edited by Lois Weis. Albany: State University of New York Press.

————. 1990. "Minority Status and Literacy in Comparative Perspective." *Daedalus* 119(2): 141–68.

————. 1991. "Immigrant and Involuntary Minorities in Comparative Perspective." In *Minority Status and Schooling: A Comparative Study of Immigrant and Involuntary Minorities*, edited by Margaret Gibson and John U. Ogbu. New York: Garland.

————. 2003. *Black American Students in an Affluent Suburb. A Study of Academic Disengagement*. Mahwah, N.J.: Lawrence Erlbaum.

————. 2004. "Collective Identity and the Burden of 'Acting White' in Black History, Community, and Education." *The Urban Review* 36(1): 1–35.

Tyson, Karolyn. 2002. "Weighing In: Elementary-age Students and the Debate on Attitudes Toward School Among Black Students." *Social Forces* 80(4): 1157–89.

————. 2006. "The Making of a 'Burden': Tracing the Development of a 'Burden of Acting White' in Schools." In *Beyond Acting White: Reframing the Debate on Black Student Achievement*, edited by Erin MacNamara Horvat and Carla O'-Connor. New York: Rowman & Littlefield.

Wells, Amy S., and Robert L. Crain. 1997. *Stepping over the Color line: African American Students in White Suburban Schools*. New Haven: Yale University Press.

Chapter 9

The Role of Peers, Families, and Ethnic-Identity Enactments in Educational Persistence and Achievement of Latino and Latina Youths

Elizabeth Birr Moje and Magdalena Martinez

In this chapter we examine the intersection of identity and educational achievement among Latina and Latino adolescent students who live in a large, urban community. In a time when achievement and accountability are the watchwords of educational practice and policy, we seek to understand the role that various academic and social, interpersonal and institutional, structures play in educational achievement as they foster and demand different understandings and enactments of identity among Latino students. We focus on Latino and Latina youths because they represent a growing ethnic group in U.S. society (Gibson, Gándara, and Koyama 2004a), even as they continue to drop out of school in alarming numbers and thus are underrepresented in higher education. In fact, Latinos and Latinas have significantly lower high school graduation rates than many other ethnic groups (Gibson et al. 2004b). Moreover, the educational attainment gap between Anglo and Latino students continues to widen (Fry 2002, 2003; Horn 1999; Kao and Thompson 2003).

Theoretical Perspectives on Identity and Achievement: Some Definitions

We take a sociocultural perspective on questions of identity and educational achievement. That is, we see identities as always situated in and mediated by social contexts and social-group memberships. Similarly, we see educational achievement as a socially mediated phenomenon.

Relational Perspectives on Identity

Our perspective is that identity is relational and enacted, rather than a stable construct that inheres within the individual. That is, identities can be viewed as socially mediated enactments of self that are shaped in the intersection of time, space, and relationships (Moje 2004). The intersection of a particular temporal, relational, and spatial moment can be considered a "context." We use the word "enacted" in our work to signal that identity is lived. It is not just talked into being or thought about by people.

Identities, however, are not only contextually defined, leaping into life in completely different iterations at each moment. To enact contextualized versions of self, people draw upon their "histories of participation" (Rogers 2002)—their experiences, practices, and past identity enactments in other activities, relationships, and spaces. Explaining identities as enacted in particular contexts, but always situated in histories of participation speaks to the concern of many social psychologists that purely contextual conceptualizations of identity cannot explain the stability of identity enactments over time (see, for example, Thorne 2004). At the same time, acknowledging the important role of context helps to explain the fluidity and downright contradiction in identity enactments to which postmodern scholars point (see, for example, Hall 1996; Hagood 2002; Yon 2000). Thus, identities are neither completely fluid nor are they cast in stone; rather, they could be considered chapters, defined and enacted contextually, in lifelong and larger stories that individuals enact (Anzaldúa 1999; Sfard and Prusak 2005). However, identities are also acted out, or enacted, in spaces (such as school), within relationships (with teachers, peers, or parents), and in particular time periods (elementary school years, adolescence, and so on; Moje 2006). Consequently, they are more than just stories we tell about ourselves, because they are also enacted, lived out in real time, and thus open to public scrutiny.

The public nature of identities draws attention to the concept of positioning, or recognition. Even as people are enacting identities in different contexts and from different histories, they are also being positioned, or "recognized" (Gee 2000–2001), by others within these activities, spaces, times, and relations. These recognitions and positionings occur within relations of power (which are produced within particular spaces), and the discourses and histories people draw on in positioning self and others are situated in and mediated by institutions. In sum, theories of identity—especially social identities—are also theories of power relations: enactments of self always produce power and are always produced in relations of power.

The articulation of histories of participation and relations of power evokes the concept of social identities. According to Henri Tajfel (1981), individuals' self-concepts—and, ultimately, their identity enactments—derive from knowing (or believing) that they are members of particular social groups. Individuals may attempt to maintain a positive social identity, but the social groups of which they are members can be associated with positive or negative values and those associations may affect the individual's choice of membership in the group. Tajfel hypothesized that the formation of social identities is the consequence of social categorization, comparison, and desire for distinctiveness. Nationality, language, race and ethnicity, skin color, or any other social or physical characteristics that are meaningful in particular social contexts can be the basis for social categorization. Social comparison involves comparing the characteristics, such as status, of an individual group with those of another group. The characteristic under comparison becomes significant in relation to the perceived difference from other groups, a point that presumes contact or interaction with other groups. Finally, Tajfel assumes that all people desire to achieve a positive sense of individual distinctiveness, even as they identify with a social group.

Complicating the categorization, comparison, and distinguishing processes is the fact that most people are members of multiple social groups and thus carry with them many possible social identities. How people think about their social identities and act on the basis of them depends then on how they make sense of and integrate their commitments to different groups as they engage in a particular activity within a given context. From this framework, ethnic and racial identities—of particular interest relative to the research we report in this chapter—are only one type of social identity, and the salience of ethnic and racial identities will depend on the spaces, relationships, and other group identities in which one is immersed (see also Galletta and Cross, chapter 1, this volume; O'Connor, DeLuca Fernández, and Girard, chapter 8, this volume). A Latina student attending a predominately Latino high school, for example, may not experience her racial identity as being as salient as her gender or social class identity. By contrast, when the same student attends a predominantly white college, her racial identity may become more salient, given the social context. The salience of social identities is not an either-or condition, however. Race or ethnicity may be only one of the dimensions of her social identification among other psychologically equivalent ones (for example, gender, social class, sexual orientation).

Perspectives on Educational Achievement

From a sociocultural perspective, achievement, while dependent on the skills, background knowledge, and resources available to students, is also a function of students' sense of self and how they are identified and identify as belonging to or in an educational setting, as well as how the educational setting makes spaces and provides supports for people to engage and persist. This sense of belonging and invitation to an educational space shapes students' engagement with and willingness to persist in the particular educational setting (see also Galletta and Cross, chapter 1, this volume). In that sense, achievement could be said to be a function of developing a school-based social identity, or an academic identity, and developing academic identities can be seen as a function of school structures and systems. And yet, social identities do not disappear when people enter schools. An important question then revolves around how academic or school identities necessary for achievement intersect with social identities to support or constrain educational engagement, persistence, and achievement (see also Oyserman, Brickman, and Rhodes, chapter 4, this volume).

A number of scholars have written about the identity mismatch that occurs for young people as they move from homes and communities into formal education institutions (for example, Heath 1983), typically highlighting mismatches between ethnic or racial identities and the "white" identities demanded for achievement in schooling (for example, Fordham 1996; Flores-González 2002; Ogbu 1987, 1988, 1994). Other scholars, however, have argued that certain family, community, and peer funds of knowledge support high achievement in formal education institutions, even as they also support and maintain children and youths' sense of an ethnic self and collective identity (for example, Delgado-Gaitan 1994; Foley 1990, 1991; Moll 1992; O'Connor 1997; Ward 1990).

Theories about the relationship between social identity and school achievement point to deeper questions about educational engagement and persistence, both of which are necessary for school achievement. The construct of persistence is most commonly used by institutional researchers and policymakers to measure student's progression from one grade, year, or time period to another. Historically, persistence has been examined by means of large-scale databases. Although important for demonstrating trends in academic persistence, large-scale studies have not revealed the nuances in *how* young people's perceptions of social identities and relationships with peers, family, and educators (to name a few) shape or mediate their persistence behavior(s) (see Oyserman, Brickman, and Rhodes, chapter 4, this volume). In particular, how does the intersection of young people's ethnic social identities with their student social identities shape their engagement and persistence in school, or in particular school classes?

When studies have focused on group practices from ethnographic or qualitative perspectives, however, researchers have tended to examine how ethnic/racial group practices are devalued by school settings (Davidson 1996). In addition, several qualitative studies have demonstrated how those practices deemed resistant or oppositional to school success actually serve as buffers against psychological struggle fostered by school settings that fail to acknowledge, or that even devalue, students' backgrounds (Davidson 1996; Flores-González 2002; Hurd 2004; and Vigil 2004). Carla O'Connor (1997), for example, demonstrated that the most resilient—and thus, persistent—youths in her study were those who had a realistic awareness of the role that racism and discrimination could play in their educational lives as black students, provided that those youths had strong role models (usually parents) for taking action against oppression (see Ward 1990). Notably, Doug Foley (1990) posited similar findings among Tejano and Tejana youths (Mexicanos and Mexicanas born in Texas) in one Texas town. That is, the recognition that racism could play a role in their lives, together with an awareness of the value of collective social action modeled by elders, was associated with educational persistence and achievement.

Other scholars have found that school structures can support educational persistence among disenfranchised youths. Patricia Gándara and Margaret A. Gibson (2004), drawing on a series of studies of Mexican-origin youths, argue that schools should create spaces of belonging, provide opportunities for youths to build social capital through interactions with peers who possess such capital, and craft opportunities for youths to learn to cross social, ethnic, and racial boundaries in positive ways (see also Galletta and Cross, chapter 1, this volume). Each of these strategies, they suggest, builds on the ethnic and racial social identities that youths bring to school and offers young people possibilities for integrating academic identities into their social identities, rather than having to cast off their ethnic social identities to take on academic social identities (see Flores-González 2002).

Constructing and negotiating social identities is complex work, as is the study of social identity and its relationship to school achievement. In a recent commentary on social identity theory, Avril Thorne (2004) argued that "one of the biggest challenges for identity research is to achieve a dynamic and contextualized understanding of how senses of self and identity are continuous *and* changing, and how personal *and* community beliefs and practices intertwine in identity making" (365; see also O'Connor, DeLuca Fernández, and Girard, chapter 8, this volume). To Thorne's points we add the exhortation to examine how personally and socially constituted identity enactments both shape and are shaped by educational achievement, particularly in research with young people from educationally disenfranchised ethnic and racial groups. Although a number of school-based interpersonal and institutional constraints and supports for academic identity development have been identified, social and community-based constraints and supports have been analyzed less frequently. In what follows, we offer a close analysis of the institutional and interpersonal supports of Latino and Latina youths who have been studied ethnographically, over time, in one Detroit community. Although we include some school institutional supports, we focus in particular on constraints and supports offered by families, friends, and the community writ large.

Research Design and Methods

Drawing from an ongoing ethnography in a predominantly Latino and Latina community in a Midwestern city, we have examined the ways that Latino and Latina youths in the community enact identities within academic and social contexts and how their enactments link to their academic engagement, persistence, and achievement. Guiding research questions for this analysis included (1) What are the identities that students construct or bring with them to schools? (2) What are the sources, or "funds" (Moll 1992), that produce and sustain these identities? (3) How do these identities appear to intersect with engagement and persistence in academic achievement? (4) How do Latino and Latina students interpret and negotiate institutional and interpersonal factors that mediate their academic achievement?

Participants and Contexts

In this chapter we present data from a focal group of six youths from the larger sample to illustrate representative patterns in how the social identities, funds of knowledge, and institutional and interpersonal supports mediate youth identity development and achievement. Although focused on resilience and school achievement, we include one additional youth participant who is currently not attending school (although she should be moving into her senior year in high school) because this young woman has articulated a desire to return to school and because she is resilient in her positive sense of self and of group identity, despite her lack of school achievement. We use her experiences as a comparative case. In addition, her experiences are representative of other youth in the community whose academic achievement has been compromised.

The youths who form our representative subsample are Celina, Chloe, Mario, Pilar, Ramiro, and Yolanda. All identify as Mexican, Mexican-American, or Chicano, except for Chloe, who identifies as "Cub-Mex" (her mother is Cuban, her father, Mexican). All participated in interviews and observations for at least one year, some for over five years. Two, Celina and Chloe, were seniors preparing for college entrance at the time of study (and subsequently entered nearby universities). Four of the youths—Mario, Pilar, Ramiro, and Yolanda—were in their junior year in high school at the time of this analysis. Pilar has left formal schooling, but intends to return to high school in the next academic year. Four of the youths—Celina, Mario, Ramiro, and Yolanda—were born in Mexico; Chloe and Pilar were born in the United States.

Researchers moved on and off of the team, and brought different ethnic, cultural, theoretical, disciplinary, and experiential (for example, teaching and research) knowledge and discourse to bear on the analyses. Three Latinas and five Anglo women have collected data across the seven-year period. A Latina, an Anglo, and an African American researcher have also participated in the constant comparative analyses with the team.

Data Sources

To address our research questions, we analyzed data from field notes collected in schools and community settings; formal and informal individual and focus-group interviews over the first seven years of the study; and written artifacts collected in and out of school over the first seven years.

Observations and Field Notes. Researchers each made classroom observations once a week, two to three visits per classroom per week each year, for six years. Youth participants were interviewed at least once during the course of the study, and ten of the youths have been formally interviewed at least thirty times over the five years.

Interviews. Interviews typically occurred in settings outside school (for example, restaurants, shopping malls, movie theaters, homes) and lasted ninety to one hundred fifty minutes each. We conducted both individual and focus-group interviews. Interview protocols included questions about what activities they participated in, what they read and wrote outside of school, what they thought of activities we engaged in together, and what their goals were for the future.

We typically selected a set of questions from the interview protocol to target in each interview, but the interviews also simply followed the lines of conversation that the youths initiated, particularly when we interviewed more than one youth at a time. Thus, the interviews generally provided occasions for participant observation as well as formal interviewing, and field notes were written to accompany verbatim transcription. Interviews were transcribed from audio tape.

Contextual data. Data drawn from the larger ethnography also inform this work. These contextual data include participant observations and informal interviews with the youth participants and their parents at festivals and community events, observations and formal interviews with a network of prominent Latinas in the community, and interviews with teachers and students at a community-based after-school program and at a charter school for middle-school-age Latinas. We have also mapped the community on two separate occasions by driving through it and recording the kinds of businesses, homes, and public spaces located in different areas. Finally, several of the research team members have participated in community organization and leadership activities.

Data Analysis

We used methods of constant comparative analysis (Glaser and Strauss 1967; Strauss 1987) to analyze our data. These constant comparisons took place individually and in our research team meetings during the past seven years, with the last year focused in part on the link between social identities and academic achievement as represented in the likelihood of postsecondary educational participation.

As part of our weekly meetings across the years, we each wrote theoretical memos (see Strauss 1987) in which we generated tentative analyses of the data collected for that week. We read each other's memos and offered additional codes and questions to pursue in the next act of data collection. Further, we regularly shared data and initial analyses with research participants, both youths and teachers, to develop and test our analyses.

As we engaged in ongoing open coding, we coded the following patterns in the data: (1) positive social identities around ethnicity; (2) family and community funds of knowledge and practice for developing positive social identities, setting future goals, and attaining academic achievement; (3) street gangs as both funds for goal setting and as distractions from academic achievement; and (4) popular cultural texts as funds of knowledge for goal setting and for academic achievement that simultaneously act as distractions from mainstream academic achievement. We also examined closely what the youths said about the different funds of knowledge that mediated their social identities, and we attempted to trace how these social identities play out in terms of academic engagement, persistence, and achievement.

Using these categories we moved into axial coding, in which each coding category is located as a central, or axial, category and all other codes are analyzed in relation to the axial code. As we engaged in axial coding with each of these categories, we found that the codes fell into two larger categories, which we identify with labels drawn from the literature: home fronts and contact zones. Home fronts were spaces in which social identities were shaped and promoted; contact zones were spaces in which youths confronted racist and discriminatory practices.

With these axial categories established, we moved into selective coding, returning to data sets and reading and rereading the data with a focus on home fronts and contact zones in the lives of these youths. We re-analyzed the data while asking how these different social identities and the spaces in which they are formed, mediated, and enacted play out in terms of academic engagement, persistence, and engagement. In our presentation of findings in the following section, we provide exemplars from individual youths' data to illustrate these representative patterns. Subsequently, in our conclusions, we turn to a discussion of patterns and their implications for the research questions we outlined previously.

Findings

We report on two key findings of the study in this paper. First, the physical and cultural space of the community provides opportunities for Latino and Latina youths to engage intergenerationally with members of their ethnic cultural community, which provided support for youths to maintain ethnic-identity tool kits that include Spanish language abilities; knowledge of Latino and Latina traditions, music, and history; and cultural values. As the youths have begun to traverse surrounding non-Latino communities, however, they have become more aware of how their identities are recognized in terms of class, race, and language, particularly within school and other institutional settings such as bridge programs and ROTC (Reserve Officer Training Corps), and in street gang and popular-cultural settings and texts. Thus, the close-knit "home front" (Guerra 1998) that supported the development of positive ethnic selves is now presenting a conflict for many of the youth as they struggle with how to present or enact these ethnic selves in "contact zones" (Pratt 1991), where cultures meet, sometimes coexist, and many times clash as a result of asymmetrical relations of power.

It is in these contact zones that ethnic identities might be considered not supportive of academic achievement and even problematic. But contact zones can also be generative spaces, in which new understandings of self and others are forged. In particular, as the youths in this study illustrate, the awareness of how racism and discrimination work in the lives of marginalized youths is often generated in these contact zones. This awareness is often theorized as an important element of resilience (Foley 1991; MacLeod 1987, 1995; O'Connor 1997). Our analysis indicates that how the home fronts provide models for positive social action in the face of racism and discrimination appears to be critical in the youths' resilience practices.

This point leads to the second pattern we analyzed. Within this home front two sets of cultural brokering resources appeared to be significant in the lives of these Latino and Latina youths. One set is interpersonal, the other institutional. Often these two sets intertwined (for example, the most successful institutional structures were led by Latinos and Latinas from the community or from similar backgrounds and experiences).

In some cases, parents and elder community members who had not experienced secondary and postsecondary educational success tutored the youths in the value of such achievements. In other cases—although these appear to be few in our sample—Latino and Latina teachers, peers, and siblings who had gone through the academic pipeline played an important role in fostering youths' academic engagement, persistence, and achievement. For other youths, academic-identity enactments were supported by older gang members who urged the youths "not to be stupid, to do their homework, go to school, go on to college."

Finally, formal institutional structures (such as Junior ROTC and bridge programs) offer human and material resources, as well as role models and information, to guide the youths toward postsecondary educational achievements. The most successful of these programs provided sustained interpersonal mentoring. In addition, as previously mentioned, they were usually staffed by potential "pipeline mediators," other Latinos and Latinas who had experienced academic success and its challenges.

All of these resources offered potentially conflicting identity resources for these youths. For example, successful high school students and college attendees struggled with acceptance in their family and cultural communities as they progressed through mainstream education settings. In addition, elders and street gang members lived what appeared to be economically and culturally comfortable lives despite their lack of movement through, or even their outright rejection of, the mainstream educational trajectory. In both sets of findings, then, the resources that guided identity enactments presented conflicts and confusion to youths as they moved from childhood to adolescence and across the education landscape.

Home Fronts and Contact Zones

The role of home fronts and contact zones in providing intergenerational models of a variety of routes to fulfill life goals or aspirations is complicated. The predominantly Latino—indeed, predominantly Mexican—community in which the youths of our study live provides access to cultural norms and practices that support their strong, positive identifications as Latinos and Latinas, as illustrated in this excerpt from Pilar's essay, written when she was thirteen years old, for the purpose of identifying herself in research pieces such as this:

> Hi, my name's Pilar. I'm proud of being Chicana—that means you're born here in the U.S. but parents are Mexican. . . . Most of the people I know are Hispanics and proud to be. . . . I think some people are just racist and I think that's wrong because no one's perfect. And you should always stand up for what you believe even if you're standing alone. And never deny your background. . . . I think being Mexican has its advantages because Mexicans have a really authentic culture. I would never deny myself because I'm so proud of being Mexican I would never deny it.

Pilar was not alone in her expression of pride in being Mexican (or Latina, Hispanic, Chicana, among other identifiers she would happily claim). All the youths we have interviewed over the last seven years have readily claimed Latino identities and have discussed the role of the community in supporting and sometimes challenging their identities, as Ramiro did here:

Ramiro: Like five years ago there wasn't that many Hispanics.
Interviewer: You're kidding. I mean, I know that the census has shown that there's been a lot of growth—
Ramiro: When I came in '96 the only restaurants that I remember was Armando's. The mercado was smaller . . . It was still the same thing except it was smaller. It was about three of them houses like that. It wasn't big. And the parking lot was small. McDonald's that was there, they didn't have any, they had black people only. The Burger King, all the little stores were black people or white people. The only Mexican Hispanic stores was Honeybee, Mexican Village, all that little stuff. . . . Pepita's. What was another one? Armando's. And they didn't have any taquerias as now. But now . . . all Virnot is all Hispanic people. . . . Before, the only Mexican bakery was the one down there by . . . um . . . there weren't that many. . . . There weren't that many so now probably about since, oh yeah. I used to live down there by Center [Street] by McCall [Street] down there . . . by where Pilar lives. . . . Well, down there, there was probably about just ten families, Hispanic families there at that time. . . . Crossing McCall by Center there was all black people everywhere. Everywhere you look. After McCall was black. Before McCall were Puerto Rican and a little bit of Mexicans, probably ten families or something. Then more people and more people started coming in and now over there is more Hispanics now.
Interviewer: . . . So when you lived there did you feel—

Ramiro: —uncomfortable. . . . I was just, like, eleven. . . . I was about ten, yeah, eleven. And then you go to the park and the Hispanics had this side and the blacks this side and they would always do fights and fights.

The sense that the community was growing not only in numbers and thus providing a safer space for Latinos and Latinas but also was growing as a cultural center and a space for community action is captured in this excerpt from a newspaper clipping (K. Kozlowski and D. Guthrie, "Tears Flow as Catholic Schools Shut: Students Protest Detroit Archdiocese's Decision to Close 18 Schools by June," *Detroit News*, March 17, 2005) that reports on recent school closures in the community:

> In southwest Detroit, residents were especially shocked to hear that Holy Redeemer High School would close. The community, which is populated primarily by Hispanics, built up around the church and school. It is in the heart of southwest Detroit and within walking distance of the numerous businesses, bakeries and taquerias.

The sheer growth in the population of the community and the increasing number of small businesses is not all that situated the community as a home front for these youths, however. Attitudes, values, and practices unite the community. One aspect of community ethnic pride is evident in the young people's wearing of T-shirts, hats, and stickers that declare, "Mi Raza Primero," "Atzlán," and "Brown Pride." These slogans are integrated with images of La Virgen de Guadalupe (see http://www.homies.tv/home.htm, "Raza Unida"), Cesar Chavez, low-rider cars, and other Chicano or Mexicano symbols. The display of these clothing and sticker items that have obvious links to major icons of the social and cultural community indicates a strong social identity bolstered by the community among these youths.

This social identity is also supported by community activism focused on issues directly related to ethnicity. In one series of events documented throughout the course of this study, eighth-grade students who protested proposed layoffs of bilingual teachers at a local school met with strong community support. In one instance, two young women who led the protest were congratulated by a parent picking up his two primary-school daughters at the school. Having seen the young women's photos in the local community paper's stories about the protest, he praised them, telling them that as a child in the 1950s and 1960s, he and his friends were punished for speaking Spanish. He concluded by stating that he was proud of them for fighting for their rights.

Thus, it can be argued that over the last five years the community has grown in ways that provide a significant and supportive home front for youths' ethnic-identity development (see also Alvarado and

Alvarado 2003). These youths did see their identities as situated within a larger social group, one that identifies variably as Latino and Latina and Hispanic, and that also claims particular national origins with pride (among the most common are Mexicano, Puerto Rican, and Dominican).

The sense of community the home front provides, however, was not always positive for mainstream academic achievement, as articulated here by Mario when he was asked why he had reshaped his identity from one of being "cool" to being "determined."

Interviewer 2: What made you feel that way?
Interviewer 1: What was the turning point for this? Was there a moment or—?
Mario: There was not a moment. It's in my neighborhood or in my family almost nobody is like go to college or finish high school. So if you finish high school and you become something you're weird. So I'm like the kind of person that don't think like that. There's a bad opinion about me. I really don't care about it and it just . . . And when I have to take things seriously . . . so what help me was my family. The way it was breaking. So I want to build my future something happen to my parents or some people in my family. . . . It's just. . . . Well, right now I'm just going to high school. *They see me and they don't see anybody.* Like, "Hi," "Hi." That's it. *So I was thinking if I go to college and do all these things every time they see me they'll go like, "Hi mister." Or they'll stop and say hi properly, not just going by and saying hi.* [emphasis added]

Mario's perspective complicates the notion of the home front. In one sense, the home front of this tightly knit ethnic enclave provided positive social identities for these young people. They did not grow up despairing of their ethnic group as Elizabeth Birr Moje has documented in some other communities (Moje 2001). At the same time, the small number of community members who had engaged in postsecondary education in mainstream academic institutions not only left the youths without actual role models and cultural brokers or navigators of such institutions but also potentially fostered the sense that the youths who pursued mainstream academic education were "weird." And yet, the drive to be seen as someone of value and importance ("They see me and they don't see anybody. . . . If I go to college and do all these things every time they see me they'll go, like, 'Hi, mister.'") mitigated the lack of cultural brokers, at least for Mario.

But what is the source of this need to be seen and valued? Why didn't these youths see themselves—their existing identities—as important and valued? One possible answer to this question lies in the exposure to contact zones via work and other activities that take the youths outside their tightly knit communities. The following interview excerpt—again with Ramiro and Mario—was prompted by their talk about negative attitudes toward Mexicans, attitudes they hoped to change:

Ramiro: But you go to the suburbs or another ethnic group and ask about Mexicans they will tell you basically that [referring to an earlier portion of the conversation, in which the boys claim that Mexicans are typically viewed as gang bangers and dropouts].

Mario: If only one Mexican who messed up they will show it on TV and they will get an opinion for all Mexicans.

Interviewer 2: Can I ask you something about that? You guys just said a couple of things about how you think about things differently now or there comes a time when you start to realize this or you think that. Did you start to think that way at a certain point that people see Mexicans in this way?

Mario: Yeah. 'Cause I've been going an hour and thirty-five minutes away from here to other communities.

Interviewer 1: What? For work?

Mario: No, just to visit and stuff. And the way I dress it's not properly but it's not un-properly. . . . They only see my belt or something hanging in my pants and they start going like, they start looking at you weird.

Interviewer 1: Do you think it's because of the way you're dressed or because of—?

Mario: Yeah. The way we're dressed and because we're Mexican.

Interviewer 1: Because you're Mexican.

Mario: All people do that.

Interviewer 1: All people do that?

Mario: Yeah, so why we're trying to do is finish high school and show that not all of Mexicans are one where they think of. . . . So we come to give them another idea.

Interviewer 2: So that sounded like that started to happen more when you left this community to go other places. And that made you—?

Mario: Because here is basically more Mexican.

Romero: Here we see Mexicans all the time.

Mario: Yeah. We don't care what these losers think or something.

Interviewer 1: Or you don't even see it because?

Mario: Before you didn't see like . . . more outside of our eyes.

Interviewer 1: Right, and outside your community too, with what he said earlier.

Mario: Getting out of our community from other communities. So basically what a person has to do to get . . . think about the whole world, is visit more communities.

This interview excerpt presents a complex view of the relative value of home fronts and contact zones. The home front is critical in establishing a positive sense of self. In this case, the irony of the home front is that it is an artifact of deep segregation (see Moje 2001, for an extended analysis of how the city space is divided among racial and ethnic groups), and yet it serves an important function in building positive social identities as youths engage intergenerationally with cultural norms, practices, and values. The contact zones could threaten a positive sense of self and social identity, but they also provide an important lens, at least for these two young men. The contact zones open spaces for them to develop an awareness of discrimination and racism in society. As Jay MacLeod (1995), Doug Foley (1991), and Carla O'Connor (1997) each argue, an awareness of the role of oppression via racism, classism, and other forms of discrimination is one important aspect of resilience. Foley and O'Connor, however, also argue that for resilience to develop such awareness must be accompanied by a sense of the need for collective struggle against oppression and of positive social models for engaging in such struggle. In the next section, we present data that illustrate how the awareness of the need for struggle and positive social models functioned in the lives of these youth.

Cultural Mediators and Brokers

In our initial analysis of the data around questions of engagement, persistence, and achievement, we examined data culled from interview transcripts and field notes for evidence of cultural mediators or brokers who supported youths through the educational pipeline via their own experiences.

Pipeline Navigators   We found very few instances of such brokering through lived experiences (that is, people who had actually worked themselves through the pipeline), but the few we did find were significant. For example, in one interview, Ramiro told of some information a friend of his who attended the research university in the nearby university town had shared with him about course work and life in the dorms. In another instance, a Latina teacher collaborator in the study reported that she regularly worked with some of the young men to provide them with information about and connections to the research university, which was based on her daughter's experience as a student there. In only two other instances did we find evidence of such cultural brokering provided by siblings and friends who had worked their way through the pipeline. Whether this lack of pipeline navigators in the youths' lives was an artifact of the youths' ages (we are only now moving into the upper grades and age levels with the youths) or an artifact of low high school and college attendance rates remains to be documented as our study progresses.

Although we documented only four instances in the overall data set of older students encouraging youth in the study to aspire to higher educational goals, these older students provided important information. They presented younger youths with a window on college life, leading to expectations as to what college would be like, as this exemplar from an interview with Celina illustrates:

Interviewer: What do you think college will be like?
Celina: I don't know, but to tell you the truth, I'm so scared.
Interviewer: Really?
Celina: Well, not scared, but I think I'm not going to make it because when I went to the [college] tour before I left to Mexico, I talked to a guy from Detroit Mercy [College] and he was a student from a private high school, and he told me this book that he had to read in a week. It was like five hundred pages long and I was like, "Oh, my God." He said it was hard in the way that you don't have anyone to tell you what to do and you have to do the things by yourself. And like in high school and middle school and everything, you have the teachers to say, "Oh, you have to do your homework," and then your mom, who says, "Wake up and go to school." And over there it's not like anymore you're a little kid, now you have to do the things by yourself. Like me, really I'm a lazy person. People have to be begging me, "Oh, do this. Go to school. Do your homework." And he said that was a big change for him because he's the kind of person I am. So I think it's going to be kind of hard, but I hope I can make it.
Interviewer: So you think the classes are going to be hard.
Celina: Well, he said that . . . well, yeah, because of what he said. I think right now he was in the engineering program . . . or I don't know what, but he was taking a lot of science classes. I know I'm not going to—well, I am but not as many as he was taking. But [to?] what he said, they are hard. If you try hard it's possible, but it was hard for him.

This kind of information, while at times daunting to the youths, seemed to hold great significance for them as they crafted and recrafted their social identities, seeing themselves as situated in their ethnically segregated home front in Detroit, and seeing "possible selves" (Markus and Nurius 1986) situated in contact zones represented by universities in nearby communities, zones that would require different sets of skills and practices than those valued in their home community.

Institutional Supports Within the Community and Schools   More often than not, the most powerful mediators of the pipeline were long-term institutional supports provided by the schools and postsecondary institutions. While Celina was waiting to hear from colleges to which she had applied, she talked about her previous experience with postsecondary education and the high school programs:

Celina: Yeah. Right now I'm not like decided, but I think I am [inaudible] but
   . . . I want to go to Detroit Mercy [College]. . . . It's a real nice school. It's
   a small school, so—I like small places. So I think I'm going to go there.
   Probably I'll change my mind, but right now that's where I want to go.
Interviewer: And so you toured the other schools too, or—?
Celina: I've been to Eastern Michigan since like middle school, it was like a
   two or three day field trip, we'd go over there and we'd take—like the
   first year was in seventh grade, and we just . . . like walk around, go into
   the classes and take a bunch of information about the classes, financial
   aid, and all that. And then in eighth grade we went to the classes, they
   gave us—well, they weren't like the classes the students there had, but
   they were like kind of similar. We did like the standard ones, like the first
   year we could stay the night with a friend, but the second we had to stay
   with someone other than from school so you could get to know or get
   used to that, so when you get there—you know, you're not going to stay
   with whoever you want. So it was a really good experience for college.
   And then I went to U of M, we went last week.

What distinguished several seniors who were going to college from
those who were not was their participation in these types of programs.
Similarly, high school programs that offered students knowledge and
resources mentioned by several college-bound students. Celina talked
about how the high school "career office" helped her navigate various
college and financial options:

Interviewer: What about here at school, who have you talked to about thinking about what colleges to apply to, what career?
Celina: Like on deciding on them, I usually go to 232 with Mr. C. and Ms. H.,
   and they're a big help, too. Like if you don't understand something about
   an application for college or something, they'll just help you. Like when
   we filled out the financial aid forms, they'll help you fill it out and they're
   a real good help.
Interviewer: And how did you learn about them, about that office?
Celina: Well, I don't think—it's been here, but not that long. The first time I
   went was because my friend went and we had to go and apply for financial aid and I was like, "Oh my God, it's time." You just think it's never—
   like when I was—it was like four years, "When am I going to graduate?
   Long time." But then you realize that you have to start applying for financial aid and colleges and everything. So we went there. It was probably like in second month we started school.
Interviewer: As a freshman or a senior?
Celina: No, as a senior.
Interviewer: So before your senior year you really didn't know about the office?
Celina: Well I did know, but I never went there. Because they'll always an-
   nounce, "This is scholarship" or award or whatever, it's here, so you bet-

ter apply for it. Because like in your junior year you're like, "Oh, next year." Well, that's how I was. "Next year." And, "Oh, financial aid. Oh, next year." But this year—yeah, we started going there. Probably like once every week just to go and see what scholarships or stuff like that. Grants and everything.

Interviewer: So you and your friends would go after school?

Celina: Well, like the first two days I went there I went with my friends, but after that like everybody went on their time. Some of them have lunch, and I don't have lunch so I go on my 6th hour. So everybody's going when they can.

The career office or "232" as most seniors referred to it was commonly mentioned among other students preparing for college. Many students had come to trust the staff in "232" to guide them in important decisions, especially since the majority of students who attended this particular high school did not have family members who could provide them with the college knowledge they needed. When asked how she knew she had to pursue an undergraduate degree before law school, Chloe, for example, recalled that, "Mr. C told me. The scholarship man. He knows everything you just ask him."

Yet another high school program identified by youths as significant in forming their career and academic aspirations was the Junior ROTC program. Indeed, on two days out of every week students proudly wore their uniforms and when probed about their experience with the program often would state that their motivation for participation was the possible college scholarships available to them. In the following exemplar, Mario talked about his Jr. ROTC experience and how it supported his determination to be successful:

Mario: Right now I'm in ROTC and I'm giving it my best so I think that's helping me a lot. That's opening the doors more and more.

Interviewer 1: Are there any people in ROTC who are particular role models or mentors for you? Is it about the discipline of the program or are there people in it who are special to you?

Mario: The discipline and the way they do things.

Interviewer 2: Is that what made you sign up to do it?

Mario: Yeah. . . . There you have to do almost everything perfect and it helps you take care of a lot of stuff. It helps you to become responsible.

Interviewer 2: You signed up thinking I really want to learn how to be responsible and work harder and I need help doing it so I need to do this?

Mario: Yeah.

Ramiro and Yolanda also talked about institutional supports, although not necessarily sustained activities as described by Mario. Ramiro described a visit from a member of the nanotechnology faculty at a research university, describing the recruiters' comments as they assured him that studying nanotechnology could be useful to his career aspirations in law enforcement. Yolanda described her own visit to the research university, the types of activities they engaged in while touring the campus and the course they were allowed to sit in on during their visit. These visits from and to campuses made an important impression on the youths, adding to the type and nature of information they possessed about college and university attendance and the role it would play in their careers. It is notable that only months before, Yolanda had expressed some uncertainty about whether college attendance was still one of her life goals, arguing that "college and all that studying, it takes so long." After the field trip, she introduced herself to a new research team member by stating that she wanted to go into "architecture or interior design," picking up the original trajectory of career plans that she had articulated in the five years prior to her sudden declaration that college might just be too long and boring for her. The field trip seemed to have renewed an interest in postsecondary education that had waned in the previous months.

Family and Community Mentors   Family and community mentors who offered advice and wisdom were another common source of support for the youths, even though such mentors may not have attended postsecondary institutions themselves. In the following exemplar, Celina talked about her parents' support:

Interviewer: Did [your older brother] encourage you to go to college? Who are the people who have encouraged you to go to college?

Celina: The most, my mom and my dad, because my mom—well, she's like, the only thing she tells me is that it's my decision and I mean if I had my mind made, she's not going to change it, because if I wanted something, that's what I'm going to do. But she says that, "If you get a good education, you're going to have a good job." She said, "You don't want to be in Detroit your whole life." And I really don't.

Interviewer: Why did she say you don't want to be in Detroit your whole life?

Celina: Well, because I've been here since I was like eight . . . and it's a nice place, but you know, you just want to improve, you don't just want to be average. My dad, too. Because like in my house, like in my family, I'm the first one to go to college. My dad, every time he can, "You're going to go to college. You get good grades," and this and that. So they're a good help.

Previous literature confirms the importance of parental encouragement and the role it plays in the formation of college aspirations; less well documented, however, is the role that other community members and popular culture play, as suggested in a series of excerpts from interviews with Ramiro. In the first excerpt, Ramiro acknowledged the role that his mother played in his educational persistence:

Ramiro: My mom said that if I'm under eighteen I have to study. After I'm eighteen or older it's my responsibility if I want to study again. Right now I'm like under eighteen so I have to study, but my mom is making me right now, but she said if you are over eighteen it's your responsibility if you want to go to college I'm not gonna force you so. . . . So right now I feel like my responsibility is to study and while I'm under eighteen I'll be deciding if I want to go to college or not, but I want to go.
Interviewer: You want to go. What do you want to study or want to be?
Ramiro: Uh, an electric engineer.

In a later interview, Ramiro makes a reference to a popular cultural text that sparked his engagement and future aspirations:

Ramiro: I want to be like a electrical engineer or like the guy in *Fast and Furious* [*The Fast and the Furious* is a movie about cars], like how that guy did the cars with and everything. I want to like do the design of the computers or cars or something.

Two years later, in an informal interview, Ramiro also described how working in construction provided him with experiences and mentoring that would shape his future education and employment choices. In an informal interview recorded in field notes, he specifically described being advised by the older men on the site to go to college:

During the summer, Ramiro worked thirteen to fourteen hours a day at a construction job. I asked him what it was like. He said that the guys at work would tell him to appreciate high school and work hard so that "you don't have to be like us." Then he went on to say: "It is kind of true, the worker guys would tell them what to do from like six A.M. to like late at night. . . . , It was real hot, it was kind of dangerous. It's kind of risky, too."…
Ramiro talked about working at a site in a nearby suburb and having a "go-car thing" flip over on him while they were working on a hill. He talked at length about the dangers of the work that he did all summer, and then said: "I'm gonna go to high school, probably go to college, and get a job in an office. . . . On construction, I'd come home, eat, probably talk to one or two of my friends, and go to bed at like nine or nine-thirty. . . . It's not complicated, it's an easy job. But it's hard work, you work your butt off, and you don't get a lot of money."

Ramiro's most recent mentors were pipeline navigators and university recruiters. Nevertheless, family and elder community members' mentoring seems significant in the course of Ramiro's development of academic achievement because they presented him with a dilemma. Consider the tension that Ramiro must have experienced as he heard elder males, his role models, telling him, "You don't have to be like us." But what were his options? Who are his models, if not the men who work side by side on his construction crew? What are they saying to him about his community and his possibilities? This experience—which is repeated for Ramiro and his male peers on a daily basis—provided him with encouragement to achieve in school, but simultaneously provided him with a view of his existing role models as disenfranchised and frustrated.

Similarly, Mario described a number of different mentors who guided his thinking about doing well in school and attending college. He mentioned, for example, that his sister was both a mentor and competitor because she was working hard in school and doing well:

Mario: Yeah. There's someone I'm competing with in my family right now. It's my sister. She's graduating this year.
Interviewer 1: I know. That's great.
Mario: That's basically, I was competing with her too.
Interviewer 1: Really?
Mario: Yeah.
Interviewer 1: She's kind of a good model, then, for you, huh?
Mario: Not a good model, but . . .
Interviewer 1: Well, she's graduating and that's something you want to do.

In the next exemplar, Mario described how his experiences in Junior ROTC provided him with mentoring via both text and personal interactions with Mexican Americans who had served in the armed services.

Mario: Today I was reading the ROTC book.
Interviewer 1: Okay.
Mario: And I'm learning about American heritage . . .
Interviewer 2: American heritage?
Mario: Yeah.
Interviewer 1: 'Cause it's an ROTC book?
Mario: Like you know when they're soldiers or veterans. Like old people who fought before in wars.
Interviewer 1: Oh, veterans?
Mario: Yeah. So we learned to think what they did.
Interviewer 1: That makes sense.
Mario: 'Cause when the ceremony was in school, there was this Mexican American guy. And I went up to him and I said hello. He had a lot of medals and he was very famous. He said he fought in both Vietnam and I forgot where else.

Interviewer 1: In the Gulf War?
Mario: Yeah. And that kind of led me thinking keeping Mexicans, like doing
   the same thing so not too much people will be thinking bad about us.

Mario's experience with the junior ROTC also represents a complex support system. The focused recruitment of young men of color for military service leads us to view such an institution with some caution. Yet Mario's experience with Junior ROTC—the discipline, focus, mentoring, and role modeling it provided for him—underscores the value of sustained and formal support systems for youths as they seek to move through the educational pipeline. Mario's rationale for his determination to succeed also illustrates the critical nature of a strong, positive home front and experience in contact zones for the development of resilience. Mario did not seek academic success simply to make something of himself and to be noticed, as he indicated in the previous interview excerpt; he also sought to change the way Mexicans are viewed in American society. His contact with spaces outside his home front brought to awareness the negative stereotypes of Mexicans that exist in some facets of U.S. society. His strong home front allowed him to maintain a positive Latino social identity. And the Junior ROTC experience provided him with specific means to foster his determination and to succeed academically.

Street Gangs   Another surprising source of mentoring came from street gang members with whom the youths had interactions:

Ramiro: Gangs can be both bad and good. They can distract you from school
   and you can get in trouble. But they can also protect you. And they can
   convince you to stay in school, do your work, go to college. And they can
   help you financially, pay our way through college.
Pilar: People think if you're in a gang, it's all bad, that you have to get in
   trouble. It doesn't. Some gang members tell you, "Don't get in fights
   when you're at school" . . . Or "You don't have to do drugs." They tell you
   to do the right thing. They don't just say do drugs and do all this stuff.

The youths in the study repeatedly spoke of the influence that gang members had on their thinking about life beyond school. In every case but one, youths spoke of older gang members as not uniformly negative influences and in some cases as positive influences on their thinking about academic achievement, arguing, like the two youths already quoted, that gang members exhorted them to stay in school, to do their homework, to go on to college. In one case, a youth claimed that his cousin was both a college student and an active gang member. The role of street gangs in the youths' academic achievement is a complicated one. The spoken message the youths heard from gang members was to follow a mainstream, safe, and legal means to achieving life aspirations. Such advice was underscored by many of the youths' observations of dangerous gang practices that resulted in young people being expelled from school, locked up, hospitalized, or killed. At the same time, however, they also saw gang identities, if not practices, as a facet of resistance against racism and oppression. For example, one young man explained to Elizabeth that the various figures represented in a sticker that he had on his notebook an Aztec warrior, Emiliano Zapata, Cesar Chavez, and a "gangster"—were emblematic of the slogan "Mi primero raza" ("My people first"). When pressed on whether gang members were representative of "mi primero raza," or Brown Pride, the young man argued that they were and equated gang members with a form of ethnically identified social activism. In addition, many youths in our study saw elder gang members as living relatively safe and economically stable lives.

The equation of gang practices with social activism and the belief that older gang members have youths' best interests for academic and social success at heart have important implications for youths' social-identity development and for academic engagement, persistence, and achievement—but not only in the negative ways teachers, parents, and law enforcement officials typically consider. Alliances with gangs as social actors or activists can become more powerful to youths as they encounter contact zones in which discrimination and oppression become more evident and in which they may be led to question perceptions of their social group (see Moje 2000; Vigil 1993, 2004). Even youths who do not actively affiliate with gang activities may adopt gang practices such as dress codes, language and literacy codes, and texts. Although not necessarily only gang-affiliated, the identities youths label as "ghetto" have ties to gang dress codes, language codes, and other identity enactments. These alliances—even if in spirit only—can serve as psychological buffers against the negative effects of discriminatory contexts and possibly as physical buffers against attack (although wearing the wrong colors can be more dangerous than not wearing colors).

Ultimately, however, these gang mentors offer confusing and troubling choices to youths. On the one hand, they tell young people not to mess up their school achievement; on the other hand, even when not actively recruiting youths for gang life, they send mixed messages about the downfalls of gang life through their access to material goods and to social power. These messages, especially about economic gain, are particularly challenging when one considers that lack of money is often a main impediment to postsecondary enrollments for this group of youths (see also Fuligni, Rivera, and Leininger, chapter 10, this volume).

A recently observed "fresa" (literally, "strawberry") identity among these youths—described by many of them as "arrogant," "preppy," "flirty," "stuck up," kids who "think they're 'all that'"—is seen as resistant to ghetto- or urban- and gang-connected styles. Youths in this study have divided on these identity lines in ways that have implications for how their identities are recognized and valued as they cross into different contact zones. Youths with "la fresa" identities have more potential for acceptance into secondary and postsecondary school settings because of their more mainstream and less urban, ghetto, gang-affiliated look. We have also noted, however, a trend for Latino and Latina youths who might easily pass as Anglo to strategically adopt "fresa" styles, thus potentially establishing contact zones within the previously Latino- and Latina-identified home front.

Popular Cultural Texts   Finally, some popular cultural texts seem to provide a type of mentoring and information to these youths, as suggested by Ramiro's comment that he drew on the movie *The Fast and the Furious* to delineate his goal of studying engineering. Popular cultural texts, however, are rarely examined in terms of the positive role models they might provide for youth, as Mario argued in the following interview exchange in which he described the surprising role that *Homies*, a website and pop culture movement, played in his thinking about Mexican identity and academic achievement (see also http://www.homies.tv/home.htm, under "The Homies"):

Interviewer 1: What else do you read?
Mario: *Homies.*
Interviewer 1: *Homies?*
Mario: It's like a new way to express Mexican, Chicano, Hispanics.
Ramiro: . . . Well there's a guy, Little Antonio, he's in a wheelchair. And he was a gang member where they shot him and he got paralyzed. He was trying to tell the other ones not to do it. Some of them they're artist so they sing. Other ones I don't know. . . .
Interviewer 2: And there's books that go with each homie?
Mario: Like labels, saying what they mean. Saying where they are and their nick-name. . . .
Interviewer 2: . . . So what do they express about being Mexican? What do you think they express? Is there anything in particular that's part of the point?
Mario: The way Mexicans live . . . . or things like sometimes these people become what they are because of problems they face. So, yeah, that's what they explain why they are the way they describe them.
Interviewer 2: . . . So the thing that makes them all what they are is that they tell you something about—
Mario: —the background of the people.
Interviewer 2: The background of the people. But they're supposed to be inspiring? They're supposed to be inspirational? Like people whose stories, they've overcome something difficult?

Mario: Yeah, because they have graduation or overcoming everything. They tell you to finish school, and stay cool and all that stuff. Stay out of drugs. Some of them try to take a message to the people.

These and other popular cultural texts that youths gravitate toward should be further explored to examine the possible role that texts can serve in fostering or detracting from youths' educational engagement, persistence, and ultimate achievement. One especially critical question—given the importance of role models, mentors, and pipeline mediators documented here—is how often Latino and Latina youths see themselves represented as successful high school and college students in various popular-cultural texts. What implicit messages do they receive about their group's academic identities? (Although the chapter is not specifically about popular-cultural texts, see O'Connor, DeLuca Fernández, and Girard, chapter 8, this volume, on the meanings African American youths make from the low representation of other black youths in their college preparatory classes.)

Conclusions and Implications for Research, Practice, and Policy

We have documented, throughout our long-term study, that this community produced, in many ways, strong, positive Latino, Chicano, and Mexicano ethnic identities among youths. The community served as a home front in which families, community leaders, and elders fostered cultural practices that valued family and community. Youths took up these practices and values in complicated ways, including taking on gang-connected identities as a form of social action and resistance to oppression. Yet these youths also took up identities of academic achievement as another means of resisting discriminatory and stereotypical views of Latino and Latinas. As Mario suggested in his explanation of his newfound determination to succeed academically, he wants to change "the way people think about Mexicans."

Within this home front, however, youths struggled to know how to enact identities that represent the multiple worlds in which they live, and they articulated themselves as enacting what they call, "ghetto" versus "fresa" identities, where "fresa" was seen by some youths as an assertion of superiority over those who align with the urban sensibility of their community. Thus, the youths drew on a wide variety of funds of knowledge and practice to construct these academically oriented and yet socially situated and culturally proud identities. They were bolstered by family and community funds, popular cultural funds, and— as unlikely as it may seem—even street gang funds, as they envisioned possible academic selves (Markus and Nurius 1986). Each of these knowledge funds represented a tension for the youths as they began to venture out of their home fronts and into multiple-contact zones outside their community. In a unique way, street gangs, popular-cultural texts, bridge programs, and university recruiters all introduced contact zones into the community home front in ways that complicated the lives of the youths and produced tensions for them to resolve as they proceeded across the educational and social landscape.

Most often these youths produced hybrid identities that wove together their strong ethnic sense of self with an urban sensibility. In some instances—particularly among the males—gang-connected identities were dominant, but they were always articulated to Latino or Chicano identities. Ethnic identities were also central to the young women for their enactments across contexts, but their social identities were also situated in a complex intersection of ghetto versus "fresa" identities, as articulated most visibly via dress, but also through cosmetics, language practices, choices of recreation, and ways of carrying themselves, dancing, and interacting. Personal role models—especially pipeline navigators from the home front—made an important contribution to the construction of the academic identities needed to succeed in school, together with the social identities to maintain home front relationships. Sustained, community-based institutional supports also made a critical difference (see Gándara and Gibson 2004). Programs such as bridge programs, the high school career office, and the Junior ROTC offered students ongoing supports, although each of these institutional supports was also a source of conflict for the youths—most notably the Junior ROTC programs, which seeks not only to educate youths but also to prepare them for future military service.

How each one of these young people will proceed through the educational landscape that awaits them remains to be seen. To date, only Celina and Chloe have advanced through postsecondary ranks. Pilar had already left school at the time of this analysis. And much like the youth Ernest and Michael represented (see Fuligni, Rivera, and Leininger, chapter 10, this volume), Ramiro, Yolanda, and Mario all have postponed college attendance to earn money, refusing to depend on their parents' resources. Although this nuanced, in-depth portrait of course does not represent a normative sample of Latino and Latina youths even in this small community, it has been documented in high school retention rates and university attendance figures that most young Latinos and Latinas do not progress through high school and into postsecondary institutions (Gibson et al. 2004b). Although our findings represent only a small step toward delineating the aspects of support youths experience and pinpointing areas for further development, their startling concurrence with several similar studies (for example, Davidson 1996; Flores-González, 2002; Galletta and Cross, Chapter 1, this volume; Gándara, O'Hara, and Gutiérrez 2004; Guerra

1998; Hurd 2004; Moje 2001, 2004; Vigil, 2004) suggests that these ethnographic findings can be generalized to larger groups of Latinos and Latinas, and even to youths of other ethnic backgrounds.

Our findings suggest that those who are interested in supporting academic engagement, persistence, and achievement among Latino and other underrepresented youth not only should look at the individual achievement of the youths themselves but also should closely examine the complex social systems in and out of school with which youths engage each day. In many cases, possible supports—whether based in schools, families, peer groups, or communities—could also serve as potential distractions for young people. When the youths in the current study were successful, their success hinged on many different facets of support that came together in sustained and deep ways.

Indeed, perhaps the most notable finding of our study is the complexity of the process of developing and maintaining ethnic and academic social identities (see also Oyserman, Brickman, and Rhodes, chapter 4, this volume). A number of studies of Latino and Latina youths' educational experience have found that the young people feel devalued and disenfranchised in schools and as a consequence fail to take up academic social identities, or they actively resist and even reject such identities (Gibson, Gándara, and Koyama 2004b; Flores-González 2002; Fordham 1996; Hurd 2004; Ogbu 1992; Vigil 2004). And yet, the youths in our study illustrate that community members are encouraging youths to take up academic identities, while at the same time implicitly communicating the sense to youths that they might be seen as "weird" or arrogant ("fresa") if they enact such identities too avidly, too often, or too convincingly. The so-called resistance that youth demonstrate in school then should be understood not as resistance to academic identities (often referred to as resistance to "acting white"), but as resistance to giving up other social identities of value. Resistance to "acting white" needs to be understood as just that: resistance to the wholesale adoption of cultural practices one does not own, not as resistance to school achievement. Recasting resistance as the refusal to give up one's social identities, rather than as refusal to achieve, demands that schools and communities take the onus of responsibility for inviting students into a teaching-learning relationship (see also Galletta and Cross, Chapter 1, this volume; Gibson et al. 2004). As Mario's comments attest, the opportunity to interact with pipeline navigators—Latino male elders—via sustained support programs in the school provided him with another way of thinking about academic identities, one that did not require casting off his ethnic identities but instead allowed him to participate in multiple communities. Schools and communities can build these sustained institutional supports to help youths navigate complex and tension-filled identity enactments and to cross social and cultural boundaries (see Gándara and Gibson 2004), rather than communicating the idea that youths must leave one community and change who they are as social beings in order to learn.

The research presented here was conducted with the support of the William T. Grant Foundation Faculty Scholars Award.

References

Alvarado, Rudolph Valier, and Synia Yvette Alvarado. 2003. *Mexicans and Mexican Americans in Michigan*. East Lansing: Michigan State University Press.

Anzaldúa, Gloria. 1999. "Nos/otros: 'Us' vs. 'Them,' (des) Conciementos y Comprisos." Paper presented at the Conference of Territories and Boundaries: Geographies of Latinidad." University of Illinois, Urbana-Champaign (October).

Davidson, Ann Locke. 1996. *Making and Molding Identity in Schools: Student Narratives on Race, Gender, and Academic Engagement*. Albany: State University of New York Press.

Delgado-Gaitan, Concha. 1994. "Socializing Young Children in Mexican-American Families: An Intergenerational Perspective." In *Cross-Cultural Roots of Minority Child Development*, edited by Patricia M. Greenfield and Rodney Cocking. Hillsdale, N.J.: Lawrence Erlbaum.

Flores-González, Nilda. 2002. *School Kids/Street Kids: Identity Development in Latino Students*. New York: Teachers College Press.

Foley, Doug. 1990. *Learning Capitalist Culture: Deep in the Heart of Texas*. Philadelphia: University of Pennsylvania Press.

———. 1991. "Reconsidering Anthropological Explanations of Ethnic School Failure." *Anthropology and Education Quarterly* 22(1): 60–86.

Fordham, Signithia. 1996. *Blacked Out*. New York: Routledge.

Fry, Richard. 2002. *Latinos in Higher Education: Many Enroll, Too Few Graduate*. Washington, D.C.: Pew Hispanic Center.

———. 2003. *Hispanic Youth Dropping Out of U.S. Schools: Measuring the Challenge*. Washington, D.C.: Pew Hispanic Center.

Gándara, Patricia, and Margaret A. Gibson. 2004. "Peers and School Performance: Implications for Research, Policy, and Practice." In *School Connections: U.S. Mexican Youth, Peers, and School Achievement*, edited by Margaret A. Gibson, Patricia Gándara, and Jill Peterson Koyama. New York: Teachers College Press.

Gándara, Patricia, Susan O'Hara, and Dianna Gutiérrez. 2004. "The Changing Shape of Aspirations: Peer Influence on Achievement Behavior." In *School Connections: U.S. Mexican Youth, Peers, and School Achievement*, edited by Margaret A. Gibson, Patricia Gándara and Jill Peterson Koyama. New York: Teachers College Press.

Gee, James Paul. 2000–2001. "Identity as an Analytic Lens for Research in Education." In *Review of Research in Education*, edited by Walter G. Secada. Washington, D.C.: American Educational Research Association.

Gibson, Margaret A., Livier F. Bejínez, Nicole Hidalgo, and Cony Rolón. 2004. "Belonging and School Participation: Lessons from a Migrant Club." In *School Connections: U.S. Mexican Youth, Peers, and School Achievement*, edited by Margaret A. Gibson, Patricia Gándara and Jill Peterson Koyama. New York: Teachers College Press.

Gibson, Margaret A., Patricia Gándara, and Jill Peterson Koyama, eds. 2004a. "The Role of Peers in the Schooling of U.S. Mexican Youth." In *School Connections: U.S. Mexican Youth, Peers, and School Achievement*, edited by Margaret A. Gibson, Patricia Gándara and Jill Peterson Koyama. New York: Teachers College Press.

———. 2004b. *School Connections: U.S. Mexican Youth, Peers, and School Achievement*, edited by Margaret A. Gibson, Patricia Gándara and Jill Peterson Koyama. New York: Teachers College Press.

Glaser, Barney, and Anselm Strauss. 1967. *The Discovery of Grounded Theory: Strategies for Qualitative Research*. New York: Aldine de Gruyter.

Guerra, Juan C. 1998. *Close to Home: Oral and Literate Practices in a Transnational Mexicano Community*. New York: Teachers College Press.

Hagood, Margaret. 2002. "Critical Literacy for Whom?" *Reading Research and Instruction* 41(3): 247–66.

Hall, Stuart. 1996. "Who Needs 'Identity'?" In *Questions of Cultural Identity*, edited by Stuart Hall and Paul G. Dugay. London: Sage.

Heath, Shirley Brice. 1983. *Ways with Words: Language, Life, and Work in Communities and Classrooms*. Cambridge: Cambridge University Press.

Horn, Laura. 1999. *Minority Undergraduate Participation in Higher Education*. Washington: U.S. Department of Education, National Center for Education Statistics, available from http://nces.ed.gov/pubs96/95166.html.

Hurd, Clayton. 2004. "'Acting Out' and Being a 'Schoolboy': Performance in an ELD Classroom." In *School Connections: U.S. Mexican Youth, Peers, and School Achievement*, edited by Margaret A. Gibson, Patricia Gándara and Jill Peterson Koyama. New York: Teachers College Press.

Kao, Grace, and Jennifer S. Thompson. 2003. "Racial and Ethnic Stratification in Educational Achievement and Attainment." *Annual Review of Sociology* 29: 417–42.

MacLeod, Jay. 1987. *Ain't No Makin' It: Leveled Aspirations in a Low-Income Neighborhood*. Boulder: Westview Press.

———. 1995. *Ain't No Makin' It: Aspirations and Attainment in a Low-Income Neighborhood*. Boulder: Westview Press.

Markus, Helen, and Paula S. Nurius. 1986. "Possible Selves." *American Psychologist* 41(9): 954–69.

Moje, Elizabeth B. 2000. "To Be Part of the Story: The Literacy Practices of Gangsta Adolescents." *Teachers College Record* 102: 652–90.

———. 2001. "Space Matters: Examining the Intersections of Literacies, Identities, and Physical and Social Spaces." Paper read at the annual meeting of the American Educational Research Association. Seattle (April 9 to 13).

———. 2004. "Powerful Spaces: Tracing the Out-of-School Literacy Spaces of Latino/a Youth." In *Space Matters: Assertions of Space in Literacy Practice and Research*, edited by Kevin Leander and Marjorie Sheehy. New York: Peter Lang.

———. 2006. "Achieving Identities: Why Youth Identities Matter in their School Achievement." In *Race and Language*, edited by Robert Jiménez. Westport, Conn.: Praeger.

Moll, Luis C. 1992. "Literacy Research in Community and Classrooms: A Sociocultural Approach." In *Multidisciplinary Perspectives in Literacy Research*, edited by R. Beach, J. L. Green, M. L. Kamil, and T. Shanahan. Urbana, Ill.: National Conference on Research in English and National Council of Teachers of English.

O'Connor, Carla. 1997. "Dispositions Toward (Collective) Struggle and Educational Resilience in the Inner City: A Case Analysis of Six African-American High School Students." *American Educational Research Journal* 34(4): 593–629.

Ogbu, John U. 1987. "Variability in Minority School Performance: A Problem in Search of an Explanation." *Anthropology and Educational Quarterly* 18: 312–34.

———. 1988. "Class Stratification, Racial Stratification, and Schooling." In *Class, Race, and Gender in American Education*, edited by Lois Weis. Albany: State University of New York Press.

———. 1992. "Understanding Cultural Diversity and Learning." *Educational Researcher* 21(8): 5–14.

———. 1994. "Racial Stratification and Education in the United States: Why Inequality Persists." *Teachers College Record* 96(2): 264–98.

Pratt, Mary Louise. 1991. "Arts of the Contact Zone." *Profession* 91(00): 33–40.

Rogers, Rebecca. 2002. "Between Contexts: A Critical Analysis of Family Literacy, Discursive Practices, and Literate Subjectivities." *Reading Research Quarterly* 37(3): 248–77.

Sfard, Anna, and Anna Prusak. 2005. "Telling Identities: In Search of an Analytic Tool for Investigating Learning as a Culturally Shaped Activity." *Educational Researcher* 34(4): 14–23.

Strauss, Anselm. 1987. *Qualitative Analysis for Social Scientists*. Cambridge: Cambridge University Press.

Tajfel, Henri. 1981. *Human Groups and Social Categories: Studies in Social Psychology*. New York: Cambridge University Press.

Thorne, Avril. 2004. "Putting the Person into Social Identity." *Human Development* 47(6): 361–65.

Vigil, James Diego. 1993. "Gangs, Social Control, and Ethnicity: Ways to Redirect." In *Identity and Inner-City Youth: Beyond Ethnicity and Gender*, edited by Shirley Brice Heath and Milbrey W. McLaughlin. New York: Teachers College Press.

———. 2004. "Gangs and Group Membership: Implications for Schooling." In *School Connections: U.S. Mexican Youth, Peers, and School Achievement*, edited by Margaret A. Gibson, Patricia Gándara and Jill Peterson Koyama. New York: Teachers College Press.

Ward, Janie. 1990. "Racial Identity Formation and Transformation." In *Making Connections: The Relational Worlds of Adolescent Girls at Emma Willard School*, edited by Carol Gilligan, Nona Lyons, and Trudy Hanmer. Cambridge, Mass.: Harvard University Press

Yon, Daniel. 2000. *Elusive Culture: Schooling, Race, and Identity in Global Times*. Albany: State University of New York Press.

Chapter 10

Family Identity and the Educational Persistence of Students with Latin American and Asian Backgrounds

Andrew J. Fuligni, Gwendelyn J. Rivera, and April Leininger

Several studies highlight the generally positive role played by minority children's ethnic identification in dealing with the challenges that they face to their educational progress (in this volume, see Oyserman, Brickman, and Rhodes, chapter 4, and Lawrence, Bachman, and Ruble, chapter 6). Converging evidence suggests that contrary to the prior assumptions of many observers, adolescents with a positive attachment to and identification with their ethnic background demonstrate high levels of academic motivation, educational engagement, and, at times, improved academic progress. In addition to the results presented in chapter 4 of this volume, in earlier work, Daphna Oyserman, Kathy Harrison, and Deborah Bybee (2001) found a positive association between ethnic identification and feelings of academic efficacy. Carol A. Wong, Jacquelynne S. Eccles, and Arnold Sameroff (2003) observed that the strength of ethnic identification was positively associated with academic achievement, and Tabbye M. Chavous et al. (2003) reported a link between stronger ethnic identity and greater motivation and enrollment in college. Although these and other studies (for example, Sellers, Chavous, and Cooke 1998; Spencer et al. 2001) have focused primarily upon African American teenagers, we recently have reported similar associations between the strength of adolescents' ethnic identification and their academic motivation among students with Mexican and Chinese backgrounds (Fuligni, Witkow, and Garcia 2005).

The consistency of the associations across studies, populations, and measures of ethnic identification leads to the question of what might be accounting for the link between ethnic identification and educational participation. By definition, social identities inhere in the social groups that children and adolescents experience in their everyday lives. Some of the processes and mechanisms that mediate the association between ethnic identity and academic adjustment, therefore, should be found in the social relations that are linked to the ethnic identity of adolescents from ethnic-minority backgrounds. Several chapters in this volume focus on the peer groups and friendships of adolescents and how these relationships mediate the role of social categories and identities in educational participation by channeling, encouraging, or disparaging education-related attitudes and behaviors of high school students (for example, Moje and Martinez, chapter 9, and O'Connor, DeLuca Fernández, and Girard, chapter 8). As a complement to these chapters, we discuss the role of the first and perhaps the primary social group in children's and adolescents' lives: the family.

We begin by first providing the theoretical and empirical basis for the link between ethnic and family identity, followed by a review of previous research that we have conducted on the associations of family identity and obligation with academic motivation and achievement. Then, we present four in-depth case studies of young adults from a variety of immigrant, ethnic, and economic backgrounds who exemplify the patterns that were observed in our previous studies and who raise additional issues involved in the links between family identity, obligation, and educational adjustment among adolescents and youths with Latin American and Asian backgrounds.

Ethnic Identity and Family Identity

We believe that families are critical components in the links between ethnic identity and adolescent development more generally, and educational participation specifically. Although many investigators have examined the impact of specific family interactions and relationships, such as cohesion and parenting behaviors, on ethnic identity and academic achievement, we instead focus on a different role played by the family. Family membership serves as a particularly important social identity for adolescents from ethnic-minority backgrounds, one that is closely linked to their ethnic and cultural identity. Family identity captures a sense of "we-ness" that goes beyond the nature of the dyadic relationships between members of the family. Applying the original definition of a social identity offered by Henri Tajfel and John C. Turner

(1986) to the family, family identity refers to adolescents' knowledge that they belong to the family as a social group together with the significance they place upon that group membership. Numerous studies have suggested that social identification with a group leads to a greater internalization of the values of the group and a stronger sense of obligation to support and assist the group (Hogg 2003), and we think that these elements of family identity are key ways in which family plays a role in the educational participation of adolescents from ethnic minority families.

Family identity is linked to ethnic categorization and ethnic identity, particularly in American society. Family membership is one of the primary ways in which adolescents' ethnic-group membership becomes established in the United States. Government institutions such as schools place children in official ethnic categories such as black, Latino, Asian, Native American, and white on the basis on their families of origin. Although children and adolescents often try to shift between different identities across time and space, the larger society limits the range of options available to them because of their ethnic categories and the social class linked to their family membership (Waters 1999). Indeed, empirical evidence suggests that ethnic identification and family identification are associated with one another, particularly in terms of the specific aspects of family identification that include an emphasis upon supporting, assisting, and considering the needs and wishes of the family. Stanley O. Gaines Jr. et al. (1997) observed that young adults with a stronger identification with their ethnic background were more likely to endorse values of family support and respect. In addition, the tendency for those with Asian, African American, and Latin American backgrounds to more strongly endorse these familistic values than those with European backgrounds was mediated by the higher levels of ethnic identity among the ethnic-minority individuals.

We have obtained a similar pattern of results in a recent study of high school students from Asian, Latin American, and European backgrounds (Kiang and Fuligni 2006). Adolescents with higher levels of ethnic-identity affirmation and achievement reported a stronger sense of obligation to support the family on a daily basis, to take into account the needs and wishes of the family when making important decisions, and to continue providing assistance to parents and siblings when the adolescents become adults. Interestingly, the links between ethnic identity and these attitudes toward family obligation were significantly stronger than the links between ethnic identity and adolescents' feelings of emotional closeness and cohesion with their parents. The tendency for adolescents from Asian and Latin American backgrounds to have a stronger sense of family obligation was significantly mediated by their higher levels of ethnic identity, above and beyond the socioeconomic differences between the youths. Finally, adolescents with a stronger ethnic identity increased their sense of obligation to the family over time.

Collectively, these results support our idea that family identity, particularly the aspects of identity that are tied to a sense of obligation to support and assist the family, are closely linked to the ethnic identity of adolescents from ethnic-minority backgrounds. A critical component of ethnic identity is an awareness and adoption of traditional norms and values associated with adolescents' ethnic and cultural heritage (Phinney 1990), and youths with a positive attachment to their ethnic background appear to adopt values of family assistance and support that exist within the cultural background of many ethnic-minority families in American society (McLoyd et al. 2000). As such, family identity and obligation may be important mechanisms by which ethnic identity plays a role in the ways in which adolescents from ethnic minority backgrounds deal with the challenges to their educational participation and progress. The specific implications of family obligation for educational adjustment likely depend upon other factors in adolescents' lives, particularly the socioeconomic challenges and strains faced by their families (Fuligni and Flook 2005). In the following section, we summarize a body of research in which we have examined the role of family obligation in the educational adjustment of children and adolescents from Asian and Latin American backgrounds.

Family Obligation and Educational Adjustment

Over the last several years, our group has done a number of studies in San Francisco, Los Angeles, and New York examining the educational adjustment of children and adolescents from Latin American, Asian, and European backgrounds. In addition to examining the role of traditional factors known to be important for academic achievement, we have paid particular attention to the impact that a sense of family obligation and assistance has upon the students' motivation, persistence, and academic performance. Our work was inspired by a number of ethnographic studies of adolescents from immigrant families that highlighted the link between family obligation and educational motivation. For example, Margaret A. Gibson noted the importance of bringing honor and respect to the family among adolescents in Sikh families in the Central Valley of California, who lived in tight-knit ethnic communities where family reputation was an important motivator for both students and their parents (Gibson and Bhachu 1991). The parents had little formal education and earned limited incomes by working in the agricultural industry, and the children in these families often noted a desire to repay their parents for their hard work by doing well in school and going to college. Carola Suárez-Orozco and Marcelo M. Suárez-Orozco similarly reported frequent references to wanting to achieve in school in order to obtain good jobs to help the family among Central American and Mexican immigrant teenagers (Suárez-Orozco 1991; Suárez-Orozco and Suárez-Orozco 1995). Finally, Nathan Caplan, Marcella H. Choy, and John K. Whitmore (1991) and Min Zhou and Carl L. Bankston (1998) reported evidence for family obligation being a critical source of the academic motivation among Vietnamese teenagers in Southern California and New Orleans.

In our work we have employed a variety of methods, including questionnaires, structured tasks, daily diaries, and in-depth interviews. Across these different studies and methods, three general conclusions have emerged regarding the role of family obligation in educational adjustment: (1) a sense of obligation to the family is associated with a greater emphasis being placed upon the importance and usefulness of education; (2) a sense of family obligation is particularly important for high levels of motivation on the part of immigrant and ethnic-minority students; and (3) although a sense of obligation is associated with greater motivation, the need to provide high levels of actual assistance to the family could present challenges to the educational progress of students whose families are in difficult social and economic circumstances.

In one study, we followed approximately one thousand adolescents from Latin American, Asian, and European backgrounds at various stages of their progression through middle school, high school, and young adulthood. These adolescents attended school in an ethnically and socioeconomically diverse district in a small city in the San Francisco Bay area. The majority of the students with Latin American and Asian backgrounds came from immigrant families; their parents came from Mexico, Central America, the Philippines, China, and Taiwan. Data collection took place at approximately two-year intervals. Participants completed questionnaires and schools provided academic records during the secondary school years, and closed-ended phone interviews were conducted at two points after the students had either left or graduated from high school.

The psychological sense of family obligation among the students was assessed with three measures, all of which were multiple-item scales that showed similarly good levels of internal consistency across the different ethnic and immigrant groups. The first measure assessed the students' attitudes toward providing current assistance to the family by asking the participants how often they should do things like take care of siblings, cook or clean for the family, and assist their parents with translation and official business. The second measure, called respect for family, assessed the extent to which adolescents believed that they should respect the authority of the family, make sacrifices for the family, and take into account the wishes of the family when making important decisions. The final scale assessed the importance of providing future support, such as financial assistance and residing with or near the family, when the adolescents become adults.

Adolescents with a higher sense of family obligation, as measured by these three scales, consistently reported greater academic motivation as assessed by a variety of measures of educational attitudes (Fuligni 2001; Fuligni and Tseng 1999). Interestingly, however, the link between a sense of obligation and motivation tended to be strongest for the students who believed in the importance and utility of education for their future lives as adults. Adolescents with a strong sense of family obligation did not report any lower levels of interest or pleasure in school, so a sense of obligation did not diminish the students' levels of intrinsic motivation. Rather, those students who believed in the importance of supporting, assisting, and respecting the family more strongly endorsed the usefulness of education for their adult lives. In fact, those with high levels of family obligation did not experience as precipitous a drop in academic motivation upon the transition to high school as that reported by their peers. Unfortunately, the students could not avoid the declining value of schooling that seems to be so endemic among American high school students (Eccles et al. 1993), but their decline in motivation was significantly less steep than that of their peers, so that they completed high school with a greater desire to attend college.

Students from ethnic-minority backgrounds, including those who tend to have more difficulty in school, often report levels of academic motivation that are either equal to or higher than those of their peers from European backgrounds (for example, Fuligni 1997). This becomes especially evident when the students are first equated in terms of their performance in school. That is, students from ethnic minority backgrounds often have higher levels of motivation than their equally achieving peers from European backgrounds. Such a pattern was evident in our own study, with the students from Latin American and Asian families having significantly higher values of academic success and a stronger belief in the utility of education than those from families with European backgrounds with the same grade-point averages (Fuligni 2001). Subsequent analyses indicated that a significant portion of this high level of motivation of the adolescents from Latin American and Asian backgrounds was mediated by their greater sense of obligation to support, assist, and respect the family. These findings are consistent with the reports of several ethnographies of Latin American and Asian families which suggest that many children in these families cite a sense of responsibility and indebtedness to their families as being a critical reason that they try hard and want to do well in school (Caplan,

Choy, and Whitmore 1991; Suárez-Orozco and Suárez-Orozco 1995; Zhou and Bankston 1998).

In a second study, over three hundred second- and fourth-grade children from New York City took part in a series of interviews about their family relationships, identities, and academic motivation. The sample included children in immigrant families from the Dominican Republic, China, and the former Soviet Union (primarily Russia and Ukraine). Additional participants included those from American-born families with European American and African American backgrounds. As described in a recent paper (Fuligni et al. 2005), we decided to employ a strategy different from the one used in the San Francisco study in order to assess family obligation at such a young age. Rather than use self-report, multiple-item scales, we developed scenarios involving a family member in need. One scenario involved a mother who needed help around the house. Another scenario involved a sibling who needed help with homework. After hearing about the child protagonist who failed to provide assistance in these scenarios, participating children were asked a series of questions design to assess the nature of their reasoning about family obligation.

Virtually all children believed that failing to provide assistance to a family member in need was wrong, but the children differed significantly in terms of their reasoning about the transgression. Specifically, the children from Dominican, Chinese, and African American backgrounds were significantly more likely to believe that providing assistance to the family was a "moral" rule, one that existed throughout the world and that required punishment if it was not followed. The children from the families with Russian, Ukrainian, and European backgrounds, in contrast, were less likely to believe that family assistance was a universal rule that should be regulated. The findings regarding, on the one hand, African American children (whose parents are not immigrants) and, on the other, Russian and Ukrainian children (whose parents are immigrants) were especially interesting, as they suggested that ethnic-minority status was more important than immigrant status in shaping the children's sense of family obligation. The children from Russian and Ukrainian backgrounds, although the children of immigrant parents, easily fit into the dominant ethnic category of white European Americans because of their appearance.

Like the adolescents in the San Francisco study, the children in the New York City study who more strongly believed in the importance of family obligation also reported higher levels of academic motivation. That is, those who believed that providing assistance to the family was a "moral rule" also indicated a greater interest in school and a greater desire to do well in school because they liked it and wanted to learn new things. These children also indicated a greater desire to do well in school in order to please their teachers and parents, which should not

be surprising, given that a source of the motivation is a sense of obligation to the family. Finally, as we had found in the San Francisco study,
the children from ethnic-minority families (Dominican, Chinese, and
African American) reported higher levels of academic motivation than
their peers from European and Russian backgrounds. These higher levels of motivation were significantly mediated by the stronger belief in
the importance of family obligation among the children from Dominican, Chinese, and African American families. Interestingly, the students
from these three immigrant and minority groups reported higher levels
of anxiety about doing well in school, but their sense of family obligation was not associated with this anxiety. Rather, it appears to have enabled them to maintain a positive orientation toward schooling in the
face of their fears about not doing well.

Across the two studies of children and adolescents from different
ethnic backgrounds in different locations using different measures, a
sense of obligation to support and assist the family was associated with
academic motivation, particularly the extra level of motivation evident
among students from ethnic-minority backgrounds as compared to
their peers from European backgrounds. Yet it is important to note that
for children and adolescents who are under particularly difficult social
and economic circumstances, family obligation also implies the very
real need to take time away from their studies and direct it toward employment or in providing assistance to the family. As suggested by
other researchers (for example, Gándara 1982; Suárez-Orozco and
Suárez-Orozco 1995), the need to provide direct instrumental and financial support to family members can potentially get in the way of the
students' efforts and desires to complete their high school diploma and
postsecondary degrees.

Although we have no evidence in our studies that providing actual
assistance to the family can account for ethnic differences in performance or educational persistence after high school, findings from our
San Francisco study do suggest that it may be associated with variability within groups according to their economic and social circumstances.
After graduating from high school, the students from lower socioeconomic backgrounds were more likely to work and provide financial assistance to their parents and siblings, which made it more difficult for
them to persist in college and receive a postsecondary degree (Fuligni
and Witkow 2004).

It is critical to remember that we have never found that the provision
of actual instrumental and financial assistance to the family explains
group differences in academic performance and educational attainment.
In fact, quite to the contrary, we observed in the San Francisco study that
although high school graduates from immigrant Latin American families were significantly more likely to provide financial assistance to their
families than their peers from non-immigrant families with Latin Amer-

ican backgrounds, the two groups of students evidence similar levels of postsecondary educational persistence. Our evidence suggests that high levels of actual assistance to the family do play a role in the variability in educational persistence within groups according to social and economic resources, as suggested by other observers (for example, Gándara 1982; Suárez-Orozco and Suárez-Orozco 1995).

Four Case Studies

In order to more richly describe the role played by family obligation and assistance in students' educational motivation and persistence, we present the postsecondary educational experiences of four individual students who took part in the San Francisco study: Ernest, May, Michael, and Carmen. These four youths from the larger study were part of a larger group that was selected to participate in an in-depth, open-ended personal interview approximately four to six years after high school. The larger group was a random sample that was stratified according to their ethnic background, immigrant status, and gender. The youths also were stratified according to whether or not they were educationally persistent, which we defined as either having received a postsecondary degree or being enrolled in a degree program at the time of the interview.

The personal interviews were intended to add the experiences, voices, and stories of the participants themselves to our understanding of their transition to adulthood that was obtained from the more closed-ended questionnaires and phone interviews. The personal interviews were semi-structured and were conducted by the third author, an anthropologist who has extensive experience with interviewing immigrant youths and families. The interviewer introduced topics from a predefined list and the participants were asked to discuss issues such as their sense of family identity and obligation and the roles that these played in their lives; their attitudes toward education, including how these related to their decision making and future goals; and how the youths balanced competing demands in their everyday lives. Questions also were asked about the participants' occupational history, such as how they obtained jobs and whether they attempted to balance work and school. The topics and questions were presented by the interviewer in a way that encouraged the participants to talk openly about their experiences, and general probes were used when the conversation strayed from the original topic. The interviews lasted from one and a half to two hours.

Interview transcripts were coded for a number of themes, including discussion of the role that family obligation and assistance played in the youths' educational experiences since high school. The four cases described were not selected randomly. We intentionally selected the four individuals because they persisted in their schooling beyond high school, albeit in different ways, and provided insightful comments regarding the role that family assistance and obligation played in their educational experiences. The four youths come from diverse ethnic, immigrant, and economic backgrounds. Collectively, their experiences illustrate the quantitative findings described earlier and demonstrate the roles played by immigration, gender, and social class in shaping the implications of family obligation for the postsecondary educational progress of adolescents from Asian, Latin American, and immigrant backgrounds.

Ernest

Before Ernest was born, his parents came to the United States from Mexico with a third-grade level of education. His parents both work at multiple custodial and cleaning jobs, including nights and weekends, and together they earn around $20,000 per year. Not a very strong student during high school, Ernest, who earned just below a C average, took five years to get his high school diploma. Nevertheless, just before graduation he reported that both he and his parents aspired for him to attend college and receive a four-year degree. Perhaps believing that his performance during high school and his family's financial situation would make it difficult for him to complete a four-year degree, Ernest indicated that despite his aspirations, he thought that he actually would go no further than a two-year college.

Ernest did not enroll in a postsecondary program immediately after high school, instead finding a job as a forklift operator at a freight company for about three years. Ernest enjoyed working at the freight company, seeing it as a good way to save money for school. While still working at the freight company and approximately one year after graduating from high school, Ernest began taking part-time courses at a local community college. He felt that he was more mature than he was during high school and was ready to take responsibility for his education.

> I just saw what I did in high school and I knew I could have done so much better. . . . I could have had it done in four years. I didn't have to mess up the way I did. . . . I can't really afford to mess around anymore, you know? I'm gonna be an adult. . . . Have to start to behave more and I have to start to work better.

Ernest enrolled in the same school that many of his friends were attending. He decided that enrolling in a two-year college and eventually transferring to a four-year college was a way to make college more affordable.

State [San Francisco State University] was too expensive. So it was a bit more of an economical idea. Plus, actually more friends I knew were going to City College anyhow, and they recommended to me City College would be better . . . to attend for four years and then transfer after four years to state college. So that would be more of [an] economical approach to it. . . . I could save up money on the side for State once I approach that.

Despite their limited financial resources, Ernest's parents offered to contribute to the costs of his schooling. Yet for Ernest, there was never any doubt that he would pay for his own education and he reported having saved up enough money to pay for his courses at the two-year college. He turned down his parents' offer, feeling that it was time for him to support himself and not to be a burden on his family. Ernest's decision to be solely responsible for financing his schooling stems in part from his admiration for what his parents have done over the years to provide for him.

My parents offered to help me out but I made a decision that I wanted to do this on my own. . . . I want to do this on my own 'cause they've already helped out enough as it is in my life and other people's lives so that I really said, I've gotta take care of this on my own. . . . They offered many times to help me out but I said, you know, it's cool, I'll take care of this on my own. You've done so much as it is, it's the very least I can do to help myself and to help you. . . . I respect them very much, not just for how they treat me but also for the fact that they also, you know, worked day in and day out to keep a roof over our heads, make sure everyone has plenty to eat.

At the time of the interview, Ernest had been laid off from his job at the freight company because of a downturn in business. Although he had saved enough money to pay for his tuition and fees at the two-year college, he was looking for a part-time job in order to cover his daily expenses and to assist his parents financially. Even while attending school and looking for a job, Ernest tries to help his parents at their jobs when he is able.

Whenever I can, on weekends, I wake up at about five o'clock in the morning, join them and work about [a] six- to seven-hour shift. You know, sweeping the carpets, vacuuming the rugs . . . like mopping the floors, scraping off the gum off the tables, you know, washing the dishes and doing a bunch of stuff there to help them out like every weekend. I've done that for, like, the last three or four years, you know, whatever chance I get. If I don't have school on a particular Tuesday or Thursday night, I go help my dad out.

Ernest also helps out around the house, where he is living with his parents, his older sister, and his sister's child.

> Whenever I can, I try to help out by cooking some fried chicken or making some spaghetti. . . . Whatever I can do around the house if I can. . . . They usually work at night, so when I can, I'll try to help them out during the day so they can sleep in and get their rest that they can't during the day. . . . So yeah, stuff like that, like little stuff. Well, what I think is little stuff compared to all the work they've done all these years to help, you know, help me out and help out my sister and everyone else in my family, that's, like, the least I can do.

When asked whether the need to balance work, school, and family assistance can be challenging for Ernest at times, he answers,

> Kind of, yeah, it takes quite a bit out of me. But it hasn't been like suffering. It hasn't been unbearable. It's something that I have been able to deal with. Just like, sometimes I just wish I could sleep in maybe now and then, but I've still been able to handle it all right.

Ernest currently is majoring in philosophy at the community college, but he eventually wants to transfer to a four-year college and major in journalism, which has always interested him since he was a child. Despite their limited formal education, his parents hope that he will complete his college degree, which they see as a key to having a good life. Ernest identifies with his parents' goals and feels a sense of obligation to pursue his education in order to repay his parents for what they have provided for him.

> I guess that's why they pushed so much for me and my sister to get an education. So that way we could get, you know, what they weren't able to get in their lives. So I can completely understand. Now, I am more than happy to comply.
> They just want to make sure I do . . . do good. They want to make sure I behave and I do okay. You know, make sure I complete my college education, have a career, have a job, have, you know, financial security and just, you know, don't mess up.

After he receives his degree and is on more solid financial ground, Ernest does plan to move out of his parents' home. But he still sees himself as helping out his family, both in small ways and in perhaps even grander ways.

> If I can ever help out, like, perhaps someday I'll buy them their own house or buy them, I don't know, a gazebo for their backyard. Something, I don't know, that would help pay them back for, like, all they've done for

me. I don't know. Maybe I'll build a huge bird bath in their backyard. . . .
I do want to help them out some way . . . don't really have a good idea
what it is yet, but I'll think of something.

Ernest believes he will be able to achieve the goal of a college degree,
in large part through the lessons that he has learned from his hard-
working parents.

I have, like, adapted to, like, their own kind of work ethic 'cause I've seen
their work ethic and I respect that. . . . I can get me some of that, so . . . I
just . . . committed myself, like, to my later years in high school and
through college. Just, you know, start working as hard 'cause I know I can
do it, I know I can do so much better and so I decided if I can, then I will.
So I have.

May

The third of four children, May has two older sisters and a younger
brother. Her parents came to the United States from Hong Kong when
May was five years old and they recently moved back there after her
younger brother completed high school and entered college. Unlike
Ernest, May comes from a family with ample economic resources, and
her father had a graduate-level education. May's father runs a successful business in Hong Kong, one that she reports brings the family over
$100,000 per year, so her mother doesn't have to work. A successful stu-
dent in high school with an A minus average, May was accepted at a
prestigious four-year public university. Her high level of academic
achievement and her family's resources led her to have high hopes for
her educational future before she graduated from high school. Both
May and her parents aspired for her to achieve a graduate-level degree
and she expected to be able to do so.

Like Ernest, May remembers education always being very important
to her parents. She cannot remember explicit pressure to succeed when
she was growing up, but it was clear that success was expected and that
one's academic performance reflected upon oneself:

When we were growing up they actually never told us to study, like they
never ever told us, "You have to get A pluses," or "You have to excel in
school." . . . But somehow us four we just, you know, tried to do well in
school and maybe it's just a personal, like, face issue or whatever.

Because May's family had more than enough resources to pay for
postsecondary schooling, the question was not whether she should attend college, but where she should go. Although May had nascent in-

terests in design and art, when it came time to decide upon a college, there appeared to be little question on the part of her parents that once accepted, May would attend the same university as her sisters did. Although she generally expresses happiness with her experiences in college, she does wonder what it would have been like to attend another type of school.

> I guess after a while like um . . . I was fine with the idea of listening to my parents, like, "Oh yeah, go to Berkeley." . . . But, yeah, there was just that pressure and then, so I went anyways, you know, met a lot of the close friends I have now from there, so I have no regrets about choosing Berkeley. I mean, I probably, I mean, I don't think I'd regret it if I chose, like, another school. But, um, I just sometimes think, "Oh, it would be so different," you know? And, oh, it would be so different if I didn't even go to a UC and just went to a design school. I think my parents would freak out, though.

Upon further reflection about her choice of college, May indicates that she felt an obligation to apply to and attend a prestigious university, just as her siblings had, in order to avoid disappointing her parents. It was a relatively automatic choice, one that she made without thinking very much about her budding interest in fashion and design.

> If I were to go to , like, . . . like a non-UC or something then, and then two of my sisters graduated from Berkeley and . . . like my brother's goal was to go to Stanford, and then the one child is just, like, the one who doesn't want to go to college, you know. . . .
>
> Even, like, beginning high school, I was really into, like, clothing and designing and things like that. . . . My parents are . . . really . . . traditional Chinese parents. . . . We should get . . . a professional, you know . . . degree, like, go get our masters and Ph.D. and things like that. And then . . . in a way we sort of . . . for me, I sorta tried to go toward . . . yeah, cause education is really important . . . but, like, in the end, deep down, . . . I'm really into you know fashion and merchandising. But I knew they wouldn't really be pleased with . . . me doing that instead of like getting . . . a B.A. from a good college.

At Berkeley, May's academic performance dipped down to a B minus average and she sounds as if she drifted in terms of her choice of major, seemingly choosing legal studies by default.

> I did legal studies . . . not because I want to go to law school, but I think because of all the things I tried the first year in college, that was the major that I liked the best. . . . But after getting in, I realized that [I] don't want to be a lawyer and it was kinda pretty hard to get into the accounting courses . . . at Berkeley, . . . unless you were the major. So, I did not

take any 'cause I never got into the course just 'cause it's a high demand type of thing. So, yeah, I still don't know what I want to do.

May graduated from college without having any specific educational and occupational plans, and spent the first two months visiting her parents in Hong Kong and traveling to China and Taiwan. After returning to California, she has floundered somewhat as she has tried to figure out what to do at this stage in her life. She has spent some time going through the motions of a job search, but it is not clear what types of jobs she is seeking.

> I came back and just started, you know, trying to get my resume and all those things in order. And then a few months ago I started doing job research, but the job market is pretty bad right now so. Yeah, and then right now I'm just, like, also in the midst of just trying to find either a part-time or full-time. Anything, basically, to pass time.

At the same time, May enrolled in an accounting class at a local junior college "just for fun." She feels that she did not get a chance to take these courses while at Berkeley and she indicated that she would likely take more courses because she finds them kind of interesting.

Although she does not feel her parents would support her desire to take courses in fashion and design, May does continue to receive financial support from her parents. Because May does not have a job and lives with her boyfriend, who just graduated from college, her parents help her to pay for rent, clothing, and food. But May does feel the need to find a job and support herself, because she is now out of college and her parents must pay the tuition for her younger brother to attend a prestigious private university.

> I know it's hard for them, . . . like my brother's tuition is really expensive . . . which is why . . . for us, when we got out of college we're supposed to go out and find our job and try to, like, help them out as much as we can or anything like that. I think it wasn't in the sense that my dad can't afford to support us, but just because you know, I guess it's just a part of growing up because they can't support me forever.

There does not appear to be much need for May to provide any economic support to her siblings or parents, but she does report that she would like to be able to do so if necessary and that this is something that is valued within her family.

> At this point I'm trying to focus on being completely independent, you know, in terms of financially, and, like, in the end, my parents want us kids to, like, support them when we're like older, like, thirties and stuff,

which I hope to do, too. . . . I wanna be able to give them spending money and stuff, like, but at this rate, I don't know.

May clearly is torn between finding a job that pays a good salary or, as she puts it, "starting over" by pursuing classes and training in the fashion industry. Interestingly, although she has a sense of responsibility to obtain gainful employment, her social class provides with her with less of a sense of urgency to find employment than Ernest's. She currently receives financial support from her parents, but she feels that the time is running out on that and the time has come for her to make a decision about her future, although what that decision will be remains to be seen.

I'm kind of, I'm pretty confused about it you know, because I want to make money, but I want to be doing something that I like. . . . So I really don't know what to say in terms of like, where I see myself in another year. I think, just, at right now, like, I just want to have a job and just make some money, and whether or not that is related to the clothing industry or not, but, I mean, I kind of think maybe any experience would be good.

Michael

Michael is the older of two children from a family of Chinese descent who immigrated to the United States from Vietnam. Earning slightly over a B plus average in high school, Michael was able to attend Berkeley and majored in both molecular biology and art. Although Michael's parents earned salaries that placed them within the middle- to upper-middle-class range, he still had to obtain financial aid and work in order to finance his college education. Michael identifies his family as "boat people," the groups of families who were displaced from their homes in Vietnam because of the war and who came to the United States as refugees. He acknowledges that his parents had to struggle to obtain a home and economic and social mobility in their new country.

I feel sorry, sometimes I feel sorry for [my mother]. I know she doesn't feel sorry for herself, but I feel sorry for her in that, I think she could have been a lot more, but, because of the fact she was with two children, an immigrant, and also a woman, she . . . didn't have the opportunity that would have been afforded to her had she been, like, here, and like, you know, just, been here. I think she's a really smart person, she's really quick, and she gets things. She's really perceptive, but, it's like, you know, there are a lot of things against her.

Michael is the first member in his family to attend college. Although his parents did have high aspirations for him, hoping that he would graduate from a four-year college, Michael feels that his parents' unfa-

miliarity with the American higher educational system has caused negative feelings and the perception that Michael is disconnected from his
family by his attainment of higher education.

> They didn't go to college. I mean, they didn't know that, I mean, if a
> school gives you money, and it's got the programs you want, you go
> there. But, they're immigrants and they're, they're not country bump-
> kins, but, you know, they're new to this country, so they're not familiar
> with how college should work, what's the best way for college to work,
> in a young man's life. [Quoting his father]: "Oh no, it's because we sent
> you away to college, and you separated from us and that's why you're
> not as close to us anymore." And I think that he was so far off and he just
> did not realize how unhappy I was. But I can't really have this in-depth
> conversation with them and they are just not that kind of people, too.
>
> They're not, they're not the kind that would go to college if they didn't
> have to. And they didn't go to college, so it makes it difficult. And I do feel
> like a certain kind of divide in terms of they didn't go to college and I did.
> 'Cause I feel like, like I can talk about things, like, global economics and
> stuff like that and have a discussion about things like that and like, when
> I ask them about stuff it's like about what's for dinner and I don't know.

After graduating from college, Michael hoped to pursue his graduate studies in graphic design abroad. At the time of the interview, however, Michael's father recently had been laid off and Michael was thinking that he might have to forgo studies abroad and pursue his
education locally in order to help his parents meet their mortgage pay-
ments. Interestingly, Michael also connects the obligation to assist his
family in their time of need to his ethnic and cultural background.

> I'm finding myself in a position where I have to possibly just start paying
> my parents' mortgage, because my father's laid off. . . . I mean I had all
> these plans to, like go to grad school and study graphic design like
> abroad. It puts a hamper on things.
>
> Asian families just have to, like, they have more at stake. They are just
> more familial orientated than, I don't know, American families in general.

Despite his belief that he should assist his parents, Michael feels a
sense of struggle to negotiate his own desire to pursue a career in
graphic design abroad with the need to assist his family in their new
economic situation. As a young adult who is just out of college and is
planning his future, he believes this negotiation will have implications
for the path that he will follow in the coming years.

> You know, like a lot of Asian people start to feel torn. There's a feeling of
> being torn.... Well, the only reason why I would stay here was if . . . the
> compromise I might make would be to, to just, help them pay for their
> mortgage. That's the compromise I might make, if he doesn't find a job in

the next couple months. I guess it's, but like you were saying, too, I guess it's like, it doesn't matter what ethnicity, I mean I do feel compelled to help them out, but yet, I also feel compelled to do what I wanna do . . . because it's like you're supposed to do that, you're supposed to go out and make a name for yourself and be the person you're supposed to be, but then at the same time, it's kind of like . . . there's this obligation there.

Carmen

The oldest of three children, Carmen hails from a family with Mexican heritage, but she, her siblings, and her parents all were born in the United States. Carmen's household also includes her grandmother, aunt, and cousin. Her parents' combined income classifies the family as working class to lower middle class. Carmen's mother and father began their family while in their teens and consequently had to work very hard to achieve their educational and economic gains. Carmen earned good grades in high school, which enabled her to enter a four-year college (San Jose State) right after high school, but she attributes her enrollment at a four-year college to a friend who was very instrumental in the application process because she herself was not informed on the appropriate steps.

When Carmen was in high school, both she and her parents hoped that she would obtain a graduate degree, and she expected to meet this goal. Carmen is aware of her parents' high aspirations for her and she has adopted these goals as her own. Carmen has used the fact that her parents, particularly her mother, were unable to continue with their own educational endeavors as a motivator to achieve her educational goals.

> I really did it for my mom and my dad. My mom, she got her GED when she was eighteen because she got married a couple of months shy of her sixteenth birthday to my dad who was nineteen. . . . They got married, she dropped out of high school, and my mom's such a smart woman. I think a lot of me does a lot of stuff because I want, it's almost vicarious for her that she sees all her dreams and accomplishments happening through me. So those are my gifts to her.

When probed about the potential pressures that may be associated with embracing her parents' goals for herself, Carmen responded by focusing on the importance of being able to share her success and to take full responsibility for her failures.

Interviewer: You've shared all your accomplishments with your family. . . .
    Has that been a burden for you at any time, or has it been positive? . . .
Carmen: You mean sharing or feeling like I have to succeed?
Interviewer: Yeah . . . feeling like you have to—

Carmen: 'Cuz it's not just your own personal success. It's the success of the rest of your family. I really do feel that, cuz, ummm, . . . I really do, it's just me doing it. It is. It's for all of them, it's whatever I end up doing with my life, I can totally share with them and say it's because of you guys that I'm here. If I make my own mistakes and fail, that's my fault, that's me, 'cuz no one else is holding my hand to do that to fail. It's me. But in terms of succeeding and making it, it because of them.

Interviewer: Does that have, I mean, is that a positive thing for you too? . . .

Carmen: It's burdensome and positive at the same time. Yeah, it's burdensome because I'm like, oh man if I don't do this, God then they're [her parents] going to think I'm a loser. Okay, then I'll do it, I'll do it, I'll do it. And now when I succeed, it just feels so good because they feel so good, so it's an all-around good feeling.

Carmen was the first in her family to attend college, so her parents were limited in the types of institutional information and resources they could provide. Although this could have made her educational pathway isolating and could have caused distance between her and her family, her mother provided emotional support and encouraged her to be independent and to become a resource for her younger siblings. The pressure that comes along with the "burden" of being the first to attend college could be isolating for various reasons, but it is not necessarily always the case, especially when family members express emotional support and convey the message that their actions will benefit the family as a whole.

Like I'm sure kids look to their parents to say, hey mom or dad, if I did this, you know, in terms of academics, my parents can't help me in that. They've been there for everything else but in terms, and my mother and father have always told me, "Honey, I can't help you with that. And I have no clue about that stuff. And I wish I knew more, and I wish I could have held your hand and did it for you but . . . " You know, she's like, "Now it should mean more to you because you've done it for yourself, and now you can do it for your brothers and sisters."

At the time of the interview, Carmen was a teacher at a private Catholic school. She aspired to more education, however, and was considering pursuing a master's degree and applying to law school, and was studying rigorously for the entrance exams. Her mother continues to express her support for Carmen's goals and tells her that she has done enough for the family and should do it for herself. Carmen agrees at a certain level, but still uses her families' hopes and aspirations as a source of additional fuel for her motivation.

But I really want my master's really bad and [my mother] already told me, "You don't need to pursue your master's, you've already given me the gift of four years and I have a degree and I can say, oh my daughter, she graduated." But this is more for me.

And now law school . . . a little bit of me has always felt, I don't know, I know she's wanted it for me genuinely, but she's living through me. She really is. She's always wanted to go to law school, never had the money, never had the time 'cuz she was always having the kids, so she never had the time to do it.

Key Themes and Discussion

Several themes emerge from the experiences of these four youths that both illustrate the quantitative findings described earlier and raise additional issues to consider in the role of family identity and obligation in the educational adjustment of students from Latin American and Asian backgrounds. It is clear that the educational attainment of their children is a cherished goal of all of the parents, regardless of their ethnic backgrounds and social class. Ernest, whose parents did not go beyond the third grade in their home country, spoke about how his parents hoped for him to go to college so that he would not face the same occupational and economic constraints that they have experienced in this country. For May, going to college was never something to be questioned in a family whose father had received graduate- level education. It was more of a question of the type of college that would accept the children. Both Michael and Carmen referred to the limited educational opportunities available to their parents because of their difficult life circumstances when they talked about why their parents pushed for them to do well in school and attend college. At this stage of their lives, the youths' ability to reflect upon their parents' own experiences and the sources of their parents' motivation leads the youths to internalize their parents' educational aspirations and to feel a sense of obligation to try to fulfill those aspirations. As Ernest put it, "I can completely understand. Now, I am more than happy to comply" with his parents' wishes.

Although social class did not limit the educational aspirations of the youths and their parents, it did have a powerful impact upon the types of actual educational choices and paths that were available to the youths upon graduation from high school. One effect of economic resources was on the timing of their entry into college and the types of schools they chose to attend. Being in a family with ample resources meant that May could afford college right out of high school, whereas Ernest believed that he had to spend a year working and earning enough money to pay for tuition. Ernest continued to work while taking classes on a part-time basis, and chose to attend a two-year college before transferring to a four-year school in order to save money on tuition and fees. This is a common strategy among low-income students in several states, including California, which has established arrangements to provide automatic transfer from two-year colleges into the four-year-college systems. Another example is the different types of schools attended by Carmen and May, both of whom graduated with high grades from the same school district. Although both attended four-year schools, May's resources enabled her to enroll in the more expensive university (UC Berkeley versus San Jose State).

Particularly evident in the youths' responses was the impact of social class upon their sense of urgency to be financially independent and to provide economic support to their families. Although Ernest, whose family had the lowest household income, does not report that his parents asked him to work, he felt a strong obligation to do so in order to become financially independent and to pay for his own education. He actually turned down his parents' offers to contribute to his education, saying, "You've done so much as it is, it's the very least I can do to help myself and to help you." May, who continues to receive financial support from her parents after college, also expresses a desire to become financially independent to lessen the drain on her parents' resources. But she clearly does not express the same urgency as Ernest. She goes through the motions of beginning a job search, but does so without much focus or direction. As she puts it, she is looking for "anything, basically, to pass time." Interestingly, both Ernest and May share the goal of financial independence that has been said to be a key feature of the eighteen-to-twenty-five-year-old age group in contemporary American society (Arnett 2000). But the speed with which they try to attain that goal appears to be largely dependent upon their families' economic circumstances.

The experiences of Ernest and Michael suggest two ways in which social class may intersect with family obligation to create situations that can challenge the educational persistence of youths from Asian and Latin American backgrounds. First, the economic and occupational circumstances of Ernest's parents make it difficult of them to provide financial support to him beyond high school and this creates the necessity for him to work to support both himself and his family. Although attending school at the same time, the need to work at both his own and his parents' job prevents him from taking a full load of classes. Ernest is working hard and appears ready to take on the challenges of both work and school, but studies of postsecondary educational persistence suggest that students who begin late, work long hours, and attend on a part-time basis are less likely to complete their degrees (Fuligni and Pedersen 2002). It remains to be seen whether Ernest will be able to continue to balance the various demands in his life and graduate from college. Second, socioeconomic status also influences the ability of families to absorb negative economic shocks and financial events. Michael's family, although financially better off than Ernest's, was vulnerable to the sudden income loss that resulted from his father's layoff. As a result, Michael feels that he will have to postpone his plans of doing graduate work in graphic design abroad so that he can work and help his parents pay their mortgage. Fortunately, Michael has already completed his college degree, but one wonders if that would have been interrupted had his father's job loss taken place a couple of years earlier.

Discussions of family obligation and support in an American society that places so much emphasis upon independence and individual achievement inevitably raise questions of whether such traditions create feelings of resentment among children and youths. Although there was some variation, the subjective reports of the four youths collectively do not present an overall picture of undue burden and resentment. Instead, family identification and obligation seem to provide meaning to the educational pursuits of these youths from diverse ethnic, immigrant, and economic backgrounds. Carmen's discussion of how her family shares in her academic successes and accomplishments shows how she sees a larger purpose behind her schooling. Rather than achieving for her own self-satisfaction, Carmen directs her efforts toward the goals of helping and providing satisfaction to her parents as well as being a role model for her younger siblings. She credits her parents, particularly her mother, for her ability to succeed. Similarly, Michael and Ernest speak about repaying their parents for their hard work and sacrifices in order to provide their children with better lives. Within the context of the cultural traditions and immediate social circumstances of many of these families, this family-based motivation helps ethnic-minority and immigrant students deal with the many challenges to their academic success that they face (Fuligni and Flook 2005). Nevertheless, these students are growing up in American society and they sometimes do experience tensions while attempting to resolve potential conflicts between their cultural backgrounds and American norms and values. This was apparent in May's and Michael's discussions of the discrepancy between their current professional aspirations and the desires and needs of their families. But even these two youth do not appear to be particularly resentful. Rather, they are trying to figure out ways to negotiate a balance between their goals and the needs and desires of their families.

In addition to richly illustrating the quantitative findings presented earlier, the interviews with these four youths highlighted two issues that have implications for efforts to assist the educational advancement of students from Latin American and Asian backgrounds. First, although families and parents provide an important source of motivation for the students, many of the families have limited ability to provide the instrumental support necessary in order to get their children into colleges. The parents of all four youths emphasized the importance of postsecondary education, but those with lower levels of education knew very little about what it took to get into college and what the experience would be like for their children once they enrolled. Both Ernest and Carmen reported relying upon their friends for finding out about the application process and for deciding which schools to attend, and Michael discussed how little his parents knew about American colleges and what they expected from their students. In contrast, May's parents, with their own college experience and having had older children who already attended college in the United States, were more able to advise her on her postsecondary choices to the point of essentially choosing a college for her.

A second issue for the educational progress of these students is that even when all members of the family agree upon the value of a college education, actually attending college can potentially create a feeling of disconnect between children and their immigrant and ethnic-minority parents who did not receive advanced education themselves. Michael rather poignantly discussed how his parents felt that college was drawing him away from them, making him less close to them. He acknowledged that his education and experiences did make it more difficult for him to share a common ground with his parents. It appears, however, that he still maintains an important connection to his parents through his instrumental support. Carmen also discusses how her mother always provided more than enough emotional support to help her through, even though she told her daughter that she could not provide any advice about how to get to and finish college. Carmen's experience is similar to that of other high-achieving Latina women who report a constant feeling of receiving support from their parents (Gándara 1982, Hurtado 2003).

Although many first-generation college students can successfully integrate their families into their new worlds of higher education, it can be more difficult for some students from similar backgrounds to maintain such connections with their families. In light of this, it would be important to provide students with tools and strategies to successfully integrate their worlds of family and school in order to ensure their continued progress through the educational pipeline. Unfortunately, much of the responsibility for incorporating the family into the socialization process that takes place in institutions of higher education is placed on the shoulders of the students (Hurtado 2003). Institutions of higher education could instead help inform parents about the experiences that their children will obtain in their academic endeavors and provide them with instrumental methods to supplement their emotional support (Rivera and Gallimore 2006). An example of a remedy is the incorporation of cultural brokers into communities that are underrepresented in institutions of higher education. Cultural brokers can help ethnic-minority first-generation college students and their families obtain information about college entrance requirements, demonstrate how they can retain their cultural values as they simultaneously become members of formal institutions, and inform parents on the ways that they can be a resource to their children (Cooper, Denner, and Lopez 1999).

Conclusion

The increasing amount of evidence regarding the positive effect of ethnic identification on the ability of adolescents from immigrant and ethnic-minority backgrounds to deal with the challenges that they face to their academic success creates the need to identify the processes and mechanisms by which ethnic identity may have an impact. We believe that one key mechanism is the link between ethnic identity and students' social relationships, particularly their sense of identification with and obligation to their families. Both quantitative and qualitative evidence that we have obtained in our research suggests that family obligation provides an important source of motivation for students from Latin and Asian American backgrounds, a source of motivation that should be encouraged and tapped into when programs to assist their educational progress are being developed.

References

Arnett, Jeffrey Jensen. 2000. "Emerging Adulthood: A Theory of Development from the Late Teens Through the Twenties." *American Psychologist* 55(5): 469–80.

Caplan, Nathan, Marcella H. Choy, and John K. Whitmore. 1991. *Children of the Boat People: A Study of Educational Success.* Ann Arbor: University of Michigan Press.

Chavous, Tabbye M., Debra Hilkene Bernat, Karen Schmeelk-Cone, Cleopatra H. Caldwell, Laura Kohn-Wood, and Marc A. Zimmerman. 2003. "Racial Identity and Academic Attainment Among African American Adolescents." *Child Development* 74(4): 1076–90.

Cooper, Catherine R., Jill Denner, and Edward M. Lopez. 1999. "Cultural Brokers: Helping Latino Children on Pathways Toward Success." *Future of Children* 9(2): 51–57.

Eccles, Jacquelynne S., Carol Midgely, Allan Wigfield, Christy Buchanan, David Reuman, Constance Flanagan, and Douglas MacIver. 1993. "Development During Adolescence: The Impact of Stage-Environment Fit on Young Adolescents' Experiences in School and in Families." *American Psychologist* 48(2): 90–101.

Fuligni, Andrew J. 1997. "The Academic Achievement of Adolescents from Immigrant Families: The Roles of Family Background, Attitudes, and Behavior." *Child Development* 68(2): 261–73.

———. 2001. "Family Obligation and the Academic Motivation of Adolescents from Asian and Latin American, and European Backgrounds." In *Family Obligation and Assistance During Adolescence: Contextual Variations and Developmental Implications*, edited by Andrew J. Fuligni. San Francisco: Jossey-Bass.

Fuligni, Andrew J., Jeannette M. Alvarez, Meredith Bachman, and Diane N. Ruble. 2005. "Family Obligation and the Academic Motivation of Young Children from Immigrant Families." In *Hills of Gold: Rethinking Diversity and Contexts as Resources for Children's Developmental Pathways*, edited by Catherine R. Cooper, Cynthia García Coll, Todd Bartko, Helen Davis, and Celina Chatman. Mahwah, N.J.: Lawrence Erlbaum.

Fuligni, Andrew J., and Lisa Flook. 2005. "A Social Identity Approach to Ethnic Differences in Family Relationships During Adolescence." In *Advances in Child Development and Behavior*, edited by Robert Kail. San Diego: Academic Press.

Fuligni, Andrew J., and Sara Pedersen. 2002. "Family Obligation and the Transition to Young Adulthood." *Developmental Psychology* 38(5): 856–68.

Fuligni, Andrew J., and Vivian Tseng. 1999. "Family Obligations and the Achievement Motivation of Children from Immigrant and American-Born Families." In *Advances in Motivation and Achievement*, edited by Timothy Urdan. Stamford, Conn.: JAI Press.

Fuligni, Andrew J., and Melissa Witkow. 2004. "The Postsecondary Educational Progress of Youth from Immigrant Families." *Journal of Research on Adolescence* 14(2): 159–83.

Fuligni, Andrew J., Melissa Witkow, and Carla Garcia. 2005. "Ethnic Identity and the Academic Adjustment of Adolescents from Mexican, Chinese, and European Backgrounds." *Developmental Psychology* 41(5): 799–811.

Gaines, Stanley O., Jr, William D. Marelich, Katrina L. Bledsoe, and W. Neil Steers. 1997. "Links Between Race/Ethnicity and Cultural Values as Mediated by Racial/Ethnic Identity and Moderated by Gender." *Journal of Personality and Social Psychology* 72(6): 1460–76.

Gándara, Patricia. 1982. "Passing Through the Eye of the Needle: High Achieving Chicanas." *Hispanic Journal of the Behavioral Sciences* 4(2): 167–79.

Gibson, Margaret A., and P. Bhachu. 1991. "The Dynamics of Educational Decision-Making: A Comparative Study of Sikhs in Britain and the United States." In *Minority Status and Schooling: A Comparative Study of Voluntary and Involuntary Minorities*, edited by Margaret A. Gibson and John U. Ogbu. New York: Garland.

Hogg, Michael A. 2003. "Social Identity." In *Handbook of Self and Identity*, edited by Mark R. Leary and June Price. New York: Guilford Press.

Hurtado, Aida. 2003. *Voicing Chicana Feminisms: Young Women Speak Out on Sexuality and Identity*. New York : New York University Press.

Kiang, Lisa, and Andrew J. Fuligni. 2006. "Ethnic Identity and Family Processes Among Adolescents with Asian, Latin American, and European Backgrounds." Unpublished paper. Los Angeles: University of California, Los Angeles.

McLoyd, Vonnie C., Ana Mari Cauce, David Takeuchi, and Leon Wilson. 2000.

"Marital Processes and Parental Socialization in Families of Color: A Decade Review of Research." *Journal of Marriage and the Family* 62(4): 1070–93.

Oyserman, Daphna, Kathy Harrison, and Deborah Bybee. 2001. "Can Racial Identity be Promotive of Academic Efficacy?" *International Journal of Behavioral Development* 25(4): 379–85.

Phinney, Jean. S. 1990. "Ethnic Identity in Adolescents and Adults: A Review of Research." *Psychological Bulletin* 108(3): 499–514.

Rivera, Wendy, and Ronald Gallimore. 2006. "Latina Adolescents' Career Choices: What Matters to Them When They Decide?" In *Latina Adolescents: An Edited Volume on Strengths and Strategies*, edited by Jill Denner and Bianca Guzman. New York: New York University Press.

Sellers, Robert M., Tabbye M. Chavous, and Deanna Y. Cooke. 1998. "Racial Ideology and Racial Centrality as Predictors of African American College Students' Academic Performance." *Journal of Black Psychology* 24(1): 8–27

Spencer, Margaret Beale, Elizabeth Noll, Jill Stoltzfus, and Vinay Harpalani. 2001. "Identity and School Adjustment: Revisiting the 'Acting White' Assumption." *Educational Psychologist* 36(1): 21–30.

Suárez-Orozco, Marcelo M. 1991. "Immigrant Adaptation to Schooling: A Hispanic Case." In *Minority Status and Schooling: A Comparative Study of Immigrant and Involuntary Minorities*, edited by Margaret A. Gibson and John U. Ogbu. New York: Garland.

Suárez-Orozco, Carola, and Marcelo M. Suárez-Orozco. 1995. *Transformations: Immigration, Family Life, and Achievement Motivation Among Latino Adolescents*. Palo Alto: Stanford University Press.

Tajfel, Henri, and John C. Turner. 1986. "The Social Identity Theory of Intergroup Behavior." In *Psychology of Intergroup Relations*, edited by Stephen Worchen and William G. Austin. Chicago: Nelson Hall.

Waters, Mary C. 1999. *Black Identities: West Indian Immigrant Dreams and American Realities*. New York: Russell Sage Foundation.

Wong, Carol A., Jacquelynne S. Eccles, and Arnold Sameroff. 2003. "The Influence of Ethnic Discrimination and Ethnic Identification on African American Adolescents' School and Socioemotional Adjustment." *Journal of Personality* 71(6): 1197–1232.

Zhou, Min, and Carl L. Bankston. 1998. *Growing Up American: How Vietnamese Children Adapt to Life in the United States*. New York: Russell Sage Foundation.

Index

Boldface numbers refer to figures and tables.

academic achievement: of Asian Americans, 136–37, 244; of Dalits in India, 59–60; economic limitations, 258–59; gender differences, 68; and intelligence theories, 126–31; learning vs. performance goals for, 171–72, 175–76; motivations for, 16–19, 148, 171–72, 240, 245–46; and negative stereotypes, 94–95; and racial-ethnic identity, 44, 67–68, 91, 99, 100–101, 153–54, 187–90, 239; and school segregation, 75; and school valuing, 154–55, 160, 188–89; self-esteem from, 161–62; Shaker Heights School District, 24–28; and social identity, 212–14; and stereotype threat, 123–25; of women, 160, 161. *See also* contingent self-worth, based on academics; family identity and educational persistence
academic achievement, of Hispanics: complexity of, 235; cultural mediators and brokers, 223–33, 235–36; home fronts and contact zones, 217–23, 233–34; negative stereotypes, 94–95; overview of, 209; research design and methodology, 214–16; research perspectives, 209–14, 240; RES model, 105–7; and school valuing, 136–37, 138, 139–40, 154–55, 244; trends, 67–68
academic achievement and race: connection with in-group, 96–97, 99–101, 117; embedded achievement, 98–101; future research opportunities, 206; Hillside High School study, 193–204; at historically black colleges or universities, 190, 195, 201, 202–4, 205; history of, 16–19; motivation, 148; Ogbu's cultural ecological theory, 183–87; policy considerations, 139; racism awareness, 97–98, 99, 100, **101**; research considerations, 67–68, 91; research methodology, 190–92; schools' influence over students' perceptions of, 203–4, 205; school valuing, 136–38, 154–55, 160, 188–89; self-schema approach, 101–7; students' conceptualization of blackness and whiteness, 187–90, 192, 198–201
academic tracks: predominantly white high school study, 194–95; and salience of group differences, 162; as segregation, 75; in Shaker Heights Schools, 23–24, 28–37, 189
achievement motivation theory, 126–31
"acting white hypothesis," 138, 161, 185–87, 191, 198–201, 235
adolescents: family identity and academic achievement, 243–44; school valuing, 142. *See also* racial-ethnic identity, of adolescents
advanced-placement classes, 28–29, 31, 34

African Americans: academic
achievement gap, 15–18, 136; as
"cultural hybrids," 43; discrimination against, 151–52; educational
curriculum portrayals, 82; female
professors, 162; geographic concentration of, 93; high school
graduation rate, 1; intelligence,
view of, 128; intelligence tests,
124; negative academic stereotypes, 94–95; oppositional identity,
15–16, 44, 138–39, 153, 184–85;
school anxiety, 148; school valuing, 138–42, 143, 144, 147–55, 161,
186; stereotype threat, 117–18, 121,
125, 128. *See also* academic
achievement and race; racial-ethnic identity
Ager, J., 96, 99, 140
Ainsworth-Darnell, J., 186
Anderson, J., 18–19
anxiety, school, 148
Arab Israelis, 105
Aronson, J., 117, 119, 122, 125, 128,
129, 142, 173, 175
Arroyo, C., 141
Asian Americans: academic achievement, 136–37, 244; family identity
and obligations, 241, 243; female
professors, 162; school valuing,
138, 139; stereotype threat vulnerability study, 119–20. *See also* Chinese students
assimilation, 43
Atkinson, P., 44

Bachman, M., 186
Bankston, C., 243
behavior, social identity's influence
over, 92
Bem, S., 71, 73–74
Bigler, R., 70–71, **72,** 73–76, 77, 80, 82,
174–75
black achievement motivation
(BAM), 18–19
blackness, 187–90, 192, 198, 200–201
Black Reconstruction (Du Bois), 17–18

blacks. *See* African Americans
Boykin, A. Wade, 61
boys, Robbers Cave study, 69–70
Brahmins, 50–51
brain transplant paradigm, 51
Brass, J. Daniel, 44
Brook, A., 172
Brown, B. Bradford, 139, 147
Brown, C., 75, 77, 80
Brown, R., 79
Brown v. Board of Education, 20
Bullock, H., 17
Bybee, D., 117, 153, 239

Caplan, N., 243
Caring Communities Organized for
Education, 27
Carter, P., 185–86, 198, 199
caste identity, in India, 49, 50–60
CET (cultural ecological theory),
183–87
CFA (confirmatory factor analysis),
108–11
Chavous, T., 239
children, 69–70. *See also* intergroup
attitudes, of children; school valuing; social identity, of school children
Chinese students: discrimination
against, 152; ethnic identification
and academic motivation, 240;
family identity or obligations and
educational persistence, 245–46,
251–54; school anxiety, 148; school
valuing study, 143–44, 147–53
Choy, M., 243
Civil War period, 18–19
Clark, K., 16
class, social, 258–60
A Class Divided, 66
classification, 71, 211
cognitive essentialism, 46
collective identity, 121, 184–85,
187–88
college education: cultural mediators
for, 223–24, 261–62; enrollment
and ethnic identification, 239;

graduation rates, 160; high school counseling offices, 224–26; recruiters, 226–27; social marginalization in, 44; women of color, 166–76

Collins, P., 44

color-blindness, 25

community, importance to Hispanic identity, 219–23

Concerned Parents, 27

confirmatory factor analysis (CFA), 108–11

connectedness, 96–97, 99, 100, 101

contact zones, 221–23

contingent self-worth, based on academics: context of, 164–65, 167–68; costs of, 170–73; definition of, 163; gender and ethnic identity as predictor of, 168–69; and identification with devalued social groups, 165–66; research considerations, 164, 166–67; research methodology, 166; strategies for educators, 173–76; within-person variation, 167

Cook, P., 186

counselors, college, 31, 224–26

counterculture, 44

Crenshaw, W. Kimberly, 45

Crocker, J., 49, 124, 161–62, 162

Cross, W., 19, 103, 189, 205

cultural ecological theory (CET), 183–87

"cultural hybrids," 43

cultural myths, 3

cultural narratives: of marginalized social groups in India, 49, 52–60; role in identity development, 47, 49, 61

curriculum, educational, 79–82

Dalits, 50–60

Dark Ghetto (Clark), 16

data collection and sources: academic achievement of Hispanics, 215–16; black academic achievement in predominantly white high school, 190–92; contingent self-worth based on academics, 166; school valuing, 142–43; social marginalization, 50–51

Davis, C., 117

Delamont, S., 44

Deliege, R., 52

Del Pilar, J., 44

DeLuca, S., 140, 154

depression, 44, 105, 173

Detroit News, 220

devaluation, of identity, 115, 118–19, 174, 213

Developmental Intergroup Theory (DIT), 71–83

developmental psychology, 70–71

discrimination: against Dalits in India, 59; and school valuing, 138, 140, 142, 146, 151–53, 154. See also racism

disengagement, with school, 124–25

disidentification, with school, 124–25, 160, 161

DIT (Developmental Intergroup Theory), 71–83

domain avoidance, 124

Dominican students: academic achievement motivation, 148; discrimination against, 151–52; family identity and academic motivation study, 245–46; school anxiety, 148; school valuing study, 143, 144, 147–55

Dornbusch, S., 139, 147

Downey, D., 186

Du Bois, W. E. B., 17–18

Dweck, C., 124, 126–27, 130, 142, 173, 175

Eccles, J., 141, 142, 239

education, social advantage of, 21. See also schools

educational achievement. See academic achievement

Educational Testing Service, 121

The Education of Blacks in the South, 1860-1935 (Anderson), 18–19

Ekalaivya, 52–59
elementary school students, 188–89,
    245–46. *See also* intergroup atti-
    tudes, of children; school valuing;
    social identity, of school children
Elliot, J., 66–67
embedded achievement, 98–99, 100,
    101
engineering students, 165
English proficiency, 105–6
enrichment programs, 24, 25
entity theory of intelligence, 126–27
essentialism, 46–49, 50, 57–58
ethnic enclaves, 221
ethnic identity. *See* racial-ethnic iden-
    tity
excellence, in education, 21, 22, 23–24
exclusion, 21
eye color experiment, 66–67
Eye of the Storm, 66

Fair Housing Act, 38*n*2
families, support of academic
    achievement, 218, 227–28, 242–47,
    260–61
family identity and educational per-
    sistence: case studies, 247–58; cul-
    tural tensions, 260, 261; ethnic
    identity link, 240–42; parents'
    goals for children, 258; policy is-
    sues, 260–62; previous research,
    242–47; research methodology,
    243; social class implications,
    258–60
feedback, 175
female feticide and infanticide, 42
females. *See* women
feminism, 44–45
Ferrari, M., 45
Flesser, D., 78–79
Foley, D., 213, 223
folklore. *See* cultural narratives
Fordham, S., 161, 185, 187
Freeman, M., 38*n*4
"fresa" identity, 231–32, 233
Fried, C., 128
friendship, 75, 76
Fryer, R., 140

Gaines, S., 241
Galletta, A., 20, 36–37, 37, 189, 205
Gándara, P., 213
gangs, 218, 230–32
Gant, L., 96, 99, 140
gender: and academic achievement
    of Dalits in India, 59–60; and eth-
    nic identity, 44–45; identification
    with as contingent self-worth pre-
    dictor, 168–69; and school out-
    comes, 67–69; stereotypes, 73–74,
    76; stereotype threat vulnerability,
    116–17, 120–21, 122; teachers' la-
    beling by, 71, 73–74
Gibson, M., 213, 242
gifted programs, 24, 28, 32
Gilduff, M., 44
Girard, B., 140, 154
goals, academic, 171–72, 175–76
Gonzales, N., 44
Good, C., 122, 128, 130, 142, 173,
    175
Graham, S., 94, 140
Great Depression, 19
group relations. *See* intergroup atti-
    tudes, of children

Harder, J., 122
Harpalani, V., 96
Harrison, K., 117, 153, 239
Harter, S., 145
helplessness, 49
Hemmings, A., 186
higher education. *See* college educa-
    tion
high school graduation rates, 1, 68
high schools: black academic
    achievement, 190, 193–204; college
    counseling offices, 224–26. *See also*
    Shaker Heights, Ohio Schools
Hillside High School study, 193–
    204
Hispanics: essentialist strategies of
    immigrants, 49; family identity,
    241; female professors, 162; geo-
    graphic concentration of, 93; high
    school graduation rate, 1; racial-
    ethnic identity of, 101–2, 219–23.

See also academic achievement, of Hispanics; Mexican Americans

historically black colleges or universities (HBCUs), 190, 195, 201, 202–4, 205

A History of Negro Education (Bullock), 17

Hudley, C., 94, 140

Hughes, J. Milligan, 82

"Human Migration and the Marginal Man" (Park), 43

identity, collective, 121, 184–85, 187–88

identity, family. *See* family identity and educational persistence

identity, oppositional, 15–16, 44, 138–39, 153, 184–85

identity, racial-ethnic. *See* racial-ethnic identity

identity, social. *See* social identity

identity bifurcation, 125

immigrants: as "cultural hybrids," 43; depressive symptoms of East Asian immigrants, 44; essentialist strategies of, 49; New York City study of elementary school students' family identity and academic motivation, 245–46; school valuing study, 143–55. *See also specific ethnic group*

incremental theory of intelligence, 127–31

India: cultural preference for sons, 42; marginalized social groups in, 49, 50–60

integration, school, 20–23. *See also* Shaker Heights, Ohio Schools

intelligence tests, 124

intelligence theories, 126–31

intergroup attitudes, of children: Elliot's eye color experiment, 66–67; and explicit curricular message about groups, 78–79; future research, 84; and group size, 77; and implicit curricular message about groups, 79–82; and minority status, 76–77; research paradigms,

69–71; and school segregation, 68, 69, 74–76; and teachers' labeling of social groups, 71, 73–74

intersectionality perspective, 44–46

interviews, 215, 247–58

involuntary minorities, school valuing, 140–42, 143, 184–85

Inzlicht, M., 128

James, W., 163

Jews, 43

Jim Crow era, 19

Jones, L., 74

Julius Rosenwald Fund, 17, 19

Kaeser, S., 38n4

Keating, W., 38n2

Kim, S., 44

Kraemer; Shelly v., 22

labeling, of students by teachers, 71, 73–74

Latinos. *See* Hispanics

Lawrence, J., 124, 186

levels system, 23–24, 25

Levy, S., 82

Liben, L., 70–71, **72,** 75, 77, 80

life-span developmental framework, for social marginalization, 42, 47–49

literal integration, 21, 22–23

Lobiner, D., 74

Ludlow neighborhood, 22

Ludwig, J., 186

Luhtanen, R., 162

MacLeod, J., 223

MAC (Minority Achievement Committee), 27

Mahalingam, R., 45, 46, 49, 51

Major, B., 124

marginalization. *See* social marginalization

Markell, M., 80

Martinez, M., 205

math, 116–17, 119, 120–21, 123, 130–31

Mehra, A., 44

men, stereotype threat vulnerability, 119. *See also* gender

mental health issues, 103

mentoring programs, 128–29, 227–30

methodology: academic achievement and race, 190–92; academic achievement of Hispanics, 214–16; contingent self-worth based on academics, 166; family identity and educational persistence, 243; racial-ethnic identity measurement, 107–11; school valuing, 143–46; social marginalization, 42, 47–49, 60–61

Mexican Americans: family identity or obligations and educational persistence, 243, 248–51, 256–58; negative stereotypes, 94, 222; schools' role in educational support, 213; school valuing, 184–85. *See also* Hispanics

Mickelson, R., 154, 189

middle class, 16

middle schools, Shaker Heights School District, 24

minimal groups, 70

Minority Achievement Committee (MAC), 27

minority status, 76–77. *See also specific racial-ethnic group*

Minority Student Achievement Network (MSAN), 28

The Miseducation of the Negro (Woodson), 16

model minorities, 99

Moje, E. Birr, 205, 221

Moreland School, 30

motivation, 148, 170–71, 239, 244–46

MSAN (Minority Student Achievement Network), 28

Nambissan, B. Geetha, 59

narratives, of Shaker Heights students, 28–37. *See also* cultural narratives

Native Americans, 67, 184–85

Nesdale, D., 78–79

New York City, study of elementary school students' family identity and academic motivation, 245–46

The North, school integration resistance, 21

novel group paradigm, 80

Obama, B., 139

observations, 215

O'Connor, C., 140, 154, 213, 223

Ogbu, J., 15, 19, 20, 37, 44, 138–39, 161, 183–88

oppositional identity, 15–16, 44, 138–39, 153, 184–85

Orfield, G., 20–21, 75

Oyserman, D., 96, 98, 99, 100, 104, 117, 140, 153, 239

Park, E. Robert, 43

Patterson, M., 75, 80, 174–75

peer sanctioning, 140–41, 145, 148–50, 186

persistence, educational, 212–13. *See also* academic achievement; family identity and educational persistence

Personal Cognitive Development, 45

pipeline navigators, 223–24

poise, 43

policy issues: black academic achievement, 139; family identity or obligation and educational persistence, 260–62

popular culture, 232–33

popularity, 140–41, 186

power, 45, 46, 210–11

prejudice: Elliot's eye color experiment, 66–67; formation of, 69–71, **72**. *See also* intergroup attitudes, of children

privileged status, 21

professional careers, 123–24

proficiency tests, 39n14

Pruden, H., 44

psychological research, social marginalization, 44

Puerto Ricans, school valuing study, 184–85

quality, of education, 21, 22, 23–24

race and academic achievement. *See* academic achievement and race
racial balance, 21, 22–23
racial-ethnic identity: and academic achievement, 44, 67–68, 187–90, 239; and connectiveness, 96–97; as contingent self-worth predictor, 168–69; cultural narratives' role in, 47, 49, 52–60, 61; devaluation of, 213; development of, 142–43; and embedded achievement, 98–99; and essentialism, 46–49, 57–58; and family identity, 241–42; influence over psychological health, 44; intersectionality perspective, 44–46; of marginalized social groups, 61; measurement of, 107–11; models of, 96, 99, 101–7; oppositional identity, 15–16, 44, 138–39, 153, 184–85; and racism awareness, 97–98; and school valuing, 141–43, 145–46, 150–51; and self-esteem, 91; and stereotype threat vulnerability, 117–18
racial-ethnic identity, of adolescents: and academic achievement, 91, 99, 100–101, 153–54; components of, 95–99; connection with broader society, 102–6; importance of, 95; incorporation into self-concept, 101–6, 107; lack of, 101–3; measurement of, 107–11; research considerations, 91–92; social context of, 92–95
racial-ethnic self-schema (RES), 101–6
racism: awareness of, 97–98, 99, **109,** 140, 213, 217–18; school lessons about, 82
Rattan, A., 130
Reconstruction period, 17–18
research considerations: academic achievement and race, 67–68, 91, 206; academic achievement of Hispanics, 209–14, 240; contingent self-worth based on academics, 164, 166–67; family identity and

educational persistence, 242–47; intergroup attitudes of children, 69–71, 84; racial-ethnic identity of adolescents, 91–92; school valuing, 138–39; social identity, 69–71, 209–14; social marginalization, 43–44; stereotype threat, 115–16
research methodology. *See* methodology
RES (racial-ethnic self-schema), 101–6
restrictive covenants, 22
return, 43
Robbers Cave study, 69–70
role models, 223–24, 229, 234
Rosenwald, J., 17
ROTC (Reserve Officer Training Corps), 217, 218, 226, 229–30
Ruble, D., 143, 186
Russian students: discrimination against, 152; family identity and academic motivation study, 245–46; school anxiety, 148; school valuing study, 143, 144, 147–53

salience, of: gender identity, 162–63; racial-ethnic identity, 153; social identity, 211
Sameroff, A., 141, 142, 239
San Francisco Bay area study, of adolescents' family obligations, 243–45, 246, 247–58
Sanskritization, 58
SAT, 130–31
Schmader, T., 116
school achievement. *See* academic achievement
school integration, 20–23. *See also* Shaker Heights, Ohio Schools
schools: building projects (1920s-1930s), 17; factors affecting children's social group identities, 71–82; and identity development, 93–95; learning environment with incremental intelligence view, 126–31; racially stratified academic hierarchies, 188–89; single sex, 68–69, 76

school segregation, 19, 68, 69, 74–76

school valuing: and academic achievement, 154–55, 160, 188–89; African Americans, 17–19; and discrimination, 138–39, 140, 146, 151–53, 154; and family socialization, 138; peer group influences, 140–41, 145, 148–50, 186; racial-ethnic differences, 146–54, 161; and racial-ethnic identity, 139, 141–42, 145–46, 150–51; research methodology, 143–46; research overview, 138–39; research sample, 142–43, 154

second-generation immigrants, 143

Sedwal, M., 59

segregation, residential, 22, 223

segregation, school, 19, 68, 69, 74–76

self-concept: definition of, 91; and racial-ethnic identity, 101–6, 107; sources of, 211; "splitting," 35

self-esteem, 91, 96, 161–62. See also contingent self-worth, based on academics

Self-Perception Profile for Children (SPPC), 145–46

self-schemas, 91, 101–6

self-theories, 126–27

self-worth, 49, 118, 163. See also contingent self-worth, based on academics

Shaker Heights, Ohio Schools: academic tracks, 23–24, 28–37, 189; community's support of integration, 21; Galetta's study, 20, 21–22; number of black students, 38n4, 12; Ogbu's study, 16, 20; proficiency tests, 39n14; quality education and excellence, 22, 23–24; racial achievement gap, 24–28; racial balance efforts, 21, 22–23; segregation history, 22; student narratives, 28–37

Shakerite, 25–26

Shelly v. Kraemer, 22

Sherif, M., 70

Sikh families, 242–43

Singhal, S., 59–60

single-sex schools, 68–69, 76

slavery, legacy of and educational achievement, 15, 16–19

social class, 258–60

social essentialism, 46–47

social identity: and academic achievement, 212–14; and behavior, 92; definition of, 240–41; devaluation of, 115, 118–19, 174; disengagement from, 124–25; enactment of, 210; high identification, 116–18; mismatch of, 212; multiple forms of, 115, 119–20, 211; nature of, 210–11; race-ethnicity incorporation in, 101–6; recognitions and positionings of, 210–11; research perspectives, 209–14; salience improvement, 120–21; and stereotype threat, 116–26; strength of, 165. See also racial-ethnic identity

social identity, of school children: and classification, 71; Elliot's eye color experiment, 66–67; and group size, 77; and messages about group status, 78–82; and minority status, 76–77; research paradigms, 69–71; and school segregation, 68, 69, 74–76; and teachers' labeling of groups, 71, 73–74

socialization, 138

social marginalization: and academic achievement, 59–60; coping mechanisms, 43; determinants of, 42; and essentialism, 46–49, 50, 57–58; experience at multiple levels, 42; in India, 49, 50–60; and intersectionality, 44–46; research considerations, 43–44; research framework, 42, 47–49, 60–61

social mirroring, 49

social psychology, 69–70

society, connection with, 102–6

South, the, school integration resistance, 20–21

Spanish language, 217
Spencer, M., 96
SPPC (Self-Perception Profile for Children), 145–46
standardized test performance, 24–25, 116–17, 119, 120–21, 125
Stark, B., 44
Steele, C., 49, 125, 161
Steinberg, L., 139, 147
stereotyped groups, identification with, 116–19, 122–23
stereotypes: and academic achievement, 1–2, 94–95, 164–65; formation of, 69–71, **72**; gender, 174–75. *See also* intergroup attitudes, of children
stereotype threat: and academic performance, 94; protection from, 126–31; research considerations, 115–16; and social identity, 116–26; vulnerability to, 116–23
stigmatization, 118
Stonequist, E. Everett, 43
stress, 59–60, 172
Stroh, K., 44
study circles, 27–28
Suarez-Orozco, C., 44, 49, 243
Suarez-Orozco, M., 44, 49, 243
summer school programs, 73–74
Swann, W., 80
Swanson, D., 96

Tajfel, H., 211, 240–41
talented and gifted programs, 24, 28, 32
task performance, 172–73
Taylor, A., 140, 141
teachers: as cultural mediators for college attendance, 223; expectations of, 155; fixed-ability messages, 130; gender stereotypes, 174–75; labeling of students, 71, 73–74; process vs. person-based feedback, 175; strategies to improve experiences of women of color in college, 173–76
teasing, 149–50

test performance, 24–25, 116–17, 119, 120–21, 125
Thorne, A., 213
Title IX, 68
Torelli, P., 140
tracking. *See* academic tracks
transcendence, 43
Triesman, U., 28
Turner, J., 240–41
Tyson, K., 188–89

Udasco, J., 44
Ukranian students, family identity and academic motivation study, 245–46
"untouchables," in India, 50–60

value of education. *See* school valuing
Velasco, A., 189
Vietnamese Americans, 243
Vincentnathan, L., 52
Virginia, school integration resistance, 20
voluntary minorities, school valuing, 143. *See also* immigrants

Wang, J., 44
Weisberger, A., 43
"white flight," 21
whiteness: "acting white hypothesis," 138, 161, 185–87, 191, 198–201, 235; schools and education associated with, 15; students' conceptualization of, 187–90, 192, 198–201
whites: school anxiety, 148; school valuing study, 143, 144, 147–53; stereotype threat vulnerability, 119
Whitmore, J., 243
women: academic achievement, 160, 161, 163; math ability, 123, 125, 130–31; professional careers, 123–24; professors, 162. *See also* contingent self-worth, based on academics; gender

Wong, C., 141, 142, 239
Woodbury, 23
Woodson, C., *16*
Working Group on Social Identity
    and Institutional Engagement, 2
work organizations, social marginal-
    ization in, 44

Yanico, B., 103
Yanico, C., 103
Yee, M., 79

Zhou, M., 243
Zigler, E., 141
Ziller, C. Robert, 44